THE INTELLIGENT HAND

To Dominic
hope you enjoy the book
regs best.
David Savage.

THE INTELLIGENT HAND

By David Savage

First published by Lost Art Press LLC in 2018
26 Greenbriar Ave., Fort Mitchell, KY 41017, USA
Web: http://lostartpress.com

Title: The Intelligent Hand
Author: David Savage
Editor: Christopher Schwarz
Copy editor: Megan Fitzpatrick
Design and layout: Christopher Schwarz

ISBN: 978-1-7322100-4-2

This book was printed and bound in the United States.

Signature Book Printing, Inc.
8041 Cessna Ave.
Gaithersburg, MD 20879
http://signature-book.com

TABLE of CONTENTS

FOREWORD

Ninety-five percent of the woodworking books out there deal with 5 percent of the things that happen in a workshop. Woodworking books – even great ones – are biased toward providing information for beginners.

This makes good business sense because there will always be more white belts than black belts. But it also creates a body of literature that is boring for anyone who already knows how to cut a dovetail, sharpen a handplane or use a router.

Plus, it is my belief that the dearth of advanced and challenging reading material prevents many of us from progressing past the well-documented basics. There simply isn't a beaten path between learning to flatten a board and becoming Sam Maloof.

Maybe David Savage can help.

When I first saw David's work – years before I met him – my reactions were typical.

• How in the holy hell did he build that?

• How did a human being come up with those furniture forms?

• Do they really look that good in person?

Whether you like David's designs or not (and I do), his work is polarizing, uncompromising and surprisingly humane. "Humane" is a weird word for objects that sometimes look like a space throne from a Kilgore Trout science-fiction novel. But it's the right word, so hear me out.

David is a socialist. A former socialist. A failed socialist. It depends on the day you are talking to him.

Despite the high-wire, high-money aspects of his professional work, David started life on one of the lower rungs of the socioeconomic ladder. (I'm not English, so I don't have the proper adjectives to offer. In America we would say he came from middle-class roots.)

Thanks to some surprising and impressive scholarships, he ended up with an excellent art-school education. And after a wild series of twists and turns (including bankruptcy – it's all here in this book), David ended up where he is today, as a top-tier woodworker who drives a Morgan to work but lives an otherwise humble and low-key life.

David hasn't forgotten what it's like to be hungry and somewhat desperate. His furniture might look fanciful or extreme. But the chairs are designed for comfort. His desks are designed for hard use. His cabinets are carefully engineered to be a joy to use. In other words, humane.

There's more. He treats his employees, customers and students well. And he's surprisingly uninterested in promoting himself as a personality. During the planning for this book, David tried valiantly to have an African student as the primary maker. This was for two reasons. He is an excellent woodworker. And it would rattle the cages of the middle-aged white men who buy woodworking books. But the timing (and his cancer) wouldn't cooperate.

So instead you have this book, which is almost as radical.

"The Intelligent Hand" is a peek into a woodworking life that's at a level that most can barely imagine. The

customers are wealthy and eccentric. The designs have to leap off the page. And the craftsmanship has to be utterly, utterly flawless.

How does one get to this point? And how do you stay there?

One answer to these questions is in this book. Yes, there is some difficult furniture in here. And David shows you the techniques used in his Devon workshop to bring his designs to life. Actually making the furniture – even the most challenging stuff – is only a small part of the process.

A lot of the hard work involves some unexpected skills. Listening. Seeing. Drawing. And looking into the mirror and practicing the expression: "And that will cost 20,000 pounds."

As you will see, it's a huge personal struggle – just like the production of this book. On the day he received a cancer diagnosis with a grim prognosis, he began work on this book. He wasn't sure what the book was going to be about (I had told David that I would print whatever he wrote). But David knew it would work out, and he attacked the work with the fervor of a much younger, healthier man.

I consider this book, like his furniture, an almost-impossible gift. It is unexpected, challenging and – if you will let it into your heart – rewarding. All of us at Lost Art Press are honored to have worked with David and the staff at Rowden on this remarkable project. And now, we are happy to share it with you.

Christopher Schwarz
August 2018

PEOPLE IN THIS BOOK

One of the many unusual aspects of "The Intelligent Hand" is that it is not entirely about the author and his work. While it would be easy for David Savage to take all of the credit for the work that comes from his workshop, that's about the last thing he would ever do.

When you first meet him, he is quick to point out (and praise) the people who work alongside him at Rowden. The only other woodworker I've ever heard do this is Sam Maloof.

Because these characters are integral to the story, we thought we'd give you a brief introduction to some of the important players.

Carol Binnington Savage

Carol was born in London and raised in the city of Southampton, but considers herself a converted country girl at heart. With little thought of what she wanted to do in life, she says, Carol fell into finance in the City of London (the historic and modern financial district), where she worked for high-powered individuals from some of the best-known U.S. investment banks.

At 28, she chucked a successful job with Goldman Sachs to study economics, then met her polar opposite in David Savage, who, she says, "whizzed me off to the country to raise children, dogs and cats." (The children are Jenny and Alex, who, as this book goes to press, are 23 and 21.)

Carol traded in the trading floor for contentment in growing fruit and veg, cooking, yoga, hiking and beekeeping.

Daren Millman

Daren began woodworking at 13, restoring a shed full of rusted tools left by his late father. With little else to do in rural Devon, he says, he began to play with any timber offcuts he could find. At 15, a week spent at a local shop to make a small cabinet confirmed his love of the craft, and upon leaving school at 16, he joined that same shop as an apprentice.

There, he worked with many skilled craftsmen, one of whom, Jeff Smith (who had trained with David Savage) inspired him to work at the highest levels. Daren later joined Smith's business, then another top-notch shop, Graeme Scott Furniture, which employed many Savage-trained craftsmen. During his five years there, he made pieces for the likes of David Bowie and Saudi royalty.

When Savage advertised for a new hand, Daren applied. Fifteen years on at Rowden, Daren is the senior maker and is responsible for the day-to-day running of the shop. He's working now with David and others to secure the future of the school and workshop.

Stephen Hickman

Stephen earned a Bachelor of Science degree in product design at Porstmouth University before graduate study led him to 10 years as a primary school teacher. But his love of design never left him. So in 2015, he began the year-long Designer-Maker course at Rowden, in which he learned not only excellent hand-tool and machine woodworking skills, but how to draw (an important component of the Rowden education) and design furniture. After completing his course, Stephen stayed on as a post-graduate "bench renter," making pieces for clients and exhibition, then worked directly with David Savage for eight months, helping to turn his designs into reality.

In early 2018, he and his wife moved from Devon to Suffolk, where Stephen is setting up shop as an independent studio furniture maker (www.stephenhickman.co.uk).

Ed Wild

Ed is an award-winning furniture designer and maker, a member of the Devon Guild of Craftsmen and has work exhibited throughout the U.K.

Ed developed his woodworking skills and a love for the craft in his grandfather's furniture workshop, making his first substantial pieces in his early teens. He then embarked on a career as an organic chemist before returning to his furniture-making roots. He trained at Rowden more than a decade ago, and now works at the school part time, passing on his woodworking skills and knowledge to a new generation of students, and teaching weekly art classes.

Ed's own workshop, www.ewcf.co.uk, is in North Devon, and is one of a cluster of furniture workshops that have sprung up around Rowden during the last 25 years. He produces commission work, and has a following as far afield as Finland and California.

Jonathan Greenwood

Jon trained at Rowden before securing a rarely available job with the top-class workshop of Graeme Scott Furniture.

Now, he works with Rowden students during their first six months at the school and serves as "the Guardian" of technical quality when it comes to handwork – he is responsible for gently (but firmly) encouraging students down a path toward future hand-skill perfection.

"It is not the critic who counts; not the man who points out how the strong man stumbles, or where the doer of deeds could have done them better. The credit belongs to the man who is actually in the arena, whose face is marred by dust and sweat and blood; who strives valiantly; who errs, who comes short again and again, because there is no effort without error and shortcoming; but who does actually strive to do the deeds; who knows great enthusiasms, the great devotions; who spends himself in a worthy cause; who at the best knows in the end the triumph of high achievement, and who at the worst, if he fails, at least fails while daring greatly, so that his place shall never be with those cold and timid souls who neither know victory nor defeat."

—Theodore Roosevelt from "Citizenship in a Republic," delivered at the Sorbonne, Paris, April 23, 1910. With apologies for the sexist language.

Fig. 1.1. Cherry nightstands. The slightly larger one is to the right of our bed, on my wife, Carol's, side.

INTRODUCTION

"Well Mr. Savage, I am sorry to tell you the results of your tests are not good. If you play your cards right you may have two years, three at best. Play them badly and we are looking at months not years."

So, I begin this book with the hope and intention to reach the conclusion before you do.

I wasn't always going to be a furniture maker; that journey is for later. For now, I want to share with you a pair of cabinets that have just been finished. They will help tell a little about who I am. They are made in American cherry, highly figured and among my more successful pieces. However, both the selection of the species and the wonderful figuring are complete mistakes for which I can claim no credit. I wanted these pieces to be made in English cherry. It has a greenish-golden heather honey colour that has an elegance very suitable for bedroom furniture. I am pretty sure I said "English" to Daren, who ordered the wood, and I was sullen and grumpy for a while when the American cherry arrived.

"I can't get English in these thicknesses," he said. "This is all I can find, and we are lucky to have that." So, we carried on – no point doing anything else – and didn't things turn out well! I could easily say how hard we looked for this highly figured stuff and how important it was to the concept, but that would be hogwash.

For most of my life I have made furniture for other people. Like the cobbler with poorly shod children, we have furniture in our home that has gone to exhibition but did not sell. What we don't have is a handmade dining table and chairs or a pair of bedside cabinets. Storage in our bedroom is a moronic piece of furniture design from Habitat that closes two large drawers together and catches them in the centre. Push, just there, and maybe the catch will hold. Push anywhere else, and this aircraft carrier of a drawer springs out toward you, whacking you in the shins. But now we have these made-to-measure cherry lovelies.

They were largely made by Daren Millman, who is the senior cabinetmaker at Rowden. Rowden is our workshop in Devon, where we have been for nearly 20 years. Rowden is also a teaching school where we cover hand-tool techniques, machine techniques, drawing, design and business skills. Rowden is a farm owned by Ted Lott, who has retired and let out the farm buildings to us. During those 20 years, we have built up a workshop with an international reputation for making fine modern furniture to order. Before Rowden, I was in a workshop in Bideford for about eight years where I did much the same, but not quite as well. The end of that, and the beginning of this, is also a story for later. (Juicy one, that is.)

Not made fast, these cabinets. When asked how long these took, Daren would give his standard answer for any serious piece: "Oh, about 400 hours." Whether it is a dining table set, or a cabinet with secret drawers, 400 hours seems to do it. Estimating times for making jobs is at the very guts of making a living in this biz, and Daren is spookily accurate.

We do price estimates in two ways. I have an arm-waving, general feeling gathered after 40-odd years of making mistakes. "Oh, it's about three months," as I visualise the piece being made from timber arrival to polishing. And I do the estimating in days or parts of days. Cutting those rails will be about half a day. I know this, for I have cut similar rails and seen others doing similar rails, and that's how long it took!

But Daren is much more meticulous. He will settle down with paper and pen to plot the progress of components and processes through the workshop. Like me, he will begin at the beginning with timber ordering, visiting timberyards, making a cutting list. Right through to polishing, packing and delivery. Each will have a time allocation. That time allocation, again, will be based on nearly 30 years' experience. He will be better than me, but I will have got there faster. So, if I need a quick price, I will use the arm-waving method and I may even ask Daren to wave his arms about. A serious job enquiry needs pen and paper, a nice comfy stool and a tidy bench. And about half of an expensive day.

But this wasn't being made for a customer so none of that mattered; we won't be getting paid for the time spent. I was once accused of being very concerned about money by one of those gutless anonymous internet trolls. This stunned me because all of our work has been for pay, but that was always secondary to making something that was special. If we could survive doing it, I would always want to make it as best we can – but to do that you need to know your numbers.

Way back in the early 1980s, I read books by James Krenov that inspired me to take up working with wood, making furniture. He inspired a generation to hug trees and to love wood, and to make as beautifully as one could, but from the position of a skilled amateur. Jim never sought, I believe, to make a living from this. That was my madness. What Jim did do, however, was touch upon the reason that is at the core of this book. Why do we go that extra mile? Why do we break ourselves on that last 10 percent? This is the 10 percent that most people would not even recognise, or care about, even if it bit them on the leg. This is the bit that really hurts to get right, both physically and mentally.

But get it right and deliver the piece and she says, "Wow, David, I knew it would be good, but not this good." Get this right, over deliver and soon you don't need too many more new clients, for she will want this experience again and again. We have been making for the same clients now for most of my working life. They get it, they like it and they have the means to pay for it. Your job is to do it well enough to get the "Wow, David," have the satisfaction of doing it right, get the figures right and feed your children. Not easy I grant you, but for some of you it will become a life well lived.

Fig. 1.2. Drawer detail.

This is the quality thing at the centre of our lives. This is the issue that brings people to Rowden from all over the world, each with what Perry Marshall would call "a bleeding neck" (something is wrong, or they wouldn't be here). Each knowing they can do more with their lives. They come with damage that they feel can be fixed with a combination of physical work and intelligent solutions. Both are essential.

Physical labour is unfashionably sweaty. We generally now sit at terminals in cool offices. We are bound by contracts of employment that would make some 18th-century slave owners seem benign. The only exercise we get is the twitching of our fingers and the occasional trip to the coffee machine. Our bodies, these wonderful pieces of equipment, are allowed to become indolent and obese. We feed up with corn-starched fast food and wait for retirement. Exercise, if we take it, has no meaning; we don't exercise to do anything. We run or jog, but we go nowhere. We work out in the gym and get the buzz, the satisfaction of the body's response to exercise, but we don't do anything. We don't use the energy constructively to engage our minds and our hands to make stuff.

White collar work has become what we do, almost all of us in the Western world. It pays the bills and keeps us fed, we get a holiday and our children are kind of OK. And that is fine for most of us. But there are some of you who know that something is missing. Something creative, some way to spend your day working physically while exercising your body and your mind. Thinking and revising what you are making, as consequence of the quality of your thoughts. This is Intelligent making, this is The Intelligent Hand.

This, then, is written for you. This is to help, encourage and support a decision to leave the world where thought and work are separated. Where they no longer exist together. This is for the brave souls who need to plough a contrarian furrow, where intelligence and making exist together and you are in control of your life. Don't be scared, but don't expect it to be dull or easy. A life well lived never is dull or easy.

FOR THE UNBALANCED AMONG US

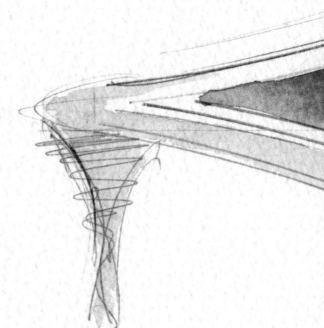

This is notionally a woodworking book, but this is not just for woodies. This is for anyone who wants to break out. This is for any one of you who feel you are living a life that does not quite fit. A life devised by someone else. I hope in these pages to help put maybe one or two of the pieces into your personal puzzle.

People of all ages and backgrounds come to Rowden seeking to make a change in their lives. They may not know it when they come, but they soon find out that the piece they are making – that chair or table – also makes them. You don't just make the piece, the piece makes you!

They come to us with that "bleeding neck" I mentioned earlier. It might be a lousy boss or a job that pays well but leaves them unfulfilled. It might be boredom or a feeling of lopsidedness. Something is missing, something that should be there. I have had a senior executive from a multi-national media company tell me of a psychopathic aggression from his old boss, an aggression that drove him to a toxic mixture of alcohol and fast cars. A scene that would soon have killed him if he had not acted to remove himself.

Techies from software companies have told me, "I can't do another 20 years looking at a screen. I love the money but my body is a mess, and I am doing the same thing I did 15 years ago. I can't work all my life to create reports that are just shredded by the next guy in."

A common thread is, "I want to make something. I want to be able to say I did that, and that, and that." Without her effort, his work, their skill and knowledge, this object would not exist. A cabinet or a dining table is harder to delete and deny than a 500-page report that can hit the shredder in seconds. It's something physical to point at and kick. Try shredding that sucker.

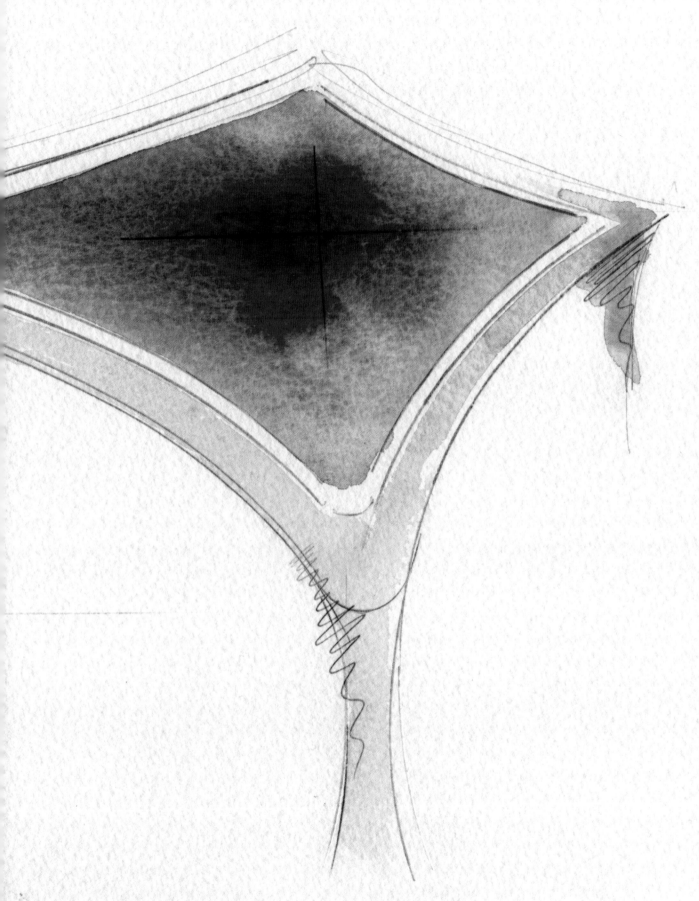

Fig. 2.1. Coffee table, version 2.

Fig. 2.2. Drawer detail.

Like our students, there was a time in my life when I was pretty stressed with the work I was doing. The Sunday Night Blues were a feature of that period, the fear of what lay before me from Monday morning for another week. The Blues would start about 5 p.m. on Sunday and go on all evening and into the night. If you get the blues, this may be for you.

Or maybe not. This is not for everyone. I know that you have to feed the family, and you have my respect. I can relate to that, and you cannot take risks. That job, well, it's not great but it does it for you. It may be like a prison sentence, I know, but it will end, you will get to your pension and there are always the holidays to look forward to. I genuinely take my hat off to you. But you are probably not reading this book.

A side of this is physical work – sweaty, health-giving physical work. A doing that makes you feel good. This is real, useful work. Work that sees something done, that you can step back from and smile.

And then there is the thinking. After all, this is The Intelligent Hand. You are not a mindless operative doing this. Again, we are talking specifically about wood, but it could be something else. I know self-employed welding fabricators, small specialist timber merchants, garden designers and green keepers who all run their own show, work physically and mentally, and are engaged in displaying skill and knowledge to serve their niche market.

The essence of this is taking back control. If you are not running your life, then someone else probably has plans on how to use your time. I once asked my son, Alex, to pack some DVDs for me during his holiday. He worked diligently, labeling and packing. At the end of the morning he asked, "Dad how much will these sell for?" I answered, "Oh I guess about $500." "And how much are you paying me to do this?" he said. "Oh, I think $15 an hour for four hours," I said. "But that's not fair!" said Alex.

Both of my children have had the benefit of an expensive education. But even there, there was no attempt to teach goal setting and life planning. Nothing was taught beyond which university to go to, and how to get the grades needed. The entrepreneurial spirit and the means to get to a distant goal are skills deemed unnecessary by most educational establishments.

To make your own life, you need dreams, goals and efforts that are out of the ordinary.

There is no shame in dreaming, but that is just what it is – just dreaming. What is needed is to turn a dream into reality. To dream with a plan that can be worked.

You have the same 24 hours as everyone else. Some of you will gain traction and move, others will spin your wheels and go nowhere. Be a mover; use every minute. Plan each day. Let no person take your attention away from the important and urgent tasks of the day. Have a goal and see it clearly. Visualise it in your head in Technicolor. See it so clearly that you can smell and taste the air. See yourself in the image. This is what imagination is for. Then think about the obstacles between you and the goal. Break them down to smaller bite-size parts. Eat an elephant a bite at a time.

Have a plan for a week, a month, three months, six months. What are the steps you can take now? Put dates on the plan to achieve this by your dates. I have job lists for each day that refer to weekly lists that lead to goals set months or years ahead. Writing it down then revising it weekly keeps you focused. Celebrate your success and work out where you didn't succeed, then carefully work out why. Then revise your list. Then work it, baby. Nobody else will do it for you.

One of the goals of this book is to discuss The Why: the reasons some of us go to such extreme lengths to achieve Quality at a time when there appears little social demand for it. To do that I need to go back to the beginning of the 20th century to set a social context, to help us understand how thought and work have become separated in our culture.

Whilst we go back I will be telling you my story, as I hope it helps explain some of the decisions and show some of the juicy failures.

But most important, I want us to visit Rowden as soon as possible, not 20 years down the road. So be aware of time warps and non-sequential chapters. Keep on your toes and stay with me. This is a journey of Doing and Thinking.

'OH, YOU'RE ALRIGHT'

I came to Rowden in 1995 not long after my workshop in Bideford had gone into bankruptcy. Now there is a juicy story, and one I will share with you at the risk of looking a complete prat too early in the book, before you know me. When I talk students through my life as a maker, they always say the best, most informative parts, are where I fall flat on my face. So here we go, face down.

Bankruptcy is little talked about. Shops disappear from the high street and old companies close, disrupting, uprooting the lives involved, but the world moves on unchanged. Behind the doors of each closure is a personal story of anguish and stress. My story was one of poor judgment on my part, and the lure of the big job.

This was the early 1990s; we had been in the Bideford workshop for about eight years. The economy was not powering along at the time, but despite that I had expanded to two workshops on the same street. This, on reflection, was huge mistake; hubris and ambition are powerful forces. We cut back once, very hard, sacking office staff and makers

Fig. 3.1. An exterior view of Rowden and some of the more rustic student housing.

PHOTO: WR PHOTOGRAPHY

who were not quick and accurate. We were good at what we did and showed a decent living, but David Savage Furniture Makers felt like a huge monster that I had to feed with work.

Then "the big job" arrived. The commercially minded among you will see this coming. I am just an ordinary furniture maker trying to do a good job and turn a penny. Mr. M saw my work at a London home and garden exhibition. I am a great one for selling direct and meeting the customer. He was American, a master of the universe, a big swinging dick in the city and they had just moved to a smart address in North London. They were looking for furniture. NOW. And a lot of it. My tongue was hanging out, and I was dribbling.

I was really up for this job. I did all the stuff I talk about in this book. I went and listened carefully. I looked at the house. I prepared a brief. I let it cook and did the drawings. I could not avoid thinking, "This job could sort all my problems" – which it did, but not in the way I had expected. They wanted several pieces; could I do them all? Well, not without pushing all my other work to one side, spreading Mr. M's work over maybe four or six benches. Madness – but that's what I did.

The work was in three phases, with three deliveries. The first was done and paid for; it was the second delivery that went wrong. Phone calls and letters went unanswered (it was the age before websites and mobile phones). When I arrived at the house it was empty. Why was that not a surprise? His company would not talk to me, suggesting only that Mr. M had returned to America.

Bankruptcy is about cash. You can have work and stock. And you can have machines. But if you have no cash then you have no business. Cash is the lifeblood of a business.

Everything in the shop had to be sold to pay the debts of my company. I did everything I could to use the little cash left to pay my staff. The group of students we had in the workshop were the worst affected. Their courses stopped, and they, quite reasonably, were pretty cross. Table saws were loaded into vans at dead of night; cramps, power tools, stones and bench lights were removed. It was like being in a maelstrom of tools and thinly concealed anger.

It was a while before I got back to furniture making,

but I had a young family to support. Wonderful clients such as Maggie Rose got hold of me and dragged me back to it.

"That table you were making for me. Can we buy the parts that are being sold at auction and have the table made up?" she asked.

"Well yes." Other clients found me at home and wanted chairs, desks, dining tables and sets of chairs.

Fig. 3.2. The entrances to the
bench rooms at Rowden.
PHOTO: WR PHOTOGRAPHY

They didn't seem phased by my bankruptcy. I love
them all.

My daughter, Jenny, was just 18 months old and my
wife, Carol, was working at a local company, bringing
in our only regular money. I was able to sell designs
and have them made locally by craftsmen that I had
either trained or worked with during the previous 10
or so years. I had a nice, profitable setup in the spare

bedroom until Carol told me, "We need that bedroom as I am pregnant and you need a workshop."

Yes. Great. But Noooooooo....

Bankruptcy is one of those few occasions when you are forced to step off the moving escalator of life. You can observe and see the workshop clearly; the moment you put your foot back on the escalator everything is moving and your image is distorted. So, I tapped the escalator with my foot. If I did this again, would I do this or that? Would I buy that table saw or buy this... again?

I had a beat-up old car, a bench, a bag of tools, my books and my portfolio. They let you keep those; everything else is sold. I had commissions to make and some cash, but not a lot.

My advert in the paper, asking for a workshop space in a local farm building, brought me to Rowden Farm, not far from home. Ted and Sheila Lott were retiring from farming and had a row of brick buildings that would make a great workshop. The buildings overlooked meadows and a lake instead of a lorry car park.

I felt that I couldn't be in a better place. My first meeting with Ted brought a quick look from him.

"Oh, you're alright," Ted said. For a man who thought he had "Bankrupt" tattooed on his forehead, that was all I wanted to hear.

Since then, for 20 years Ted and Sheila, and more recently their son, Edward, and daughter, Rachel, have closely supported the idea. And, I think, they have some pride in having Rowden Workshops on their property. I certainly could not have done this without their warm encouragement and friendship.

Feeling that you are in the right place, and knowing that this is where you should be, is a great part of contentment. Rowden does this for me. I could much more easily be working on a grimy, miserable trading estate in a London suburb and be much nearer to clients. But this is better. Way better. It was an instinctive move to get out of London all those years ago (before Bideford). I was laughed at and criticised by nearly everyone we knew. My bank manager called me a fool to move away from all my customers and the centre of

Fig. 3.3. The machine room (left).
Fig. 3.4. The school's drawing studio (above).

PHOTOS: WR PHOTOGRAPHY

all my potential income. But I was right. It wasn't until much later, however, that I understood why I was right.

It's all about the contact with nature and the effect this has upon one's work – being open to the influence, on a daily basis, of the shapes and textures of the natural world about us. The seasons get me. I walk my dogs around the lanes to see it, each year, again and again. Ah, the snowdrops are out, then a few weeks later the little purple flowers, then something else.

I have always been influenced by the Arts & Crafts movement (more of this to come). The influence of William Morris was not so much the wallpaper and the fabrics, but the way he looked at the English garden and natural forms and adapted those forms and shapes to his work – the natural forms and structures that are the essence of growth and regeneration, the bones of nature in all her beautiful ways.

And the thinking and the doing. Morris was always thinking and inventing, but alongside this he was always "doing" something. Almost on a daily basis he was playing about with weaving looms or some

historical technique he sought to revive and employ in his current designs. If it wasn't that, it was special printing methods to get his wallpapers to the intensity of colour he required. He must have been a pain to work with, but his working practice lives with me to this day.

The essences of nature and the structures of the natural world, learnt from Morris, bring us to the proportional systems that underpin all Rowden designs. Classical proportions and the development of skills to make design look "right" are paramount. Euclid, Pythagoras and Fibonacci have all contributed to our understanding of growth in nature, why leaves and trees and bushes look the way they do.

The other thing was the political ideology of how we work together. I have never been comfortable as a boss. Having been a socialist, it seemed a wrong thing

Fig. x.x. One of the top-floor bench rooms at Rowden, usually occupied by the more senior students.

PHOTO: WR PHOTOGRAPHY

to do – but I was never going to do this alone. The Bideford workshop taught me how to go about this. But it also told me that I had come close to a system of exploitation and oppression that I did not feel totally happy with.

I was providing work and paying decent money. I hope I was giving some satisfaction in the work simply by asking for the work to be done to high standards. Where we could, one or two makers saw the job through from start to finish. That seemed important.

but cut that from solid we could save half a day."

This raw intelligence, this force of nature owned by the maker. She has the kind of brain that runs a mainframe CAD programme between her ears. A conversation with her about a making issue would be like a tennis match. We are discussing a solution in three dimensions.

"What are we going to do at this junction?"

"No idea; what do you suggest?"

"Well, we need some kind of fixing."

"I need these two components to be slim and slender."

"There will be some stress on that joint."

"What do want to do to give it the strength?"

"Well, if we can get two Parnham fittings, about 5mm, into each spaced 20 mill apart…"

"Can we cut that back to 4mm and keep the dimensions?"

"Yes, we need it to flex."

And so it goes on. Making on the edge of material structure. I have been blessed to work with makers of considerable intelligence who throw that care and knowledge into the work they do. This, for me, is what the Arts & Crafts ideology was all about. This is something that we cherish at Rowden.

I have very occasionally seen young makers developing high-value art furniture in workshops that could be compared to the most exploitative sweat shops in India. I have sent Rowden graduates to them and heard their reports. It's not a happy experience. This is always the designer misusing the skill and trust of his workshop in pursuit of his own ambition. It is hateful.

"A hand" used to be in industrial terms a unit of labour.

"He's the charge hand."

"We need an extra hand to do that."

This is a different notation. This is the Intelligent Hand. This is a person working physically and giving all – head, hand and heart – to the making of a piece. To the making of a piece worth making well.

But too often we found ourselves doing a batch of successful chairs that got too big. Sure, it paid well – very well – but the repetition was not what I wanted. It dulled the edge too much.

I had come to see the raw intelligence of the wonderful makers I worked with. This became visible when resolving designs and construction issues, or improving an older method. They brought ideas to the job in surprising and valuable ways.

"Why don't we do it this way?" "If we laminated this

AND THEN THERE IS LUMBER

This is the killer. This is the element that gets you. It could have been metals – hard cold and nasty – or plastics. No – never plastics. A house full of brightly coloured children's plastic toys leaves me feeling very ill. Or glass, maybe leather, or even mud.

But it's wood. Lovely, warm, intractable and cursed wood. Ed Wild, who works with us, says that, for the right person, if she can do a week working wood properly with good sharp tools, she'll be sunk. She will never be the same again.

Which is why we begin with hand tools. Stuffing boards of oak or ash through a machine will get you a nice surface, but it will tell you nothing about oak or

ash, or the difference between them. A speculation sheet will tell you notional differences. But hands responding to the material, feeling the action of a blade on fibres – that tells you a lot. A handplane will begin to inform you with the first shave you take.

As you see more timbers, you learn there is more and more to know. Each species has its own characteristics. Each log can be different: top of the log, quartersawn, late wood, early wood. It's literally a moving target.

Fig. 4.1. Mistreat your lumber and it will literally disappear (left).

Fig. 4.2. Weathered and wild (above).

The damn stuff is expanding and contracting with the weather as I type.

And it has the benefit of being relatively inexpensive to set up as a woodie. You don't need a massive factory with expensive machines. Many small workshops I know of that operate at the top of the market are small and highly skilled, but they buy time on expensive machines. What they have is the knowledge to form this material in all its complexity, to add shagreen inlays and exotic polishes to create perfect surfaces for expensive products.

We work now mostly with native hardwoods: elm, ash, oak, cherry, yew. What we hope is to find that special log you see once a lifetime. The log that should never, ever go anywhere near a factory.

Imagine this: You have a board of pear. It's 2" thick, rare English-grown and air-dried. Swiss pear is wonderful, but lumberyards steam the timber to remove wood borers, and this changes the colour. Unsteamed pear is rare and best, as the pinky flesh colour is maintained. There are hints of a dark purple-red figuring toward the end of the board.

You take this board to the band saw to resaw it. That is, to stand it on edge and cut it into two 1"-thick boards. This is slow, difficult, noisy work that needs patience and a delicate touch. The band saw slowly chomps down the edge of your board CHA CHA CHA CHA Cha. As it reaches the end, you can at last open the board. There is a purple-red flame of colour flickering over the two surfaces. You are the first to see this; no other eyes have been here before you. Timber contains joy and heartache, almost in equal measures. Some boards open and are as dull as the England football team.

I have a mate, Stephen Bedford, whom I met nearly 40 years ago. At the time, he was a joiner with a passion for oak. With that passion, he set up a small one-man timber-supply business in the disused railway yard at Bishops Nympton railway station.

He had little stock but he liked his timber, and as a joiner he knew what good timber was. I kept going back year after year. Soon he would put stuff back for me.

"I've got a nice stick of yew," he'd say. I rarely had the money to buy it "on spec," but I knew where it might be when a job came up.

Through the years, Stephen's business flourished with his hard work. He moved his stock to a yard in front of his home. When I visited, one of Stephen's many tow-headed children would come out and shout "Daddy! Daddy! It's a customer!!" They developed a business supplying natural oak floorboards, and one of Stephen's tow-headed brood now runs the yard.

To show his engagement with this process, Stephen bought land and planted saplings, walnut, for another generation.

When I was with my mentor, Alan Peters, I saw great stacks of air-dried timber around his workshops. Alan invested a great deal of time and effort into these supplies. But if you don't know what you will be making, it's difficult to plan like this. We could be doing cathedral doors in oak or tiny boxes in yew. I didn't follow Alan's example. I didn't have great stacks. I bought in (usually kiln-dried) material as we needed it. This, on reflection, was another mistake. Kiln-dries stuff works differently to air-dried. Air-dried timber is a nuisance; you need to plan months ahead. I remember Alan cutting air-dried stuff and bringing it into the warm summer bench room to dry down to 15 percent moisture or less. This was stuff for a job that wouldn't be started until the autumn.

Although handling it requires the entire workshop to trip over the stuff for most of a summer, working it is considerably easier than working the kilned stuff. Air-dried oak comes off the blade like a paring of hard cheese. It's lovely to work. Kiln the same board and you have to fight to get that finishing shaving.

It is this variance of material, the truth that even with nearly 40 years playing around, that proves you don't know everything about it. Each log is different – warm, responsive, bloody-minded and difficult. Oh yes – work this carefully for a while and you are sunk; completely sunk.

Fig. 4.3. Walnut slabs waiting in the Devon sun.

WHEELWRIGHT

ALL HAIL THE 863

I need to take you back in time to the beginning of the 20th century. I need to do this in order to explain what I think has happened to us, and why. As Henry Ford set up his first production line in America in 1913, the Arts & Crafts Movement was being established in the sunny fields of England. Ford developed an existing (brilliant) idea to "bring the work to the worker." In truth, it was more complex and more revolutionary than that. What Ford was did was to create a system of activities.

Until then, vehicle manufacture occurred in small workshops and factories with relatively skilled engineers doing varied and various work – the stuff we celebrate. What Ford did was analyse that work and break it down into a series of steps. Each step could then be carried out by a relatively unskilled person. The steps were put in sequence, and the partially complete vehicle was brought to the worker.

This is one of the most famous examples of what

Fig. 5.1. Before. A 19th-century wheelwright shop from Edward Hazen's "Panorama" (1846).

was to become a major management process in 20th-century industry, not only in the factory but also the office. The "Knowledge Engineer" systematised skills and created processes that became the management's property. All that was left after their passing was the script and the process.

To fill 100 jobs on his new production line, Ford was forced to hire 963 skilled workmen and women (863 did not stay on). And he had to double his wages to achieve his goals. Rather than hissing and spitting, Ford described this as one of his best business decisions. The extra cost for wages was recouped straight away by increasing the speed of the production line, instantly doubling, and later trebling, production. This was new. Before this, paying extra for piecework didn't increase production and may in fact have decreased it. Ford had workers working at a speed he could choose. This could not have been achieved just by paying people more money.

Fig. 5.2. After. Henry Ford's assembly line in 1913.

The 863 who could not stomach Ford's new factory are, for me, the interesting ones. Where did they go? History consigned them to the rubbish dump of the past. Like buggy whip makers in the age of the automobile, they were no longer needed. But my hat is removed in honour to their instincts. I would have been amongst them. For they knew that their skills and knowledge were part of a balanced and well-lived life.

This was called "scientific management" and was outlined in the monograph "Principles of Scientific Management" (1911) by Frederick Winslow Taylor. Taylor writes:

"The managers assume the burden of gathering together all the traditional knowledge which in the past has been possessed by workmen and then of classifying, tabulating and reducing this knowledge to rules, laws and formulae.... All possible brain work should be removed from the shop and centred in the planning and layout department."

In this way, Taylor, whose work was hugely influen-tial in the early 20th century, was able to encourage the concentration of scattered craft knowledge into the hands of "the process managers." The "time and motion analysis" was born. The objective was to create a process that, once designed, needed no further thought or tinkering.

In that situation, skilled workers could be replaced at machines by unskilled ones. Labour and cost were thus reduced as production increased. Skill once observed and analysed was no longer needed.

Soon after this, the age of consumer spending was upon us. Thrift and avoidance of debt – a mark of prudence and good management – was to become a thing of the past. Consumption engineers such as Claude Hopkins, one of the early leaders of marketing, sought to bring consumption under the hand of scientific management. Now we could earn money building cars, and maybe, if we paid over 10 years on the "Never Never" (aka an installment plan), we could drive one as well! Aren't we smart all of a sudden! All we needed to do was to give up the personal skill we earned over 10,000 hours. Plus, the personal pride in the achievement of making, of doing something complex and difficult and doing it well. For there was no real skill required on Ford's line – just hard manual work, day after day, after day, after day. The 863 who could not take up Ford's offer could not do that. All hail the daft old 863!

Who can deny the enormous prosperity and economic comfort that this scientific management has brought us? We work, we earn money, we have holidays and we pay taxes. Then we get a pension and die. And don't think that being a smarty in an office will save you. The same "expert systems" are coming your way. In the book "The Electronic Sweatshop: How Computers are Transforming the Office of the Future in the Factory of the Past" (1989, Penguin), Barbara Garson writes:

"The modern knowledge engineer performs similar detailed studies, only he anatomizes decision making

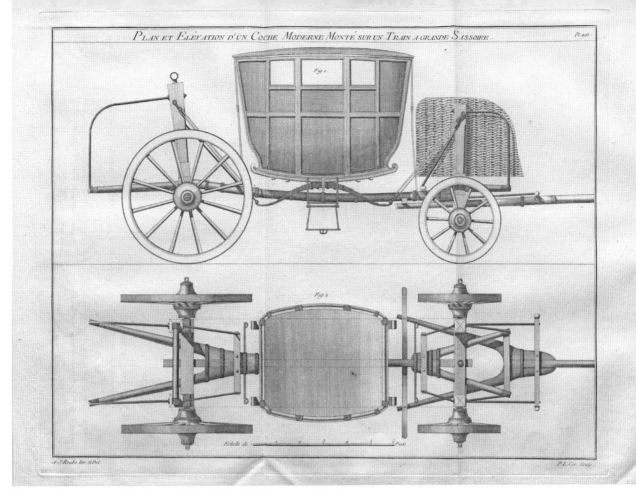

Fig. 5.3. Early automaking. From A.J. Roubo's "l'Art du menuisier."

rather than bricklaying. So, time and motion study has become a time and thought study.…To build expert systems, a living expert is debriefed and then cloned by a knowledge engineer. That is to say, an expert is interviewed, typically for weeks or months. The knowledge engineer watches the expert work on sample problems and asks exactly what factors the expert considers is making his apparently intuitive decisions.

"Eventually, hundreds or thousands of rules of thumb are fed into the computer. The result is a program that can 'make decisions' or 'draw conclusions' heuristically instead of merely calculating with equations. Like a real expert, an expert system, should be able to draw inferences from 'iffy' or incomplete data that seems to suggest or tends to rule out. In other words it uses (or replaces) judgment."

My wife, Carol, worked recently in an office in Bideford. She spent her day on the telephone reading prepared scripts to prospective clients, who were owners of holiday cottages. Carol has a degree in economics; she has worked on the trading floors of some of the world's most famous investment banks. Carol could sell

ice to Eskimos. But their scripts were what the company wanted spoken; Carol was only a mouthpiece. Her ideas of what they were doing wrong and how it could be improved were of no interest to the company. She was cheap local female labour that came and went while the system controlled by the company remained intact. Its image as a small family company remained unchallenged, but the truth is very different.

I do not suggest that this is bad. I cannot ague that this systemisation, this splitting of thinking and doing, has not resulted in huge economic benefit. We are all vastly more wealthy and more secure than previous generations. This is good; nobody can argue with that. But there is a type of person — and I see them coming to Rowden year after year — who does not quite fit this pattern. Someone who wants a bit more from life than a job, money, holidays and a pension. She wants something else; she wants to use her head and have responsibility for what she makes. She wants to make a thing about which she can say, "That's mine; I made that." And she wants to sell it for money, decent money.

All hail the 863.

JOHN RUSKIN & 'HAPPENINGS'

I was fortunate; I was not destined for the production line. I was lucky enough to go to the wonderful art school at the University of Oxford that was set up by John Ruskin, the great theorist at the centre of the Arts & Craft Movement. Ruskin believed that art should be taught at places of great learning, that art students would benefit from being at the centre, right in the hum of the academic process, and that in turn those universities would be enriched by their presence.

Ruskin set up three art colleges: The Ruskin School at Oxford, The Fitz William at Cambridge and The Slade College at London University. Although The Slade has since prospered and gone on to become one of the greatest post-graduate art schools, I don't believe that all three were universally welcomed by "the Dons." The Fitz William is no more, and my own experience at Oxford suggested that The Ruskin School was not entirely loved by the University. We were always damned by the idea that as art students we could not be given a proper

degree because we were "not academic enough." The intelligence that we displayed daily was of the wrong kind for the Dons (the professors).

William Morris and his buddy Edward Burne-Jones were at Oxford at Exeter College. They shared lodging in the same street as me, but many years earlier and probably in much greater comfort. My time at Oxford was the late 1960s, concurrent with the brand-new contraceptive pills, very, very short skirts, the very beginnings of feminism and all the fun that entailed.

The Ruskin School was then situated in a wing of The Ashmolean Museum. We had three large studios, one of which was devoted entirely to life drawing and painting. Before you were allowed to draw from the

nude you needed to serve a full term's apprenticeship in drawing plaster casts of Greek statuary, mostly from the Parthenon. This was mind-numbingly dull, but it gave you great discipline in the simple task of looking very, very hard.

We were in a gallery in Walton Street about 200 yards from the Ashmolean. An ancient but much loved and respected tutor named Geoffrey Rhodes would slowly, very slowly, make his way from the school to the cast gallery. He was a small man who took tiny, painful steps. I was the only student diligent enough to be drawing at three in the afternoon. It was silent in the gallery. The outside door opened; I could hear Mr. Rhodes' approaching footsteps. Tap, tap, tap. It took ages.

"Ah, there you are David," he said. Slowly, he looked at my drawings, then put his whiskery head next to mine to see what I was looking at. To see exactly what I was looking at. "Ah well, not much I can help you with there, carry on." He then turned and tapped his way back to tea and cakes in the staff room. Drawing is like that; there are times when words just don't do it. Mr. Rhodes knew that, which is why he was universally loved and respected.

This was at the time of "The Hornsea Art School Revolt." The school's studios in London were being filled with dry ice, smoke and writhing naked bodies. "Happenings," laced with LSD and weed, were "what we did now." If you painted, it had to be a kind of Mid-Atlantic Expressionism: big vacuous canvases, lots of sloshing about and full-on freedom of expression.

I didn't work this out until much later, but all these developments were about de-skilling young creative minds. The Conceptual Art that won the "Salon" and that has become the Official Art of my generation needs no skill – just ideas. For it, skill is a restriction and inhibition to creative expression. Which is, of course, nonsense.

What I came to learn at art school was how to draw, how to look, how to think visually. This was slowly, gradually being devalued and removed from the curriculum. All the skills were being chucked out of the art school window to the point that now, a generation later, we have few capable teachers left to teach the basic drawing skills.

I had come to learn to draw; I felt this in my waters. I loved the daftness of all this at Hornsea, especially the writhing nakedness, but something within me wanted to have the skill to draw and draw well, which meant practice. Ten thousand hours, they say, to achieve any skill or competence. Like a pianist, I knew that it was necessary to practice.

The Ashmolean Museum is a wonderful place for a young, visual mind to explore. In it, there's everything from Egyptian sarcophagi to Samurai armour, from Minoan figurines to Classical Greek statues. The classical Greek dudes were a big deal for me. They were in a long gallery between the drawing studio and the front

door. A small ragged group of us would gather at the front for a cigarette every time the model took a break. We sat on the stone walls outside the main doors, got piles (hemorrhoids) and had monumental snowball fights. We really were a scruffy nuisance to have in a museum, but it was the best place to be. I absorbed the Ashmolean though the pores of my skin. In three wonderful, full years I knew what the artefacts of world culture felt and looked like. My eyes had wrapped around and embraced everything, whilst probably I knew very little. What I did know, however, included a small collection of Raphael and Michelangelo drawings of which I devoured every line and every nuance. It was BBBBBBBbrill. Did I tell you I had a stammer?

Stammering was an affliction I carried with me throughout childhood and school into my middle years. It was an invisible affliction. I didn't look like I was crippled in any way, but to a large degree, it stopped me from speaking. My mouth would jam up with words beginning with "B" or "M." I could see them coming up ahead in the sentence. It was like lockjaw – I was left humming, buzzing and dribbling, trying to push out a word that had jammed in my mouth. The more effort I put into getting the word out, the tighter the lockjaw.

To say this affected my life would be an understatement. Think what your life would be like if you couldn't talk. That's unfair. I could talk – it's that I chose to not talk very much. It was irritating when it came to girls and no doubt restricted my sex life when I could have had much more fun. But isn't that always the case? We all could have had much more fun when looking back. Much later, I was able to get past this obstacle, but that is another story for later.

I wonder if Burne-Jones and Morris got piles from sitting on the same stone walls outside the Ashmolean? They certainly inhabited the same space. For Morris, brotherhood and comradeship was a big deal. He gathered about him members of a group of young painters who were to become the rather pompously titled Pre-Raphaelite Brotherhood. They later went on to paint up a storm. Then, they painted with startling lack of success, the walls of the Oxford Union.

Morris was always wrapping fellow artists and writers about him like a warm cloak. Blessed with a background that meant a few shillings were not a problem,

Fig. 6.2. I had come to learn to draw, I felt this in my waters. I loved the daftness of all this at Hornsea, especially the writhing nakedness, but something within me wanted to have the skill to draw and draw well.

he could focus on ideas and ideals. Here, Ruskin came to influence both Morris and his group. "The Stones of Venice" was a powerful and popular thesis published in three volumes between 1851 and 1853. The books examine Venetian architecture in detail. In "The Nature of Gothic," a chapter in book two, Ruskin gives his view on how society should be organised:

"We want one man to be always thinking, and an-

other man to be always working, and we call one man a gentleman, and the other an operative; whereas the workman ought often to be thinking, and the thinker often to be working, and both should be gentlemen, in the best sense. As it is, we make both ungentle, the one envying, the other despising his brother: and the mass of society is made up of morbid thinkers and miserable workers. Now it is only by labour that thought can be made healthy, and only by thought that labour can be made happy, and the two cannot be separated with impunity."

Wow. Tell that to Henry Ford.

I have worked night shifts at Black & Decker. I worked a machine that bored a part of the casing for an electric drill. These were the industrial "top of the range" drills. Learning to do this well took about two shifts. After that, what could I do to keep my mind occupied? I had a total number of casings to do in a shift; too few and I had the charge hand on my neck. Do more than this, however, and the union guy was going to give me earache. So you play: How fast can I go for an hour? Then how slow? How few could I make in the next hour? I needed the money but after a while, when I had paid my bills, I joined the 863.

Morris picked up Ruskin's social ideas and ran with them. Known initially for his poetry, Morris again assembled a group of trusty creatives to create William Morris and Company. The goal was to create, improve, make, have made and sell stylish artefacts for the burgeoning middle-class home.

The Muse came to Morris and found him working. (The muse has always got to find you working!) His inspiration was the English countryside, not just the generality but the very core of how nature fits together. I believe this is why the movement has so much resonance for us now. Not what Morris did – his shapes and forms, the wallpaper and fabrics – but why he did it, and the way he was looking at nature. Morris gave us a Victorian response. Why can we not look at nature and give a 21st-century response?

Morris rented Kelmscott House near Oxford – a beautiful, warm, stone house with a mature garden full of perfumed summer. During his time there he

developed something that touches the essence of nature herself. His drawings were cleverly arranged into repeated images that could become wallpapers or woven tapestries.

It was typical of Morris to spend a part of the week "in the doing" – weaving, drawing, printing. The making was important to him, and he was not afraid to bring back old techniques. His textiles needed skills, looms and processes that could be found abroad and recovered from obsolescence.

The Arts & Crafts Exhibition Society poster below shows in part the ideas that were evolving – the artist and the maker shaking hands as equals, with mutual respect.

"Let you have nothing in your home that is not both beautiful and useful." That was the strap line of Morris and Co.

Oscar Wilde answered that with: "The definition of Art is that it is useless."

First-class, Oscar. His argument (which has little historical validity) in the following years won the day. The creative force of the 20th century has very largely created an art that defines itself as useless.

Leaving this battle (yet to be lost), the Arts & Crafts movement encouraged a new generation of makers, often young men and women with sufficient resources, to set up small workshops outside the cities that were close to nature. These were jewelry makers, potters, weavers, silversmiths. The new railways would take their product back for Morris and others to sell, and they could live the rural idyll.

It was the furniture makers who particularly affected me. They were part of a small group that settled near Cheltenham. Each year, I take a group of Rowden students to see their work at the Wilson Museum in Cheltenham. I do this to show them the freshness of

Fig. 6.3. Rowden students examine a table base by Ernest Gimson at The Wilson Art Gallery in Cheltenham.

the workmanship and to remind myself of the essence from which Rowden has come.

For me, their move to the countryside was most important. It was the closeness to nature, having it around you every day when walking the dog, seeing the changes in the hedgerow as season followed season. Remembered changes from last year become marked in your work. You get closer to the raw bones of nature, and your work benefits. You bring home bits of hedge and draw, not knowing why, but feeling that it is part of the process – and you trust your feelings.

Two brothers, Sidney and Ernest Barnsley, and a good friend, Ernest Gimson, all young, all recently trained as architects, took to this idea of living and making out in the sticks. They came to the quiet Cotswold village of Sapperton (not far from Cheltenham) and set up small workshops. Sidney Barnsley worked alone, always. Ernest Barnsley spent a little time with Gimson, but soon gathered a commission for work at Rodmarton Manor and became engrossed in that. Gimson is my hero. He worked not alone but with the help of both local and imported craftsmen. Probably learning as he went, Gimson, with his assistants, created a place that turned out extraordinary furniture.

The table shown above is made in solid English walnut with black Macassar ebony and pale green holly detailing. The boards of the tabletop are secured with a decorative dovetailed key. The hide glue would probably have secured the joint, but these were joints to express, to show off the workmanship.

Each year I delight in showing the freshness of the workmanship displayed in the wide chamfers worked in the hard black ebony. Tool marks are evident; they could only come clean off the spokeshave or drawknife. This is stunning work.

The goal of this small group was to make pieces with integrity, very largely by hand. There is almost no veneer from the early Gimson workshop; what you saw was what you got, all the way through. Gimson worked with local craftsmen, notably Henry Clissett and Edward Gardiner, who were skilled chairmakers. Clissett was notable for aiming to make chair a day and rush the seat in an evening. Gimson aimed to take these traditional chairs and improve the product, using his design skills in conjunction with the craft skills of Clissett and Gardiner.

Here is an example that blows me away at left. This is a chair reworked by Gimson but made by Gardiner. Look at the chair back. Look at the arrangement of the back splats. Five of them all different, each getting larger as our eye climbs up that back. This chair is aspirational – it seeks to pull the eye up, a positive upward movement. Look at the chair legs. They cant outward toward the top, welcoming the body into the chair. See how the back splats are arranged on the chair. Look hard. The centres are each wider, one from the next. The ends are each wider, one from the next. The splats are fixed with a negative space that is wider, one from the next. But look at the centre. The top of each splat is the same distance from the splat above. It's as if all is upward energy, every element is up – but this is like a string in the centre of the chair back that pulls down. You don't see it until you hunt – but it's there.

This is what a good chair design does; it teases the eye to find the hidden logic. It is just there. You could not change one element without binning the whole lot. Gimson must have driven Gardiner mad (until the orders came in and the money followed).

It was not so much the work that grabbed me by the throat, it was the activity. These men and women were contrarian counter-culture beings, and I liked that. They set themselves up in the wilds of rural England when transport and communications were ridiculously hard. The move to the country was a serious decision and one I support, working at Rowden in the heart of rural Devon, with a lake to chuck the dog in and fields to walk.

Although Gimson is my role model, it was the other guy, Sidney Barnsley, the guy who worked alone, who had another most serious effect. He had a son, Edward Barnsley, who, confusingly, also became a furniture maker. Edward Barnsley came to work at and later own a workshop at Petersfield in Hampshire. The man who founded the Petersfield workshop was Geoffrey Lup-

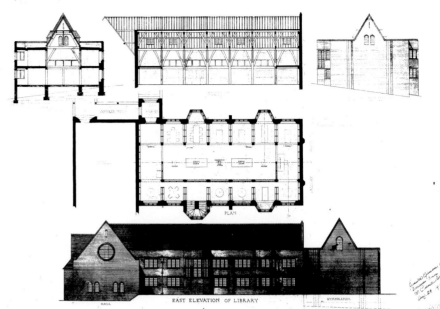

Fig. 6.5. The library at the Bedales School, which involved the talents of several great designers and woodworkers.

ton, a former apprentice of Gimson's who was largely responsible for the library at the nearby Bedales School (above). The building was designed by Gimson, the tables in it are by Sidney Barnsley and the chairs are by Gimson. The building was started by Lupton but was completed by the workshop under the direction of Edward Barnsley.

I nearly wrote "finished by Edward Barnsley," when really it was the team that he led – a group of clever intelligent makers, probably capable of telling the lad, "No boss, it's got to be this way." Our culture doesn't allow us to name everyone; it's bad enough to acknowledge they are even present – but they damn well are there. And it's this presence, a team working together, with different skills pulling together, that makes something extraordinary.

The Edward Barnsley Workshop continues to the present day. In 1950 they took on apprentice Alan Peters, who went on to open his own workshops at Cullompton in Devon. It was this man who gave me a model to follow. I admired him so much. With a lovely Devon long house, the barns converted to workshops, the stacks of English hardwood drying in the sheds, and his two skilled assistant makers, he made beautiful, saleable modern furniture. He was the man I wanted to become. But that's another story.

Fig. 6.4. The Edward Gardiner chair, also at The Wilson.

Fig. 7.1. Mural detail.

Fig. 7.2. Work. These murals explored the drudgery and exploitation of workers.

GIVE NOT A STUFF

The Ruskin School at Oxford gave me a great start; I loved my three years there. I learned loads about looking and was coming to know the difference between great art and OK art. I learned that most of it is just OK; getting to great is hard and unusual. This was part of what pushed me — I always chased that last 10 percent bit where the quality lived. What the three (and following) years did was give me a firmer hold on identifying "the great." Confidently knowing the difference between the great and the OK has been important in my life. But more of that later.

The next step in my Rake's Progress was to take this young man to London Town. Again, I was fortunate. During my second year at Oxford, the wife of Peter Greenham, professor of the Royal Academy Schools in Piccadilly, was invited to speak at the Ruskin School.

I had that autumn crashed and burned the first love of my life. Sandra was a stunner; I met her just as I was going up to Oxford. I remember her seeing me off on the train, tearful and distraught. I had to look away, to the shocked annoyance of two women in the same

Fig. 7.3. A new home. Burlington House at the Royal Academy of Arts.

carriage. I couldn't believe I was loved so warmly. I was going away to a grown-up world far from Bridlington railway station. I neglected Sandra shamefully. Instead of going home the following summer to dull old Brid, I had another adventure planned. I was going on a cheap, 50-pound flight to New York, on an exchange student scheme for the whole summer. I got my just desserts later that year when I was back in Oxford; I was dumped by that lovely young woman, who was in turn going off to explore the world and go to college.

I was in bits. I had no language to express this. I still stammered like a lunatic. I had never experienced such intense loss. It took me months to work through it. The drawing pad, a 2B pencil and squidgy oil paint were to become my therapists. I drew and I painted what it felt like. Toward the end, I did a huge 5' x 8' diptych (two panels joined together). It was a huge, expansive blast of bright red paint. I was doing this in the studio adjacent to the life room where Mrs. Greenham gave her wonderful lecture. I think the painting was very near completion. "Mmmmm....." she whispered to the principal. "He should apply to the Royal Academy Schools."

Now this was the Premier League, a bit like being invited to play for Manchester United. That spring, hundreds of art students from all over Europe put in portfolios of drawings for examination. I think 15 painting students and four sculpture students were admitted each year to a three-year post-graduate school. And I was one of them!

Let me explain: This is the oldest art college in the world! It exists, a line of glass-roofed studios, at the back of the Royal Academy in the heart of London's art world. Corks Street, with its line of sniffy private art galleries, and Bond Street were right behind the studios. Fortnum & Mason was across the road. Here was the best life-drawing studio you could find anywhere. Blake, Turner, Reynolds – all had been students at the Royal Academy Schools. I had three years of this. WOW.

I remember having a row the first morning I arrived. I parked my car in the front courtyard much to the distress of the attendant.

"You can't park there, young man."

"Oh, yes, I can – and if you want to, you take it up with Professor Greenham." This worked a treat. The attendant had, I guess, been selling it and other parking spaces in prime central London to office workers nearby. I didn't hear a squeak from him for the next three years. In year two, he even said, "Good morning, sir."

Greenham set the tone for this extraordinary place. He was an extremely sensitive and kind man. I remember when he interviewed me for the place that we sat on a bench in the sun in the front courtyard.

"David, what painting in the Ashmolean really impressed you?" he asked.

I stuttered on about a Claude Lorraine landscape, and I could see in his eyes that we shared a love of the same great painting. A shambolic dresser, Greenham would be seen in Picadilly with his waistcoat buttoned to his shirt. His works, highly regarded, were small, sensitive landscapes – beautifully painted, but not of the current age. Greenham was not on trend, and I believe that he didn't really give a stuff. Most of what I learned at the Royal Academy Schools came from this example. Do what you believe to be excellent, and give not a stuff. History, not fashion, will determine whether your efforts are just OK or really great.

Today, young artists would be encouraged to have a CV – a list of magazines that had mentioned their work and exhibitions in which they had participated. You would be encouraged and taught to network. None of that was encouraged at the Royal Academy. In the temporary outdoor exhibitions on the railings of Piccadilly hung the "pot boiling" examples of art that had succumbed to commerce. This was the worst disgrace. Yet across the road, in the swish galleries of Cork and Bond streets, we could see exactly how art was marketed to the wealthy – a rare desirable product – not reproducible and so, of consequence expense. This is the Art Market that the great Australian critic Robert Hughes described as, "the second largest unregulated market after heroin."

We have seen during my lifetime the centre of that art market switch from Paris to New York and the development of a market from discrete exploitation to massive profiteering. Don't you just love it?

Two distinct influences at that time were fellow students Desmond Rochfort and Andrew Turner. Des became a great friend and partner in our later mural painting escapades. Andrew for a short time became a dominant influence.

An older man, Andrew came from a strongly held Scottish communist background. He was passionate about his beliefs and his work showed that passion. To me this was very attractive. For a very short time, less than two years, I even joined the Communist Party of Great Britain (CPGB). There was a great Labour party minister, Denis Healey, who said, "If you failed to join the party in your youth it was a sign that there was something wrong with your heart. And, if after two

years you were still there, it was a sign that there was something wrong with your head." I followed that pattern.

The leading comrades in the local party branch were Di and Val Bolton. Middle aged, they had been in the party for years but didn't really look the part. Vladimir Ilich Lenin and Rosa Luxemburg they were not. They looked instead like a sweet couple that you could meet buying vegetables in North End Road Market. Di had a car, an old Austin A40, on which he would lift the bonnet and put old carpet over the wings to lean in from either side and tinker about. My dad and I used to do exactly this almost every other weekend. Saturday morning was for washing the car, then a little bit of tinkering. Never did he make it run better, but we always enjoyed doing it. I liked Di, if only for the way he cared for his old car.

Then there was Deanne Burch, a young woman who had a curious background in the military. She joined at about the same time as I, and was straight away given the job of membership secretary. As dangerous revolutionaries we were probably being watched by the authorities, and quite rightly so. I wonder if Deanne was there to assist this observation. Though why they bothered is beyond me.

Revolutionary work consisted almost entirely of weekly meetings to organise. We organised jumble sales to raise money, and we organised to sell a dreadful, thin, expensive and unreadable newspaper called *The Morning Star.* I remember on one occasion several of us gathered to sell the paper at Hammersmith Tube station late one Friday night. We had the early Saturday edition, which should have attracted the crowds. It was instead a bit like a scene from Federico Fellini's "Satyricon." Drunks, druggies and the simply abusive slowly filled the streets. Encouraged by the alcohol and the dark night, they became, little by little, more attentive. The silly paper sellers were the outsiders; we were the mad people and we obviously needed abuse, and they were there to help provide it.

It is a sign of the feebleness of this organisation that after a very short period of membership and for a few weeks only, I became party secretary of the Hammersmith and Fulham branch of the CPGB. Now understand that "secretary" is the duck's guts. Perhaps the only event whilst I was branch secretary that had a real consequence involved a young South African couple.

They came to me for advice; they wanted to return to South Africa at a time when it would have been very dangerous for them to do so. I later learned the young man spent some time on Robbin Island for distributing leaflets. Brave people.

The Communist Party of Great Britain was a wonderful collection of eccentric idealists, each wanting a better world and who failed to see the failure of socialism. I have written that name of the organisation in Capitals, very carefully, as there were at the time several similarly named communist parties, and they all curiously spent a great deal of time knocking spots off one another.

Desmond and I wanted to paint. The spirit, if not the talent, of Michelangelo flowed through us. But we

Figs. 7.4 and 7.5. Still standing. One of the now-vandalized Royal Oak Murals (above) and a detail of one section (left).

didn't want to do it in the art market. Murals – public art – seemed a good idea. We met a young couple who showed us exterior murals currently being done in Chicago that encouraged us to do something similar in London. We found our nice, dry walls on two adjoining buttresses that supported the urban motorway in Paddington, West London.

Technically, this was a challenge. As properly trained painters, we wanted the damn thing to last, and we knew that emulsion paint was not the medium to use. We researched and located Keimfarben, a German paint company that made a paint system based upon water glass. That paint had a history of successful outdoor use for more than 100 years, so this was the way to go.

One problem – Keim was expensive and required a porous render to be applied to the wall before we could start work. So, we embarked on a money-raising venture. We built an accurate scale model of the two walls and made as close a representation of the images on the model as we could. We typed up a sales document that was presented to any London Arts committee that sat still long enough. That damn model was humped around to meeting rooms all over London. Some gave us money; some gave us ridicule. In the end, we raised about $18,000. I had not (until writing) this realised how formative that process was in helping me develop a sales presentation that I later used to sell furniture.

"The Royal Oak Murals" were one of the first of a series of public art works of that period. For a short time after their completion, they were at the centre of the London art world's fuss and controversy. They have since been comprehensively vandalised. I don't like looking at the images now, but odd bits of the wall

Fig. 7.6. The Battle of Cable Street in 1936.

that have escaped the local spray can artists tell me that I wasn't doing too bad a job. I now get earnest young academics writing theses about the subject, pestering me for valuable time.

Royal Oak led me to "The Battle of Cable Street Mural," my first real catastrophe.

When I tell this story to students they always say the catastrophes and failures have been the best bits. Each time I tell the story I get the courage to look a little closer at what went wrong. It helps to see each failure not as a falling down, but as a stage of personal development. It's how you get back up that matters. Creatives are good at failure; we do it all the time, and we know there is no good work without it. But it helps in the telling if the blood and gore gets drippy.

The Battle of Cable Street happened in 1936 when Oswald Moseley attempted to lead a band of the British Union of Fascists through the largely Jewish East End of London. They were prevented by a large crowd from going along a main route, so they were diverted down a smaller parallel road, Cable Street. The group was so deeply provocative that this road, too, was blocked and the march was prevented from proceeding. Hurrah!

This area near the London docks has always been where immigrants would first settle. It had been the home of Huguenots and, in turn, Jewish people flee-ing pogroms in Europe. As immigrants settled, gained stability and a little prosperity, they would all move to other areas of London. (In the 1970s and 1980s, the new Bangladeshi immigrant population was threatened with fire bombs and daily racial intimidation from a small but vocal far-right political group in the same way that the British Union of Fascists had done to Jewish East Enders in 1936.)

Remembering the Battle of Cable Street seemed an important thing to do. Especially as the side wall of the Stepney town hall on Cable Street had a public garden in front of it and seemed to have PAINT ME written all over it.

I began the selling process all over again. I made drawings and large watercolour designs, showing as much as I could what the wall would look like. The proposal had considerable local support, but most people, quite reasonably, couldn't see the sense of spending any money on art, especially this art. Going against a majority opinion for what seemed to be right was becoming a silly habit of mine.

The local authority was the Tower Hamlets Council, and as owners of the building, they were responsible for its repair (rendering the wall paintable). Getting this done took years. In my proposal, I asked for two assistants to speed up the job. This never happened. I was

Fig. 7.7. Failure at 80'. The Battle of Cable Street mural.

PHOTO: JO MARSHALL; WIKIMEDIA COMMONS

on my own. The scaffolding was nearly 80' high. My plan was to work from the top of the wall down, which may have been foolish. At some stages I would put a projector on top of a nearby tower scaffold and project drawings onto the wall. Working on the top of it meant my work was obscured from view by the scaffold board I trod upon. To see the area I had worked on from the ground meant removing the boards and climbing down, spying the errors, putting the boards back and making the change. And on and on. I was running up and down those ladders all day long. It was exhausting and dangerous work; twice I fell a short distance.

But the wall was going well; I had spent two winters and a summer on it, and most of the top part was near finished. The image was beginning to emerge. I didn't

realise it, but this was the dangerous time. This is when the wall was comprehensively vandalised.

That and the exhaustion got me. My body told me that if I went on that wall I would probably fall again, and this time I might die. It was a move I am not proud of, but I pulled out. I quit. I knew the mural would be finished, as the political will (and the money) was now there to do it.

A team of three, including my old mate Des Roche-fort, along with Ray Walker and Paul Butler, were commissioned to finish the job. Well done fellas. Hurrah! This mural, unlike the "Royal Oak Mural," has been protected from vandalism and become a well-loved part of the area. The repair and restoration has been periodically and lovingly done by Paul. Well done, Paul.

FLAILING ABOUT WITH WOOD

So, what next? I spent a few months licking my wounds and faffing about the house. I had no idea what to do; I felt useless and an incompetent failure. Giving up is not a good feeling, but I knew that was what I had to do. I had no more juice in the tank. No power on earth would get me back on that scaffolding.

I made a wooden bookcase – nothing special, just six bits of pine screwed together. Then I made a plant stand for outside. What struck me was that I took some small pleasure in doing these simple constructions. When I was at school, I was compelled at the age of 13 to give up woodwork. I could not do both art and woodwork, though I was quite good at both. My choice was woodwork until mum steamed into school and changed all that. You will do art! So now, 15 years later I wondered: Could I make things?

Memories of my school woodwork master and Ken Bulmer, my girlfriend's clever dad, came back to me. It seemed attractive that I could maybe use my brain and body at the same time. After running up and down that scaffolding all day, I enjoyed the way my body functioned. I enjoyed the sweaty work. The rewarding glass of cold beer. The stammer was SSSSSSSSSstill with me, and this made me remain pretty silent. So where could I find out more?

The colleges didn't help. This was mid-winter and courses had already started. *Woodworker* magazine and Charles Hayward's books and articles became a source of gem-like pieces of information. Hayward taught me through those pages, though his fine diagrams, some of the essence of Great British Woodworking. And, let's remember, we had been pretty good at it. In America,

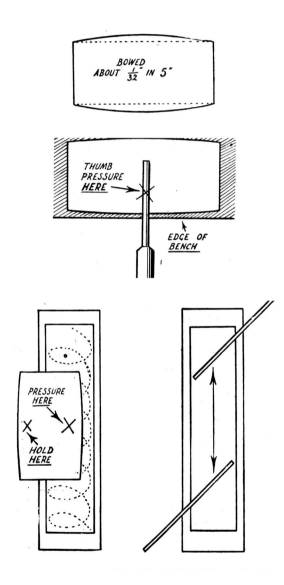

Fig. 8.1. One teacher. Charles H. Hayward's writings helped, but hands-on work was required.

SHARPENING THE SCRAPER

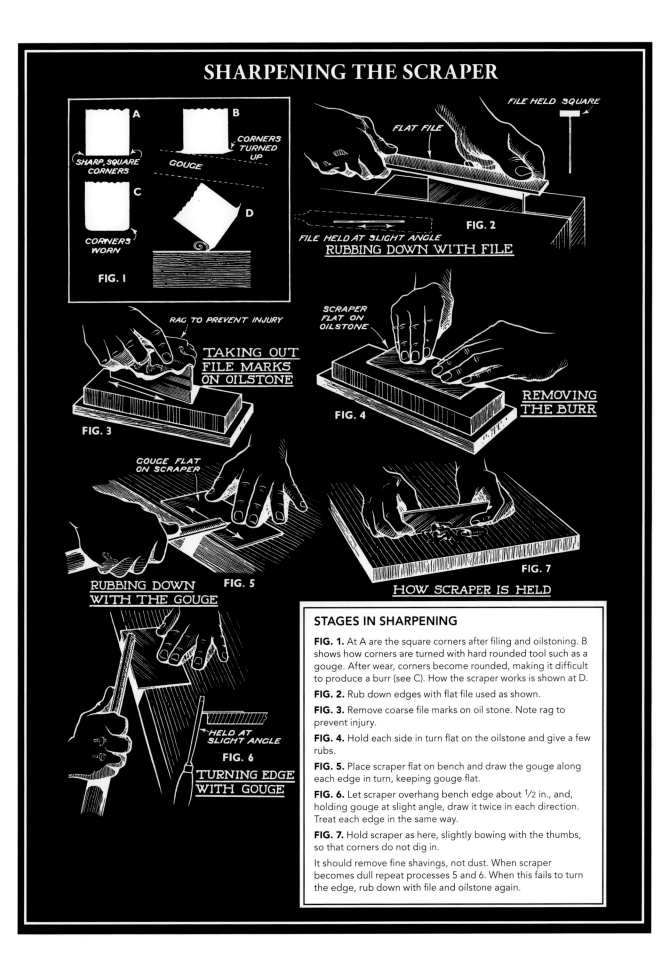

FIG. 1

SHARP, SQUARE CORNERS — A

CORNERS TURNED UP — B

GOUGE

CORNERS WORN — C

D

FLAT FILE

FILE HELD SQUARE

FILE HELD AT SLIGHT ANGLE
RUBBING DOWN WITH FILE

FIG. 2

RAG TO PREVENT INJURY

TAKING OUT FILE MARKS ON OILSTONE

FIG. 3

SCRAPER FLAT ON OILSTONE

REMOVING THE BURR

FIG. 4

GOUGE FLAT ON SCRAPER

FIG. 5

RUBBING DOWN WITH THE GOUGE

FIG. 7

HOW SCRAPER IS HELD

HELD AT SLIGHT ANGLE

FIG. 6

TURNING EDGE WITH GOUGE

STAGES IN SHARPENING

FIG. 1. At A are the square corners after filing and oilstoning. B shows how corners are turned with hard rounded tool such as a gouge. After wear, corners become rounded, making it difficult to produce a burr (see C). How the scraper works is shown at D.

FIG. 2. Rub down edges with flat file used as shown.

FIG. 3. Remove coarse file marks on oil stone. Note rag to prevent injury.

FIG. 4. Hold each side in turn flat on the oilstone and give a few rubs.

FIG. 5. Place scraper flat on bench and draw the gouge along each edge in turn, keeping gouge flat.

FIG. 6. Let scraper overhang bench edge about 1/2 in., and, holding gouge at slight angle, draw it twice in each direction. Treat each edge in the same way.

FIG. 7. Hold scraper as here, slightly bowing with the thumbs, so that corners do not dig in.

It should remove fine shavings, not dust. When scraper becomes dull repeat processes 5 and 6. When this fails to turn the edge, rub down with file and oilstone again.

Fine Woodworking magazine was just starting to publish.

I was good at learning from books; all were devoured. I had a friendly local librarian who showed me how to borrow books from anywhere in the country. I would go home with more woodworking books than I could carry.

I had a workroom that had been my studio. Soon it turned into a workshop. I got a small Startrite table saw and a tiny Startrite band saw. The planer, a solid cast 9", could be used only when Betty, my neighbor, wasn't needing a nap. At this time I had no income except an unemployment payment. The authorities didn't see my attempts to retrain myself as being supportable in the long term, but thankfully they didn't stop giving me a few quid. My long-term partner, Jan Savage, put up with a great deal from me, and I have to say a huge "thank you" to her for the financial and emotional support she gave me at this crucial time.

Nothing came easy. My dad had given me a really good tool box with proper tools when I was a boy. But the metal plane in that didn't work like the lovely wooden planes we had in the school woodwork shop. The chisels were blunt, and I learnt then that having really sharp tools is so very important. (For those of you impatient to get to Rowden and the woody tool-sharpening bit, I will talk about that very soon. I love going out of sequence.)

I was keen to learn the right way to do things. Authenticity of process, going about it the best way, seemed important. I saw that most clearly in the makers who came from the workshops of the English Arts & Crafts movement, such as Ernest Gimson.

Then I came across people like James Krenov and John Makepeace. Very few woodworkers of my generation could fail to be affected in one way or another by Krenov. His books put meat on my bones and fire in my belly. They were the first woody books that talked about the "why." Why the heck do we spend an extra half-day fiddling to get that corner right, not nearly, but damn right! Jim got me going, but his whole attitude was that of the amateur. Nothing wrong with that, but My Madness was: Could I do what Jim had done, in the way Gimson had done it? Could I do this maybe with a small team and turn a penny?

Makepeace was also a considerable influence. He suggested that if you did it right, you could turn a penny, which is what I wanted to hear. He took the doing of craft furniture making and added two more dimensions: good business management and good contemporary design. This concept of standing on three legs, not two, was one that sustained me, and one I now suggest to students.

But still I was struggling with making. I didn't know if I could do it. The books and magazines taught me a great deal, but I really needed some help.

And here I have a problem…what do I call him? I can't use his real name because – how do I put this? – he may have not been entirely honest in his woodworking. And he has family that could well read this book. Let's call him Fred. I came across Fred because of the partner of one of Jan's old girlfriends. That partner was a dealer in long case clocks, and Fred was one of his restorers. I knew that the antiques business was full of rogues and vagabonds, but Fred seemed on reputation to be very skilled. I was given an introduction to Fred.

"Go see Fred if you want to make things in wood; he may help you."

Well he didn't help. I banged on his door twice then couldn't utter a word. FFFFFFFF…… Fs are difficult, as well. This stranger just looked at me and slammed the door. And he did it twice. Until I showed him a note.

"Why didn't you show me this sooner? Come in."

Fred had a very small workshop with a back room. I never got to see inside the back room; Fred kept that locked up. I'm sure for the first few visits he thought I was from the Inland Revenue. "I don't teach," he said again and again. "But FFFFFFred, I will work for you and I don't need paying." "Hmmmm….This is unusual. You are telling me that you will work for me for nothing?" "YYYYYEs." "See that tabletop? Scrape it down," he said, chucking a cabinet scraper at me. He then walked away, but he watched me for a while. I saw him clearly struggle with an internal battle before he came over. "No, not like that; like this," he said, slightly bending the scraper and immediately getting not dust, but a ribbon-like shaving.

Fred had the Japanese concept of teaching. He sometimes ignored me for days, until my struggles convinced him that he really should help – that it would be the kind thing to do.

As the morning wore on, my thumbs became scorched with the heat of working this thin piece of steel in the mahogany. Fred watched and let me get to

Fig. 8.2. The traditional English workbench and tools were a ways off in the future for David.

the point of chucking the scraper across the room.

"Here – wrap your thumbs in tape; that will keep them cool." I guess he tested me for ages. I couldn't go there every day, just now and again. I didn't tell Jan I was going to see Fred. I sensed that his position "in the trade" made him someone she would not approve of.

But over a period, I guess Fred got the idea that I wanted to learn, and that I could help out, and that I was not from the Inland Revenue. Sometimes I would turn up and he would throw a blanket over a piece he had been working on. Long case clocks were Fred's thing. I guess that if you brought Fred a 17th-century long case clock for restoration or repair, what you got back would be beautiful and polished…but it might or not might not have been your clock case. Fred was that good at "restoration."

It was this misuse of great skill that made me swear to never get involved with reproduction or antique re-pairs. (Which was a shame because I was thinking that both were valid ways to turn a jolly good penny. But it seems that it was not for me.)

Fred taught me about things other than woodwork. One morning, I came in with his post. There was a

white envelope that he picked up with great suspicion.

"This, David," he said, rapping the envelope on the bench, "this is trouble." He put the envelope down on the bench and ignored it for the rest of the day. "Are you going to read that letter Fred"?

"No, they want money; they can wait 'til I earn it."

It was a letter from Inland Revenue.

It took a long time to work out that I could do this woodwork lark, that making was what I was here for. But making wasn't enough. The design had to be an integral part of it, for there was no point in spending three months making unless it was worth that time. And it was the design that determined whether it would end up in the great dumpster of history in 20 years or be kept because it was "quite nice." And then it had to turn a penny. Not as a primary thing; I have made lots of things that have lost money, and I am still pleased that I made them. Money is a good thing to make with your hands. So three legs, not two. Making, Design and Business Management.

MOVING TO DEVON

London had been great. I had lived there since coming up to the Royal Academy Schools in 1971. But it was 1983, and the shine was going off the place. This was Margaret Thatcher's Britain, with no place for small business, and that's what I was becoming – a small-business person. I tried selling small desk sets to big stores with a little success. I tried making furniture for friends and relatives with a little success. I wanted to make designs for industry but found that copyright issues gave me little protection. I could work for months to bring a product to market only to find a copy made very quickly.

The short time I had with Alan Peters was eye-opening, and it urged me to move toward Devon. The bombs were going off in London. The IRA were intent on reminding the English of who they were. I remember shopping near Harrod's when a bang made my ears ring, and it made me wonder if I was in the right place.

My partner of many years, Jan Savage, was a newly qualified teacher, so moving nearer to her family made some sense. A job came up in Bideford in North Devon. Jan went for the interview. I looked around the estate agents, and we arranged to compare notes at half-time. She liked the school and I liked the town.

All my life, saying my name, saying who I was, introducing myself, had been a huge hurdle

Fig. 9.1. A bit remote. With its narrow (very narrow!) sunken lanes, Devon is a world away from London.

that kept me not locked away, but reluctant to put my hand out and say, "Hi I'm David Bbbbbbbbbb." For the stammerer, B bbbbbbb is right on the front of the lips; they are pursed hard together, and the more you try the worse it gets. Saying a word beginning with "B," or "M" or "F" or "T," seeing it coming up in the sentence was high stress. David Binnington was who I was. Saying who I was was a Bbbbbbbbbbitch.

I don't want to moan about this. I didn't ever let it get me down. But imagine a stammerer making a phone call: "Hello, I'm David Bbbbbbb," and then a curious, strangled, buzzing noise. I used to say it was like trying to talk whilst eating a very dribbly bacon and egg sandwich. I almost never made phone calls, but I would pick up the phone if it rang. I hated those kind souls who would want to finish my sentences.

"I am trying to find some Mmmmmmmmmmmmm-mmmm, dribble."

"Do you mean Marmalade?"

"No, thank you. Mmmmmmmmmmmmmouse traps."

The stammer had to an extent framed my existence thus far. When I was young, I attended speech-therapy sessions each week. Usually, they were kind ladies who saved me from the double period of maths, which I hated. They had no effect on my stammer whatsoever, and I did try to help them. When I asked one kind lady, "Do you knnnnnnnnow what causes a stammer?" Her reply was very frank and honest, "No, I am afraid we don't." I gave up with speech therapists. Even double maths wasn't as futile as that.

I had chosen art as an area in which to shine – an area that was mute, that had no language and now that had bombed. I was looking at a change of life that also allowed me to sit quiet, or run around, but work without much language. I hope I didn't let the stammer dominate, but it was a surprising relief when this cloud lifted a little.

My task was to go around all these estate agents in this new town, Bideford. Savage was easy to say; Binnington was not; So, I used Jan's surname: Savage. "Ah, Mr. Savage, we may well have property for you." That's interesting. I was able for the first time in my life to freely introduce myself, and if a little stumbly and dribbly, I could engage with folk and chat away.

Much later, with the help of Jan's solicitor father, I changed my name to David Binnington Savage, and dropped the Binnington. It wasn't smooth, but the

Fig. 9.2. One of the many models at the Rowden studio.

change was positive, and the more I talked, the better I got at it. Within a few years, the stammer was no longer an issue. I would stand up in front of small audiences and babble away without blocking. I still stammer if I am tired, but mostly I am now fluent. I can stand on a stage with an audience and wave my arms about like an idiot. BbbbbbbBinnington, however, still scares the hell out of me.

The essence of this is that I was training neural pathways basic to human existence. This talking lark should have been sorted out when I was a child. But it wasn't. There I was, a grown man in my 30s, learning to talk. And doing it with some success. When I came much later to seek to teach people to draw, I remembered this. Skills and practices such as drawing and talking can be learned and taken up at any age. Provided you are determined enough to do the practice, drawing will come. Those neural pathways will open up. (More on this to come.)

It's a bit like broadband – use it more, pay a bit more, get a bigger pipe, download those movies faster. Have more fun; use it more. The more practice, the better you get. That rings a little bbbbbell with me.

Fig. 9.3. A Devon sunset, 2015.

ALAN PETERS:
THE MISERABLE MENTOR

Alan Peters wasn't really that miserable, but it felt like a cold wind when he was looking at your work. I first met Alan when I went on a residential short course at his workshops. I think it was two weeks, and a group of four of us were making a small cabinet with doors and a single drawer. Typical Alan, he assumed we could do all that from scratch in a short a time because he could do it in his sleep.

The workshops were wonderful and they were in Devon, where I later moved, largely to be nearer to this man. Three old barns around a quadrangle formed the workshops. The barn on the right was a machine shop, the left barn was a timber store and ahead a long bench room with views over the fields. The sun came in the afternoon though multiple roof windows, and we either closed the curtains in the afternoon or moved the work out of the way. I was there during a workshop holiday so we were with Alan, not his staff. But it was brilliant to be in a commercial workshop, feeling what it should be like. I later worked hard to create that atmosphere in my bench shop – one of focus and intense concentration.

I think this was the first and last summer school that Alan offered. I can accept full responsibility for that. I was the one scratching on the studio doors at seven in the morning and the last one at night asking damn silly questions. This man had all the answers. I put him through the mangle with my pestering questions.

There's a joke about cabinetmakers and light bulbs

Fig. 10.1. Elm stool. This stool, designed by Peters, was made in batches by his apprentices.
PHOTO: DAVID BARRON

that was told at Alan's funeral: "How many cabinetmakers does it take to put in a light bulb? Ten – one to put in the bulb and nine to work out how Alan Peters would have done it!" This was the reverence he was held in by many makers of my generation.

The thing wasn't just that he made so well, or that he made contemporary furniture. Others were doing that. But he was selling it and employing two makers, seemingly without compromise. I may be wrong, but you never saw a kitchen being made in his Cullompton shop or restoration work done for a local antique dealer.

This was, however, at the beginning of the 1980s. There were precious few small workshops doing this, and recent exhibitions had turned up the volume of potential enquiries. Although I could not see this at the time, we were at the beginning of wave that David Savage Furniture and many other small furniture makers rode into the next century. People were fed up with high street pieces and were content to pay more for a nice dining table, well-made from good, solid, native hardwoods. What was more, they would wait. They would come and visit the workshop and get involved in the process of having a single piece made just for them.

As my questions became more probing, Alan didn't flinch, bless him. "How much do you sell those tables for, Alan, and how long do they take?" His responses were straightforward and clear. I remember one time he encouraged me to include a lot of timber in a design

Fig. 10.2. At the bench. Alan Peters
was a legendary craftsman in the
U.K. and had direct links to the Arts
& Crafts movement.
PHOTO: COURTESY OF FURNITURE & CABINET-
MAKING

for a low table. "They seem to think it's much more valuable, having a great slab of ash, but you only paid so much a cube."

The guts of what he knew, however, was bread and butter Arts & Crafts making. He knew how wood expanded and contracted, and his contemporary designs worked within these restrictions. He was fast and accurate, though in later years when I knew him, he was not as fast as his makers. Keith Newton, one of his assistants, once complained to me of Alan coming down from his drawing studio and messing up some pieces that would have been perfectly fine if left alone to them. This, as I know, is the penalty of not being on the tools every day.

Fig. 10.3. Serving table. Wenge and yew.

PHOTO: CHRISTOPHER SCHWARZ

I remember Canadian furniture maker Michael Fortune telling me that he had a grant to come to England. A part of that visit was to spend time with Alan. Michael had training at a college in Canada and was aiming to design for the emerging furniture industry in Canada. He told me that the trip to England and his time with Alan helped him toward seeing the possibilities of designing and making in the small workshop, his workshop. Michael was stunned not only at the speed and fluency with which Alan worked, and often just with simple hand tools, but by the fact that Alan didn't seem to need all the giant machines. At that time, Alan didn't even own an electric drill. Neither did he see the need, as a brace and bit did a great job.

I never worked directly for Alan, but I saw him quite a lot. When I got established, he would come to Bideford and show slides of his work to a room full of makers at events I organised. Once, I got a phone call

from Alan: "David, the Devon Guild needs you." I was delighted; I was not yet a member and had hoped one day to become one. The Guild had recently purchased a huge former mill house in Bovey Tracey, and they were in the process of creating a shop and gallery. Being a member was a big number to me at that time.

"Come down Saturday, early, and I will show you what's up," Alan said. What happened was that Alan and Trevor Pate, another senior member and former shipwright, were in the process of fitting out what was to become the Devon Guild gallery and the shop. My job, as I was left behind in Alan's machine shop, was to plane up a stack of Devon ash, bigger than I could look over and nearly as wide.

"Get this done for me by tea time will you?" Alan said. "Good lad. Lock the door when you're done. Laura is out. See you later." I loved that man. I would have done that work with my teeth if that was all I had.

But he could be a stern critic. He would have hated some of the pretentious furniture made in the 21st century – eye-popping pieces made for the digital file rather than the human being. He believed, and I think he was right, that quiet integrity would eventually win the day.

"People will remember your mistakes far longer than your success."

"Don't go rushing to exhibit. Do a special piece each year if you can afford it, and show that locally."

"You really send the most awful Christmas cards."

These were all things he said to me. Like his furniture, he was honest through and through.

Fig. 10.4. Chest of drawers. Made in elm, it's typical of Peters' work. Notice the subtle curves to the rails between the drawers. This gave a finger grip to either top or bottom of the drawer and eliminated drawer handles.

PHOTO: DAVID BARRON

THE BIDEFORD WORKSHOP & DEREK PARKES

The Bideford Workshop was a great time for me. Situated in Westcombe Lane opposite the refuse lorry park, I had 2,000 square feet of space that had been used as a metal refinishing factory. It was a horrible, stinky, dark, cheap mess. I spent weeks putting in roof lights and electrical wiring to make it as much like Alan Peter's workshop as I could. I had little money and little paying work, but I could put my labour into making this place shine.

It's easy for me to say now, but it's important to work out what you will and will not do in the form of work. It's less easy to do this with no work and little money. It's that thing about knowing where you want to go. I said I would repair old furniture but would not do reproduction copies. I would not work in the antiques trade. I would not do fitted kitchens but I would do joinery work, doors and windows. Though there seemed little chance of that. Next door were the professionals. Des and Ginger were proper joiners, not imposters like me. Ginger would strangle a 1/2" router, cutting trenches in staircase stringers. You could hear it going from a scream to a low moan as Ginger dug it into the timber.

Des was, however, to remain a permanent reminder to us of the danger of woodworking machines. One Friday afternoon rushing to get done, he took the top of two fingers off on the jointer. These machines are Very Patient Meat Eaters.

Two thousand square feet of space on two floors was way too big for me, I thought. I arranged to rent out the ground floor and put all my machines upstairs in

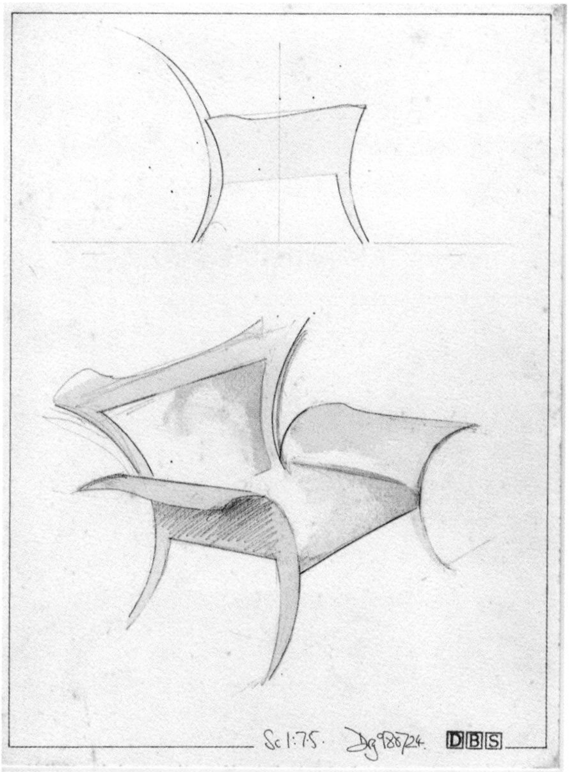

Fig. 11.2. Images now are bouncing around the world in moments. Then it was different. If you had any new-looking piece, you could get it featured in a glossy magazine for nothing!

what was becoming a nice, light-filled bench room with a lovely varnished solid-wood floor.

I found work soon enough making big Gothic solid-oak doors for a builder, and a regular task of assem-

Fig. 11.1. Though the Internet has changed many things about making a living at woodworking, it hasn't changed this: Good photography is important.

bling kitchen cabinets from flat-pack once a month. I made a small walnut bureau for a neighbour and a maple desk for a doctor in London. This was a good commission; the deal was I had made them a dining table for the cost of the timber whilst my pal was a medical student. When he qualified, I made him a desk for his office for real money. This was like being a real furniture maker.

There were disasters, as usual. (You are, I hope, beginning to expect that with me.) Des sent a local lady to me to who wanted a pair of beds. I did a lovely watercolour that sold the idea, but then couldn't make the bed ends look like the watercolour. She wanted her money back. I learned that what you show the client in the watercolour should be pretty much what she gets. My "in laws" helped out by buying the unwanted beds from me, bless them.

Getting pieces photographed was harder than it is now. It involved a studio and a man with a huge wooden-plate camera to make 5" x 4" transparencies. "Dupe Trannies" (duplicated transparencies) were then sent to magazines with a 300-word "who, what, where, when" blurb. Images now are bouncing around the world in moments. Then it was different. If you had any new-looking piece, you could get it featured in a glossy magazine for nothing! And that brought more work. For several years this was my major form of marketing. Free PR was sent to magazines and published regularly. Almost no month went by without David Savage Furniture Makers being featured in one glossy magazine or another.

The most important arrivals at that time were Malcolm Vaughan and Jim Duthie. They came to me from a local maker who needed to take a break from teaching. The trouble was, this was right in the middle of the courses Jim and Malcolm were taking.

I hated the idea of students and said "no thank you" when first offered these two students. I then returned to my labours. I was assembling a pile of kitchen cabinets that a local builder wanted done by Friday. Well maybe it would be better than this.…

This put me, only very recently part-baked, in the uncomfortable role of teacher. But I remembered an old saying: "In the land of the blind the one-eyed man is king." And I attempted manfully to stay one page ahead of my very clever students.

I had a precedent to follow. Edward Barnsley had

apprentices and fee-paying students. Among them was Oliver Morel, who first paid Barnsley then took a job with him as a maker after a year's training. Morel took the model and set up a teaching workshop, first in Wales then in Morton in the Marsh. It was this model of a commercial workshop with makers, apprentices and fee-paying students that I emulated. I didn't plan it, but it seemed to work.

The future would see this as a part of non-existent business plan. I would have a half-dozen employed makers, one or two apprentices and maybe three or four fee-paying students. The aim was to never to allow the students and apprentices to outnumber the skilled makers. The advantages were cash flow and potential skill. Like Barnsley with Morel, I could find good staff amongst my students. The thing I learnt about staff is that it's not what they know that matters, it's who they are. After a year, you have a pretty good handle on that.

On the other side were the apprentices. I trained a number of local guys in the Bideford workshop. Two of them, Neil Harris and Chris Hayward, have become exceptional makers. Neil was my first apprentice. He was straight out of school on a Youth Opportunities Programme. I was stunned by Neil's abilities on one of the earliest jobs I gave him: clean the greasy parts of a disassembled veneer press I had bought. Neil and I then set about assembling the beast. We had no instructions, just an A4 photocopy of what it looked like assembled. Whilst cleaning those parts, Neil had this thing assembled in his head.

"No, that goes over there, this fits in here." Neil Harris has gone on to become one of the best furniture makers I know. Fast, clever, efficient, he also trains spaniels to do amazing things at Field Trial Championships.

Malcolm, who stayed on as staff after his course, was also brilliant but in a different way. After his time as an executive at a paper manufacturer, Malcolm wanted to leave behind his experience with a large corporation. He brought to the workshop a wonderful sense of humour and a keen eye for business. The pine assembly bench became the boardroom table, and we each acquired corporate parking places – rank and position beyond our years. Malcolm made doing this fun. But as Malcolm was putting the briefcase away, I was getting one out. Not yet totally liberated from stammering, I had furniture to sell. It was Malcolm's experience in

Fig. 11.3. A photo competition. The photo of a chair (based on one from the Doge Palace) that changed everything.

public relations and his marketing wisdom that helped the place to tick more than anything.

About this time, I learned a valuable lesson about wealthy people. It began with a walnut desk that had been commissioned by a London architect friend. This was a prestige job for a building conversion in London's Covent Garden. It was right on the Piazza – a prime spot. My desk was to fit diagonally across the reception area. Malcolm and I worked and worked to get this spot on. Table delivered, everyone delighted, craftsmen paid.

A few weeks later I get a call: "The building has been sold. The new owners don't want your table, so it has been taken by the managing director of the developing company for his Dorset house. We suggest you get in touch with Derek's wife, Mary."

WHAAAAT!!!!…. I hated this. Malcolm and I had made this table for a specific place in the centre of London. Now it was going into some rich dude's country house – a disaster I sulked over for days. It turned into something unexpected.

Getting hold of Mary Parkes was not easy, and I didn't really want to do it. Making the phone call took me ages. When I did talk to her it was, "Oh I love your table! We are restoring a house in Dorset and we have put it there. We need some special dining furniture. Can you help us?"

I remember feeling extremely scared before I met Mary. I went trembling to a very smart address just off the Kings Road in West London. I came with some draft ideas of chairs and tables. Derek arrived later; he was genial and friendly and very much the worse for a few drinks. We settled nothing but agreed to meet at their Dorset house sometime later.

When we met again, Derek was on great form. He spent a whole morning showing me around a wonderful old house. He proudly showed me some of the restoration work. It was incredibly expensive but almost invisible. Derek took great pride and pleasure in what he was able to do to restore that beautiful old house. He introduced me to the gardeners and household staff; he knew each by name and knew about their

Fig. 11.4. The new owners don't want your table, so it has been taken by the managing director of the developing company for his Dorset house. We suggest you get in touch with Derek's wife, Mary.

families and children. This man was operating socially on a completely different plane to the rest of us. To me, he was amazing; I was bowled over. He liked making things, and enabling things to be made.

Mary and I worked on her ideas. Derek wanted chairs in which he "could have a great dinner party, consume a bottle of claret and not damage himself falling out of the chair." I remember Mary doing sketches of chair backs that I recognised from chairs in the Doge's Palace in Venice. I picked that up and developed it.

We made a table in solid English cherry and a set of chairs. It was the biggest job I had every done. I remember Malcolm and Neil sweating blood over it. Mary wanted holly and dyed blue veneer details to match her fabrics.

"We can do that," I said with complete conviction and total ignorance. We would find a way.

We delivered the pieces, the bill was paid and the client was happy. I brought over my photographer, John Gollop, to take a shot of the pieces in location. John did that, then did something that was to me extraordinary. He picked up a chair, carried it into the next

Fig. 11.5. Do the job well enough and you will be working for a small group of clients for 40 years.

room and put it in front of a full-length window. There was a huge potted plant behind it. The photo he took changed everything.

Derek and Mary were happy if I made versions of their chairs. I thought I might make two or three. John's photo and versions of it were in every glossy magazine for what seemed like months – the 1980s equivalent of going viral. It was an early confirmation of what furniture maker Garry Knox Bennett much later told me: "Dave, we are all in a giant photographic competition."

We were making these damn chairs in various timbers for clients all over the country for the next few years. But more important, it told me that I could do this: I could talk with people, nice people, such as Mary and Derek Parkes, and come back with ideas for furniture that would make their homes better places to live. I could listen to what they wanted and translate that into an image that fitted them like

a good suit of clothes.

Thankfully, I was a good listener; the stammer had taught me that. The first quality of a designer is to be a good listener, to take the brief and hear what is not always said. Then take the idea back to the workshop and make it. The making would be done without compromise; we would make as well as we could. Mary and Derek hadn't quibbled over price; they wanted something special – something like the house they were living in, something new but worthy of the place. IKEA wouldn't quite work here. The idea of "designing for clients" came directly from this job.

When I met Derek again nearly 30 years later, he was still at Blackdown House. His life has become a tribute to a wonderful English country house. We made another piece for the same room. I love that – do the job well enough and you will be working for a small group of clients for 40 years. They will always want you to make another piece.

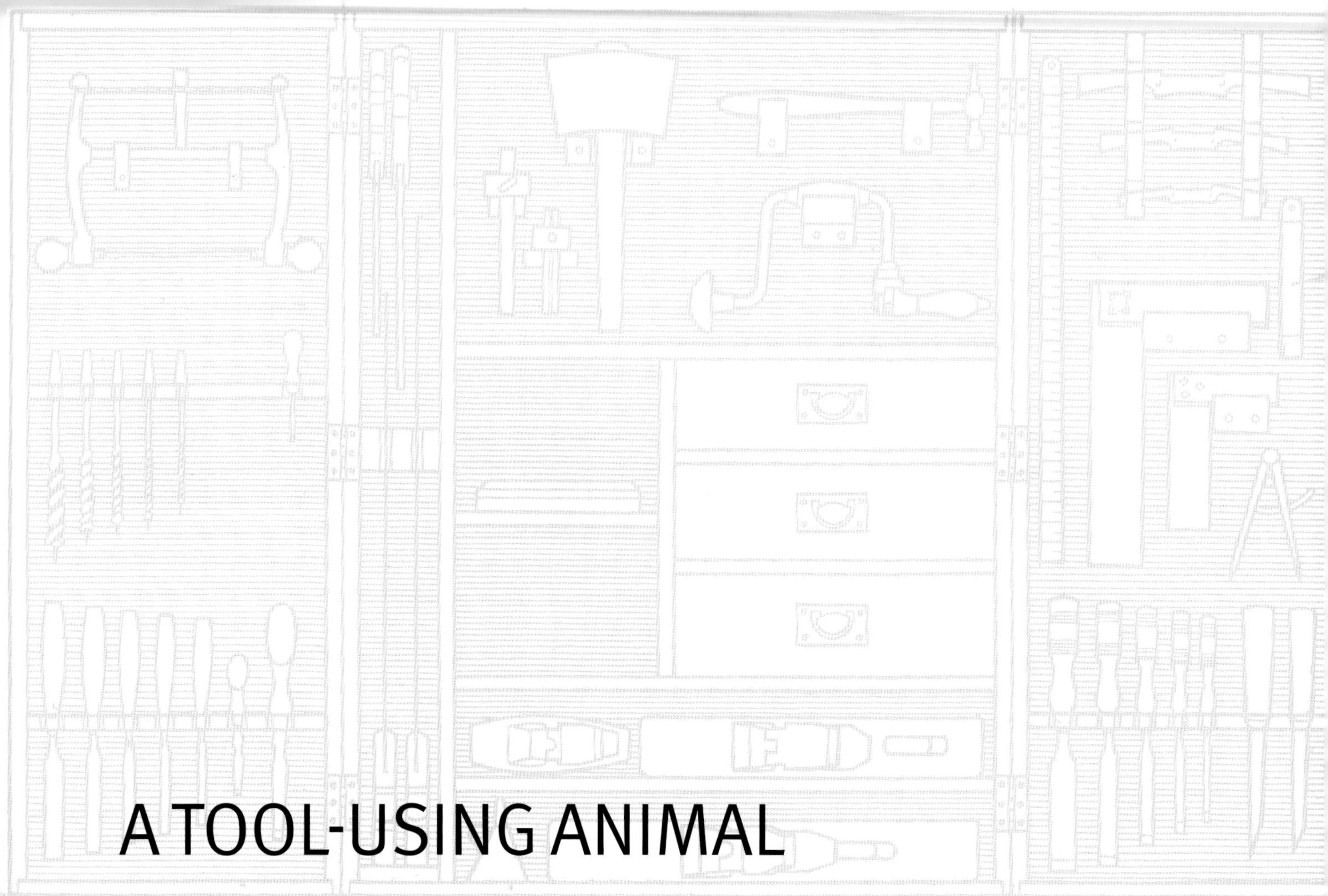

A TOOL-USING ANIMAL

I first learned what tools were from my dad. We were one of those families lucky enough to have a car. This was the 1950s, just after the war, and cars were less common in the United Kingdom than today. Dad had, I think, a Rover, and he was proud of it.

Saturday morning was car-looking-after time in the driveway of our house in Bridlington. Generally, it was a wash and polish; some weeks it was tyres to be checked and pumped up with a foot pump. He would put a gauge on the tyre to read the pressure then either let out air or pump it up furiously. I watched, and held the gauge as needed.

The best jobs involved lifting the hood and fiddling beneath. Nowadays there is little to fiddle with in a modern motor. German cars are reputed to have considered placing a notice under the hoods saying "Nichte Ge Fiddle Finger." But we are now back with Golden Age of fiddling about.

Dad would do this almost once a month, and I was there to help. He would lift the hood and place two pieces of old carpet on the wings so he could lean over one side, and I could learn over the other. I was about

7; my job was to hold the spanners that he needed, and point an electric lamp into the gloom. The rocker cover came off first and was carefully put aside. We were now into the oily innards of the beast. "Tappets" are where the valve head is pressed down with the rocking arm on the top of the engine. Dad would turn the engine with the fan belt until the valve was not in compression, then he would measure and set the gap between the top of the valve and the rocker arm. This was technical stuff.

This was where I came in, as dad had a floppy, thin feeler gauge, a screwdriver and a small spanner to manipulate around each valve head. The gap was critical. The "feeler gauge" was correctly named because this shim of steel felt the drag as the two surfaces were pulled down together and released. Dad needed it spot on. Each cylinder had two valves and there were four

Fig. 12.1. Toothing a panel. Using the teeth of a dovetail saw to prepare a panel for veneering.

cylinders, so this was a good morning's work. This was very bloke-ish stuff. Mum would never fiddle with the car. She had her own tools in the kitchen; the garage was where men did their stuff. I am not sure how effective Dad was; the engine always seemed to rattle. But I don't think Dad worried too much about it. He liked doing it, and Mum said it kept him out of her hair and out of trouble.

I cannot conceive of life without a shed or a basement. Somewhere to just be. Somewhere where my wife, Carol, would never come and tidy me up. (Never come, full stop, except to call me in for supper.) This is my space.

DIY in Britain has acquired a bad reputation due to appalling self-assembly furniture that doesn't self-assemble (included screws are too cheap to not burr over), and shelves that never go up straight because the walls they are fixing against are rubbish. The whole event is to be avoided if possible, unless you know enough to do it right — and that's a different game.

Dad gave me a toolbox when I was about 9. It wasn't a toy toolbox, but proper woodwork tools: a smoothing plane, chisels, a marking gauge, rules, a tenon saw and a small panel saw. All in a nice wooden box. I was speechless, literally.

The tools, though I loved them, caused me nothing but frustration. The plane didn't plane, the chisels were blunt and the saw nearly cut my hand off. Dad didn't know how to make the tools work, and I didn't have a bench to work on. Holding a job whilst working on it was a real problem. I played with the tools for a while until mum stepped in, put them in the box and made me wait for big school.

That's where I met the man in the brown coat — the woodwork master at Bridlington Grammar School. I think his name was Arthur Capewell. He could command a room full of 11-year-old boys simply by chucking a small offcut of pine across the room with deadly accuracy. He kept a modest supply of ammunition in the tool well of his bench. Mr. Capewell was a Lancastrian and had a reputation as a cricketer. Playing cover point, he would field a ball hit in his direction, see the attempted run and with deadly accuracy throw the ball at the wicket. This, I know, means nothing to Americans — but it impressed the heck out of a great number of small boys.

In his school workshop he had beech handplanes that hissed across the wood. They made a shaving, an eel-like electric band of thin pine that wriggled around in our hands. And there was the aroma like fresh antiseptic. Pretty, soon I was ankle deep in happiness.

This bliss, however, was not to last for long. Art and woodwork were what I did best. I was never a really clever child like some of my contemporaries. Year three and, "You can do either art or woodwork, not both." I did woodwork for two days until mum steamed into the headmaster's office and demanded I do art, not that messy, sweaty woodwork — it's so working class!

I carried on at home with my making. Model airplanes in balsa, covered in tissue paper or nylon and tightened with something even in those days called "dope." This became a hobby and a great source of satisfaction, making sleek, fast, functional flying machines. I even had a shed for it, and my hobby took all my evenings and weekends. I got plans of airplanes. I dug the garden to earn the money to buy a small 2.5cc petrol engine. A wonderful local man, Peter Warner, set up an aero modeling club that became the centre of my young life. But the life-cycle of the model plane seemed to me to be a little short. I would spend all winter building a sleek machine only to see it crash to destruction within a few moments of flight. Others in the club were better pilots and eventually I learned how to keep a plane airborne for longer than 20 seconds.

Peter played an important part in my growing up. He was headmaster of a local school and the father of Andrew, one of my good school friends. My own father died when I was 10, and Peter was happy to play a part in mentoring me. As I grew older, he would invite me over, I would be sat down in the living room with a glass of whiskey, and Peter would argue with me for the rest of the evening. Whatever opinion I presented, Peter would take up the opposite view, arguing with precision and clarity. It took me years to work out that he was just exercising my mind and my stumbling vocabulary. A firm believer in the Socratic tradition, was Peter. I owe him a great deal.

It was at about this time, when I was leaving for university, that I saw tools in use again. Sandra, my first real girlfriend, had a dad who was a highly skilled joiner. Ken Bulmer blew my socks off one evening at

Fig. 12.2. Truing a panel. A Japanese smoothing plane levels the border around a panel.

their place. We had just had tea and I was saying how I needed to buy a secondhand cabinet to store all my textbooks. Ken looked at me and said quietly, "Don't go spending your money lad; we will make you one this evening." Note the "we."

Ken took me out to the back where he had a shed and timber. Most of the wood was secondhand, reclaimed from years of making. Ken pulled out a dark veneered sheet and two thicker boards that matched the colour. "This will do it," he said. He then went for a bag of tools. He had a couple of trestles to work on, and I held the long boards as he marked out then sawed the components. He used a white chalk line on the faux rosewood polished surface. His saw shot down that line. He then picked a sharp smoother out of his bag and with two stokes that edge was smooth and straight.

"We can put a bit of stain on that edge to bring it together," he said. The sides and top were mitred by sawing to the line. He put three shelves into stopped dados on either side that he cut quickly with tenon saw, a chisel and an "old woman's tooth" router plane.

Fig. 12.3. Vintage Marples chisels.

Fig. 12.4. Note the thin edges on the side bevels on this vintage chisel.

The whole assembly was glued and pinned together, a back was fitted pinned and the edges were stained. All by 10 p.m.

"I want to see the news," Ken said. I had done little but hold the odd board, drive in a few pins and watch in stunned amazement at the skill of this wonderful man. "There yer are lad, that should do the job." It certainly did, Ken. It certainly did that.

There is no doubt that the tools in Ken's tool bag were not made as well as those we can buy now. I have seen a huge improvement in hand-tool manufacture in my working life, led by Lie-Nielsen Toolworks, Lee Valley/Veritas and others. There was a time when you bought a new Record plane in the late 1980s and you would have to flatten the sole every month for a year to get a plane that was nearly flat. It was a really bad time to become a maker.

But it's not totally better – the greatest market for hand tools is in the amateur American market. Amateurs are not great at sharpening, so jigs and sharpening systems abound. This leads us to A2 steel. It is pretty sharp, holds an edge for a long time and is easy

to manufacture. But it has led us away from O1 high-carbon steel cutting edges.

I fuss about this point because the cutting edge has control over the work. Sharpness is a key stage in understanding of your material. More sharp, less shove and better feel.

I guess I am losing this one. Many of my students do pretty well with modern A2, but I have had O1 carbon steel edges all my life and have seen and used the very best edge tools made in Sheffield before World War II. That for me is where the very best edge tools have been made. I have a chisel drawer filled with a mixture of narrow-neck Marples blades made in the 1960s and handmade Japanese chisels.

When I started buying tools, it was at a secondhand tool shop on Islington High Street in North London. I would spend hours there. The owner had all kinds of hand tools – not just woodworking tools – and he knew a lot about them. It was like first year at university all over again. I loved the idea of a tool that had been used and bore the handprint of the kind of man I wanted to become. I learned about companies such Ward, which had a reputation of making the hardest steel in Sheffield. A Ward paring chisel at huge expense became "a precious." (What the man didn't tell me was that the flatness of the back of that blade was not great, and that it would be the devil's own job to get flat!) I admired the balance of a long, thin, light blade against a boxwood handle. I loved the way the bevels created a thin edge down either side, diminishing to nothing at the cutting edge.

What I didn't realise at the time was the human cost that went into making a blade like this. "Ah, you can't get the grinders to die of lung disease in their late 30s any more," said Ray Isles, son of a Sheffield toolmaker. Apparently, they would sit on a bit of wood called an "arse board" with a water-cooled grindstone spinning between their legs. The blades were hand applied to the free-running stone. The work was better than we can achieve now, but at what a cost? I look at some lovely high-carbon spokeshave blades made now in China and wonder at that human cost.

I learned here about metal planes from the 1930s and 1940s – Spiers and Mathieson and, best of all, Norris. These were planes not manufactured but handmade. Heavy, beautifully forged blades, close-fitting

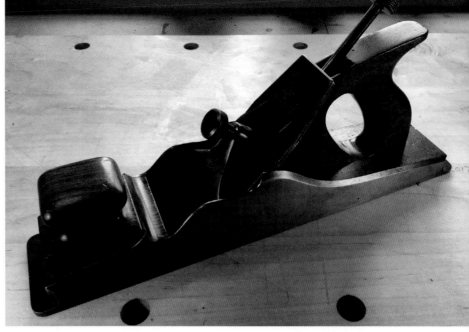

Fig. 12.5. A Norris infill panel plane.

back irons, small mouths and rosewood handles. These were the duck's guts of woodie hand tools, and I bled internally until I was able to afford one. I bought a pre-war Norris, 14" in length with a rosewood infill, a patent adjustment mechanism and a carbon-steel, thick, hand-forged blade. That plane has been with me for more than 30 years, and it would be the one thing I would grab were the workshop on fire. The blade is nearly shot, and it's way too heavy for an old man like me to use now. Light, super-efficient Japanese planes are putting it out of work in my bench shop. It is a great sadness that I no longer have the energy to use these lovely, precise handplanes.

We are suckers for tools – at least I am. All the shiny things on the shelves – we hope they give us identity as a maker, but they never do. However, I notice a different, more pragmatic approach from makers I greatly respect. Daren Millman could never have afforded a Norris plane in his apprenticeship, but he took the trouble to find and set up an old, flat, Bailey-frogged Stanley No. 6. Daren keeps very few tools about him and he knows at any moment where they all are. He knows that speed and accuracy comes with putting down and picking up tools efficiently. You never see Daren scrabbling about looking for a blade he has lost. He can see what tools are out and where they are. His benchtop is clear. But for the job, tools and stuff go in the tool well. That's why it's called a tool well. At the end of the day, he sweeps things clean and tidy, sharpens his tools and puts them away. Professional practice. We try to teach this at Rowden. At times it's like bombarding cabbages with gamma rays, but we try.

"Can I have a list of specific hand tools that I need, that tells me where to buy and which brand you recommend?"

It's not an unreasonable question, and it's one I am asked time and again. I shy away from it, as I know that once we give our recommendation to this or that manufacturer, our independence is compromised. I also know that hand tools have to fit the hand. For this reason, we have eight or nine toolboxes at Rowden that we loan to students. They all represent different manufacturers' offerings of saws, planes and marking-out tools. I suggest that each student try different brands and compare notes before making an informed purchase. You only want to buy these things once, so take some time to get it right. This does not stop students from abusing the system and hanging on to the loaner toolbox for much longer than they should. And it doesn't stop visitors from stealing small tools. But they know who they are, and they know that a woodworker version of Hell awaits them.

So this is Daren's list, developed in response to the question. It includes specific brands that we have found popular amongst Rowden students. Quite a few of the suppliers are British (as you would expect), but we are aware that some of the best hand tools are now being manufactured in Canada and the U.S.A. Daren, being Daren, avoids the "shiny tool syndrome" and sticks to the mantra of having the fewest tools around him that do the job.

Planes

No. 6 or No. 7 Bench Plane

No. 60-1/2 Block Plane (Lie-Nielsen Toolworks)

These are what I would buy were I a young maker (and they are popular in our workshop). I would try to get a carbon steel blade for finishing work to supplement the workhorse A2 blade supplied. There is still is a little bit of work to be done on these long. Dressing the sole

on fine abrasive attached to dead-flat glass will sometimes show a sole that is very slightly hollow in the
centre. This hollow can be taken out with careful work.

You need a special setup to do this, and quite expensive equipment to check flatness. A granite slab about
18" square and 3" thick is what we use for general
flattening. On this working stone we use water and
abrasive sheets of #180-grit wet/paper. The stone
backs up the abrasive sheet and provides a flat reference surface. We have another granite slab that is used
only for checking with light and feeler gauges. This
slab is reverently kept under a foam-lined box cover.
You do not damage this surface; it has been prepared to
atomic flatness and we have a certificate to prove it.

The mouth can be filed to give a relieved 80°, which
allows the shaving to pass when the blade is tight and
forward in the mouth.

The back iron can be fettled with a flat Japanese stone
to sit nice and tight. Research has shown that Japanese
planes have a tiny 70° stoned bevel at the point the
back iron comes down to back of the blade. My own
Japanese planes confirm this, and it suggests that this
small bevel is a good improvement to polishing performance. We should also note that for polishing work,
the back iron in a Japanese plane is pushed within a
hair of the edge. The Western 1/16" seems clumsy in
comparison. It seems to me that the back iron could be
improved in all Western planes.

No. 410 Shoulder plane (Clifton)

We have had great results with this plane, though we
also see people buying both the large and small Lie-
Nielsen Toolworks shoulder planes.

No. 80 Scraper Plane (Stanley)

This is another example of a simple tool doing a great
job. There are more complex and expensive versions,
but we don't see many of them here at Rowden. The
sole may need to be flattened on a glass plate and the
scraper blade sharpened to the specification provided
with the tool, but that's it.

Scrapers

Set of three Cabinet Scrapers (Clifton)

The hardness of the metal used for some scrapers is a
bit of an issue. Clifton seems to have it about right.

Fig. 12.6. Stanley No. 80 scraper plane.

Scraper Burnisher (Clifton)

Same thing goes for the Clifton burnisher — it has just
the right amount of hard surface on the burnishing
blade to do the job.

Chisels

Set of six Bevel-edged Chisels (Ashley Iles)

These light bench chisels have nice handles and the
blades are well shaped with bevels down to a thin edge.
By and large, they seem to get a good, flat, polished
back relatively easily. These are preferred because they
are light and sensitive to use; the heavier Lie-Nielsen
Toolworks blades are good and can be better when hit
hard with a mallet, but we advocate a slender blade that
will deal with gentle malleting.

Layout Tools

2" and 6" Engineers Squares (Moore and Wright)

I have used these metalworkers' squares for 35 years,
as a result of the poor quality of squares when I started.
Now, however, companies such as Starrett make high-
quality adjustable squares that are accurate enough
and have greater versatility. All our squares are checked
against a workshop square that does no work and is
known to be "spit bonk." (I should also admit that we
have considered making our own squares as a part of
the course. Light wooden tools are great thing to have.)

Fig. 12.7. Adjustable square, double square and square.

Fig. 12.8. Marking gauges.

Fig. 12.10. Marples marking gauges.

Beveled Straightedges, 450mm and 750mm
This is where we cheat. A genuine straightedge from Starrett would cost a huge amount. We suggest that students buy a relatively cheap straightedge from Axminster Tools & Machinery, a local supplier. We do this knowing it will not be straight, but that the bevel-edge design leaves us with a very thin edge to get dead flat. This we can do with equipment in the shop. We use a dead-flat bench with a long, thick sheet of glass. On this we fix relatively fine #180-grit abrasive and carefully dress the straightedge. We then compare it to the expensive 2' square, dead-flat checking stone to make sure the edge is true. If you lack this fettling equipment, you may want to get a Starrett.

Four No. 2 Marking Gauges (Joseph Marples)
You will need a number of marking gauges. These shown above are relatively inexpensive and can, with a drilled hole, become a pencil gauge. There are many other more expensive ways of gauging a line than this. A steel and brass gauge with a small cutting wheel is an example. I have had experience teaching with the latter and find it an easier tool for the beginner to use. Bear in mind that in both cases, you need to have two tools: one with the cutter's bevel edge facing in and another with it facing out. You then use the most appropriate tool.

1,000mm, 600mm, 300mm and 150mm Rules
We are a metric shop and you may be Imperial (United States Customary Units). Just make sure you have good, accurate rules that all tell you the same measure down the entire length. Having a square that is out of square and measuring tools that are not accurate is like having a traitor in the camp, constantly undermining your quest for good work. I like the metal rules that have the measurements engraved in the surface; you can feel them with a fingernail.

250mm Sliding Bevel (Veritas)
This is an important tool, and I would not dispute Daren's suggestion that Veritas (a Lee Valley Tools brand) makes a good version. Whatever you buy, make sure

Fig. 12.11. Blue Spruce Toolworks spear-point marking knives.

Fig. 12.12. Pax dovetail saw.

Fig. 12.13. Knew Concepts (red) and Groz coping saws.

the means to lock the blade is easy to use and works to really lock the damn blade.

Dovetail Marker
There are lots of dovetail markers on the market; we even considered having one made. Be aware that the surface will wear as you run a sharp marking knife against it. Dress it with #180-grit sandpaper on a flat benchtop.

Japanese Marking Knife (Axminster Tools & Machinery)
This is Daren's best advice in a complex area. The Japanese knife is made of very hard steel and holds a good edge. I have a favourite Blue Spruce Toolworks marking knife that might be considered a bit "unnecessary" – I like the thin blade that will click into a line and send a message back to the hand. But I have always been picky about marking knives.

No. 3 Scalpel and Blades (Swann Morton)
This is where Daren goes against common practice in recommending the use of sensitive surgical sharp cutting knives. He overcomes the bevel on both sides by slightly angling the blade. When it dulls, he just fits a new blade in the handle. These inexpensive and high quality scalpels are an excellent substitute for a more expensive marking knife.

150mm Digital Calipers (Axminster Tools & Machinery)
These calipers are almost too accurate. We have had students take a measure in one studio, go upstairs and take another, and get two readings. This way madness lies. My advice is buy the cheapest plastic calipers with a dial clock that you can find. These will be accurate enough and allow you to drop them without too much expense.

Saws

Dovetail Saw (Lie-Nielsen Toolworks)
The Lie-Nielsen saw is very popular at Rowden (but the little Pax saw is very good, and it's one I would also recommend).

Coping Saw and Piercing Saw (Groz)
Both of these saws have become pretty standard at Rowden and get a fair amount of use. The coping saw,

Fig. 12.14. A veneer saw.

Fig. 12.15. A variety of Japanese hammers.

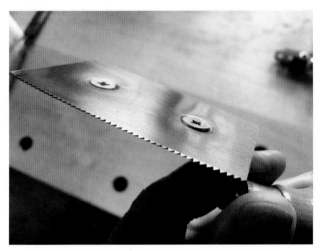
Fig. 12.16. Here you can see how the face of the veneer saw needs to be flattened before use.

when coupled with good blades, is a good tool. The red piercing saw is a new addition and an improvement on previous versions. Just be sure to release the blade tension when you store it.

Veneer Saw (Victor)
This is a cheap veneer saw so expect to do some work on it. Remove the blade and stone the blade dead flat where it attaches to the handle. Then take the blade and stone a bevel on one side of the blade. This brings the teeth to a point and helps the saw to cut a clean, sharp line across a bundle of veneers.

Miscellaneous Tools

Wooden Spokeshave (Woodjoy)
I don't know this brand, but if Daren rates it pretty good, it's good. I have seen nice, small Chinese spokeshaves. Look for high-quality carbon steel blades; they take a great edge.

Hammers
Daren has on his list a white rubber mallet from Thor, and a Stanley claw hammer, Warrington hammer and pin hammer. This is a modest start. I have a separate drawer in my tool chest for hammers and have gathered all sorts over the years. My favourites are Japanese hammers of all sizes and weights. I love 'em.

Screwdrivers
Same with screwdrivers – I have a drawer full of those. Power-driven screws have nearly taken over, but in top-quality work there still is the need for a brass screw with a slotted head. It is proper to fit a screwdriver to that screw. It need not be a new driver, but take it to the sharpening bench and stone the sides of the blade until the screw head just sits tight on the blade. Then stone off the corners that poke out. Now you are set.

Veneer Roller
Daren likes the 40mm stainless veneer roller from Axminster Tools & Machinery. If you are going to do any amount of veneering, a veneer roller is essential. I

Fig. 12.17. A drawer full of drivers.

see Daren using it to knock the tape down onto the job when taping up.

Dividers

While not on Daren's list, I feel dividers are essential. These are marking and measuring tools used when developing proportions within a design. When we want a relationship of 5:8, the question is five what? Inches? Feet? Miles? Or is it just the gap between these sharp pointy ends? This, I believe, was the way artisans developed designs without calculators or great mathematical skill. Starrett makes the dividers shown here.

Waterstones

We have looked at all sorts of sharpening systems but kept with Japanese waterstones, as they are the quickest and most effective. Also, in a teaching workshop, they tend to be the least expensive to replace. We recommend two stones: a brown stone to turn a burr (a grit of about #1,000) and a gold stone (of about #4,000) to polish. You can also get a Nagura stone. Use this to

Fig. 12.18. Starrett dividers.

Fig. 12.19. Safety equipment, such as ear defenders are essential for machine work.

PHOTO: WR PHOTOGRAPHY

work up a slurry on the gold stone that will help you get a quick polish on the blade.

This is enough at the start. Get used to these two stones before going higher. (I have natural waterstones in my personal setup and they are spectacular – but they are not for the beginner.)

Safety Equipment

Daren lists safety glasses and ear defenders from Uvex, and a cup mask respirator from Alpha Solway. We also suggest that boots have steel toe caps.

Safety stuff is dull and it's long-term protection. If you are young now and in a workshop for the next 30 years, you won't notice your hearing going for another 10 to 20 years – but by then it will be to late. Protect yourself now.

SHARP SHARP

This is a wonderfully controversial subject, and one that will have the trolls thundering about. This isn't a system; it is just a way of doing it quickly, without unnecessary jigs and other tools that always get lost or slow you down.

We use the tool in your hand that needs touching up and the stones on the sharpening bench – nothing else.

Sharpness is a fundamental thing to making with wood. If you want to cut timber, you need to grind an edge tool that is sharp and at the correct angle; without that you will be exerting more effort than you need. What we want is control of the edge. To exercise control you need to use less effort.

A description of a really sharp edge that I like is "keen." Now there is an adjective to conjure with: An edge that is keen is eager to get into that timber to slice and pare away, and it tells you about every fibre before it. That means short but frequent visits to the stones. An edge might get slightly dull, but it should never get blunt. That would be neglectful. It's professional practice that benches are cleared at the end of the day and all tools are put away sharp.

The sharpness is there to give you sensitivity, a feel for what is happening at the cutting edge. There is no better way to learn about timber than through a selection of sharp hand tools. Stuffing that board through a machine may be what you have to do later, but right now, learning about that board means sharp edge tools.

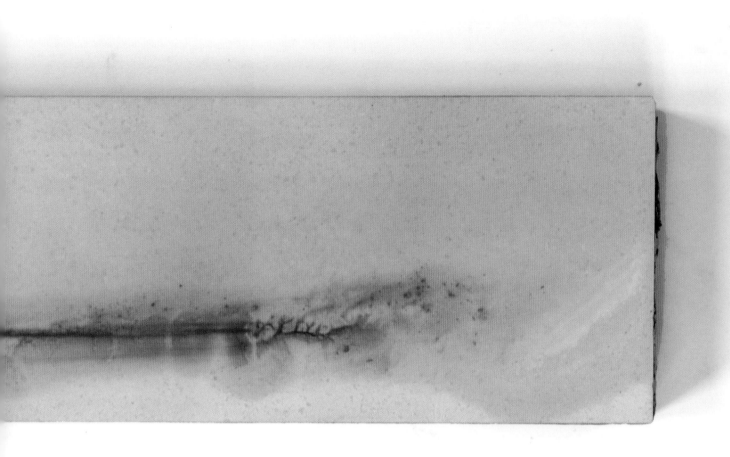

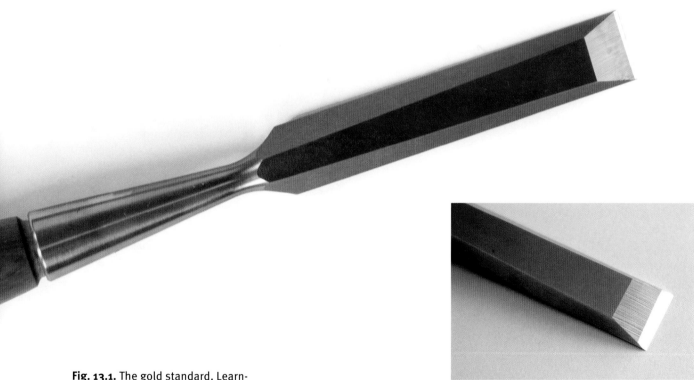

Fig. 13.1. The gold standard. Learning to sharpen is the gateway to many other woodworking skills.

Fig. 13.2. A polished chisel edge is a joy to behold and use.

Fig. 13.3. A set of six Marples chisels.

Look at the design of this tool – a nice wooden handle and a blade. The blade will probably have bevels from the top of the blade down to the sides. We like a bevel-edged chisel; it means that we can see more easily where the corners are cutting. You will find out that it's the corners of a chisel that do most of the work. We like and advocate looking for some of the older Sheffield steel chisels where the bevels have been hand ground to give slender sides and great visibility.

We have used all sorts of sharpening stones over 35 years in practice, but we keep coming back to manufactured Japanese waterstones for general use. Waterstones are soft, and with use, they quickly go out of shape. So you need a way to keep your stones flat. We use a 15"-square granite slab with a dead-flat surface upon which we place fresh wet/dry #180-grit sandpaper. Water holds the paper

flat to the granite and the abrasive cuts the stone. Water is the lubricant. Rub the stone face down on the wet abrasive; you can see a hollow in your stone – the dirty blackish area in the middle that with each rub gets smaller and smaller. In our busy workshop, this flattening method seems to work. (I have natural waterstones in my personal studio; these I keep flat with a small diamond-embedded plate.)

Let's start the sharpening talk with chisels. These are primary hand tools and need to be nicely kept. We have leather tool rolls to store chisels in our beginners' toolboxes. When students build a bench, they include tool storage that keeps sharp edges from clanging together.

Look at the back of the blade; this is where sharpness begins. You need that blade to have a back that is flat enough to stay in contact with a dead-flat sharpening stone. Bumps in either the stone or blade make sharp-

Fig. 13.4. Granite flattening stone.

Fig. 13.5. The hollow back of a Japanese chisel.

Fig. 13.6. The brown stone for coarse work,

ening difficult.

Your aim is to get the back of the chisel flat enough to contact the stone across its entire cutting edge. Start with the brown waterstone to see how flat the back is.

Start by rubbing the back of the blade on the #1,000-grit stone, making sure the stone is supported well on a flat surface. An even greyness should show up across the blade's back to soon tell you how flat its surface is. Add water regularly and change the position of the stone so you rub the blade on it in different areas. If your blade is very uneven, you may need a coarser stone or move to #180-grit wet/dry sandpaper on a granite surface before coming back to the stones. Most modern blades are pretty good and come flat fairly quickly.

Don't rub for more than three minutes at a time, because the waterstone can hollow in three minutes.

We use a kitchen timer to stop people from doing that. Go to the flattening setup after three minutes to keep your stone flat.

Your gold stone (#4,000 grit) will take the grey away and give a lovely shine. That will also quickly tell you how flat the chisel back is or is not. Getting the backs of the blades to an even shine, corner to corner, is the basis of sharpness. You need your chisel's back flat to have intimate contact with the equally flat stone when you are sharpening; this is WHY you are doing this. That surface, the chisel back, will now need only to touch the gold stone during future sharpenings – so do the flattening job once and do it properly.

Before I go much further, I'd better write about steel and get myself into trouble. The process of hand-tool development in my lifetime has been away from O1 carbon steel toward the harder A2 steel for chisels and

Fig. 13.7. The dry grinder at Rowden.

for plane blades. This harder steel is popular because it holds an edge for a long time. For those who find sharpening a difficult chore, this is no doubt attractive. There are all kinds of nifty sharpening gauges that bring these tools to the stone at the precise angle. They are generally slower to set up and cumbersome to use. I gave up using mine when Alan Peters saw me using a honing gauge and gave a low moan. They are like training wheels on the kid's bike – great to get you going but shameful after a few days of use.

At Rowden, we take a different view. We believe that O1 carbon steel is superior and urge students to use it – if they can get it. This is because it gives us a sharper edge than A2, which hold a duller edge for longer. It is also easier to learn to sharpen with O1, as the burr comes off more easily and cleaner, often in one piece. With A2, the burr hangs on and comes off in small clingy clumps. (More on burrs to come.)

We teach people to use their bodies as a sharpening jig and to go to the sharpening bench for a short time and often. Sharpening should become routine when your back aches and your eyes cloud after 15 minutes of paring – this is when that edge in your hand should be touched up, meaning a quick rub on the stones then back to work.

One of the ways we assess makers who want to work at Rowden is to look at their tools. If Daren sees evidence of the use of sharpening jigs, he generally does not offer the job. A professional maker can be at the sharpening bench several times a day. The speed and efficiency of that process is critical to economic viability and the overall economic viability of the workshop. Sharpening at Rowden should be a quick routine every day, a multiple-times-a-day activity. If you regularly find yourself taking a bundle of dull and blunt blades to the sharpening bench, begin questioning your practice.

Now let's look at the other side of the chisel, the bevel side. You will see two surfaces here: one is a ground surface made by a machine, a grinder of some sort; the other is right at the cutting edge, a polished, honed surface. We want to work on that ground surface and make the honed surface as small as possible, but leave part of it.

We have two grinders at Rowden: a water-cooled slow-cutting grinder that students new to woodworking use; we also have a dry grinder that more experienced students quickly get the hang of. Not many professional makers would use the water-cooled grinder because it's too slow. But an amateur, for whom time is of less importance, could be on there all morning and

Fig. 13.8. Waterstone holder with stops to restrain the stones. Note the Nagura stone on the gold stone.

get a very good result.

The dry grinder is a dangerous tool. Always wear eye protection and treat this machine with respect. Ours has a cool-running white wheel that's about 1" across . The secret to using a dry grinder is to dress the cutting surface of that wheel to a slight dome. It should never be flat. We use a diamond dressing stone with which we dress the grindstone to removing all debris from it and leave a slightly domed surface. This is done at least once a week. Friday cleanup usually sees this wheel and other stones on the sharpening bench checked out.

There is danger to yourself, but the other danger is to your tools. The heat created in the removal of steel from the blade builds up in the steel. Alarmingly quickly, the thin edge of a blade can become over-heated. "Blued" is the term, and blue is what you will see appear. It comes as fast as light. Keep a pot of water by the grinder and dunk the blade before you see this happen. If you feel heat, back off, slow down. The dome in the wheel will mean that it cuts only in the centre. Move the blade to the left and then to the right, and don't neglect the corners.

With a solid, accurate shop-made tool post (jig) fitted to your grinder, you can take the blade off and put it back at exactly the same angle. So what is the angle? We grind chisels and plane blades pretty much at 25°. Some Japanese tools and some A2 steel chisels come in to Rowden at 30° (A2 does not like low grind angles); we usually regrind them at 25°.

There are occasions to use a higher or lower grind angles, but these are unusual. A fine paring chisel that will never be struck with a mallet can be ground to 20° and honed to 25°; a chisel that will be whacked hard can be taken up to a 30° grind and honed to 35°.

Now let us understand honing. This is where you put a polished surface on the bevel side to meet the polished surface on the back of the chisel. Let me repeat that – it is important. We are bringing two polished surfaces together to meet at an angle of just a bit more than 25° – but not more than 30°.

The surface from the grinder is rough like a ploughed field; you need to turn it into a smooth, flat shiny top. You do this with two stones. Stones that you keep flat and lovely.

Place the brown (#1,000-grit) with its narrow end about 2" from the edge of the bench and running away from you. Find a way to secure the stone to the bench-top (we have two stops that the stones fit into, or we use a non-slip cloth). Make sure the stone is damp (we usually keep them in a water bath). Now, and this is the good bit, your sharpening bench should be relatively high so that when you stand and press the concave ground surface of the chisel against the stone at its far end, you don't find your shoulders hunched up and you are not on tippy toes. This should be a natural stance for you.

Settle the blade on the stone at the far end of the stone. It will sit on two points because it is a concave surface – that's OK. This sets the angle of 25° that we want. That is the angle at which the grinder tool post is set. Tuck your elbows into your body and draw the chisel back toward you. There should be a black mark on the stone where the chisel has left steel particles behind. You are the honing jig; as you pull back, the chisel slightly lifts. That is good; that is what you want.

What we are looking for is contact with the honing stone on the very front of the blade only. The lifting will increase the honing angle, and it should be the smallest amount you can get away with. Each time you sharpen, you will lift a little higher. I estimate that after three or four hones it's time to go back to the grinder.

The key thing to grasp is that the total cutting angle is 25° from the grinder and no more than an additional 5° from honing. I see loads of hand tools at Rowden and elsewhere up to 35° or 40°, which is only good for hitting with a big mallet. Stay under 30° to retain the sensitivity of the edge.

Now, having pulled back, lift the blade and go back to the far end of the stone and pull back again. You may need to do this on the brown stone three, maybe four, times. Without changing your stance, poke an index or middle finger out and feel the surface just at the tool edge, running your fingers down the back to the edge. Can you feel a tiny but slightly rough burr running from corner to corner of the cutting edge? Good. Well done. This is "the

Figs. 13.9 & 13.10. Settle the blade at the far end of the stone (far left and middle).

Fig. 13.11. Pull the blade straight back.

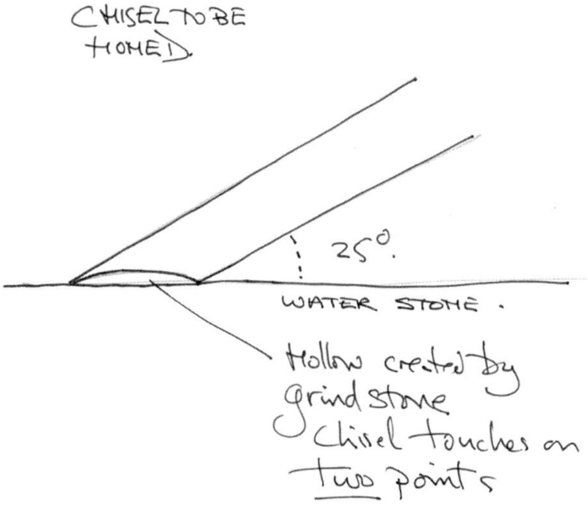

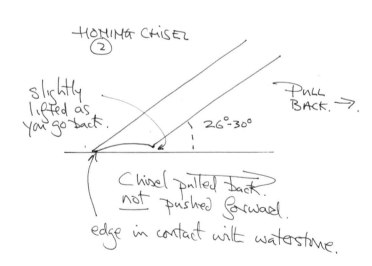

CHISEL TO BE HOMED

25°

WATER STONE.

Hollow created by grind stone Chisel touches on two points

HOMING CHISEL 2

slightly lifted as you go back.

26°-30°

PULL BACK. →

Chisel pulled back. not pushed forward. edge in contact with waterstone.

Fig. 13.12. The grinder creates a hollow grind.

Fig. 13.13. Lift slightly as you pull the blade back, so the rear arris of the hollow grind is off the stone.

burr." If not, worry not, – just repeat and slightly lift your heel as you pull back. This will slightly increase the honing angle. You are the sharpening jig.

The Burr

Sharpness: the coming together of two polished surfaces to create a junction that will not reflect daylight.

You have to have a burr. It is a vital step that cannot be omitted toward a honed edge. You can knock that burr off by stropping it on the palm of your hand, or on a bit of scrap, but that will leave an edge that is raw and rough – good for some really good work, but not for us. We are after an edge that's not perfect, but pretty good and quickly done. As perfect as we can obtain quickly. (We will look later at some Japanese planes and natural stones for a more perfect sharpening, but that is not necessary for now.)

Remove the burr with the polishing stone (#4,000 grit).

Gold stones are soft and need to be kept flat in the same way as the brown #1,000-grit stone. These two sharpening stones, and a small Nagura stone, will be all you will need for the first couple of years. The Nagura stone is a small stone that helps to flatten the gold stone by rubbing it over the surface, particularly on parts your blade hasn't touched, while at the same time working up a cutting paste up on the stone's surface that can be left in place as you hone your blade's edge. See how you get on with it; it is used with a light, delicate touch to help the gold stone cut more quickly, but it creates a mess that can stop you from seeing what is going on. Seeing is helpful if this is new to you. If you like, leave the Nagura until later, after you know what you are doing with the burr.

Pull the gold stone out of the water (though we keep all stones in a water bath so they are ready for work, some can be used with just a squirt of water), put it in the same position as the brown stone, and put the brown stone back in the water (after ensuring it's flat).

After sharpening on the brown stone, you have a blade with a delicate burr on the edge. What you are aiming to do here is polish both sides, the back and the bevel. In so doing, the burr is moved left and right and the junction with the blade edge is weakened. Polish the burr off, don't break it off – in so doing the edge will be sharper.

Start by honing the burr exactly as you sharpened on the brown stone. Next, turn the blade over to work the back. The burr will be pointing down toward the stone. (Remember: You created this burr with the blade facing the other way on the brown stone – didn't you?) Carefully bring the burr into contact with the gold stone. To do this, I lay the blade on the side of the stone with the chisel handle down and the burr above the stone's surface. As I pull the blade toward me down the stone, I slightly raise the handle to bring the burr into contact with the stone. Read that again; it's important.

Now that the blade back and the burr are in the same plane, you can work away on that chisel back on the stone like crazy. This is where you save time by weakening that junction and getting the burr to fall away. Press evenly over the whole surface; work the blade backward and forward. Don't stay in one place. You can see that black of the steel coming off on the stone. This is where Nagura slurry and a more delicate touch can speed things up. With a good, flat blade and a nice stone, this should not take more than 10 to 15 seconds. You can double, but not treble that.

Now turn the blade over; the junction between burr and blade will be greatly weakened by your polishing. Carefully wash the stone clean. Now hone the bevel again. Starting at the top of the stone, use your honing action to draw the blade toward you, with the bevel on the stone – being careful about that burr. Keep a nice grip on the blade, your elbows in, and draw back the blade. You may well now see that burr fall away from the edge of the tool.

If not, turn it over and polish the back again. Seeing the burr come off the blade is one of those moments of understanding. I suggest that you keep the stone clean and your eyes open for this. Later, you can use the Nagura and delicate touch to speed up this process.

The burr may come off in one whole piece or in two or three smaller bits. Where the burr stays on the edge, polish it away; don't rub it off with the thumb. Use your eyes to look for the burr. "Sharp" is the intersection of two polished surfaces; you know it's sharp when you can literally see nothing on that edge. It's a visual test; light will not land on that edge. Look at it in daylight or with a good bench light. If you see sparkles on that edge, it means there is a flat of steel or bit of burr, and it's not damn sharp enough.

Fig. 13.14. The Rowden stones stay in water baths between uses, so they're always ready for sharpening sessions.

Doing this the first few times will be slow and careful work. When you get used to it, honing an edge can be done in less than a minute. A well-ground blade will take a honed edge three or four times before you need to go on the grinder again. Keep the polished bevel narrow; it will increase each time you hone, as the angle you take to pull the burr will increase. Four hones and I am usually up from the initial 25° to a hefty 30°.

O1 carbon steel blades sharpen more quickly and more easily that A2 which is one reason we like O1. With O1, the burr tends to come away in large pieces; with A2, the burr clumps up and comes off in tiny pieces more slowly. When you are learning, you may find it easier to learn with O1 steel then move to A2 later. A2 is a useful steel for work that demands removing a deal of stock. Having said that, from the point of view of a man who has used carbon steel blades for nearly 40 years, I see most of Rowden students using good quality Lie-Nielsen Toolworks planes with A2 blades. Well, there you go.

Having learned to avoid the honing guide, you will not be worried by having to sharpen tools that don't fit the standard honing guide. Drawknives, carving tools, spokeshaves, adzes – all will take an edge from your hands. Sharpness, the bringing together of two polished surfaces, will be in your intelligent hands.

Fig. 14.1. The fetish joint. Modern woodworkers tend to pay a lot of attention to dovetails compared to their forebears. Still, there is nothing more satisfying that a row of well-made tails.

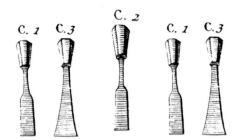

SAWING, PARING & CHOPPING

Machines play such a huge part in our modern workshop that it's easy to focus on developing machine skills – which is what many colleges now do, assuming it will make the student more commercially viable. It does not; it just makes a person more dependent on a machine to cut a straight line.

We aim to have our machine surfaces bang on. Then we refine the joint as needed with hand tools. For example: Can two edges coming together benefit from one stroke of a handplane to slightly hollow the joint?

Our bench saws don't get a great deal of use; the machine shop does this so much better than we can. Crosscutting on a table saw to a perfect size is a given. But it's good to have small saws for carcase joinery and drawer making. I have two dovetail saws: a 20 tpi saw with very little set on the teeth that results in a narrow kerf; this is for small work and drawers. My second saw is slightly longer with 15 tpi and more set to cut a more aggressive kerf. I use this as my carcase saw – it won't bind in 3/4"-thick stock, and it cuts nice and fast. These two saws get quite a bit of work around the bench.

I have two other saws that are set to cut a more aggressive kerf – a big old Disston panel saw and a good Stanley tenon saw. These get used when I have to snip off an end and save myself the walk to the machine

Fig. 14.2. Dovetails saws.

Fig. 14.3. Shop-made saw vice; we call it a saw chop.

shop. It's important to not be limited by your skill. Sawing a straight line is not hard; it just takes a little bit of thinking and a bit of practice.

Sawing

Let's start with a saw. It has to be sharp. Look at the tops of the teeth. If you see shiny tops, it's a dull saw. When I worked with Fred (remember the long case clock maker from earlier) he said: If you cannot sharpen a saw you don't really own it. I think he is right. I used to watch him every Friday night. All his tools were sharpened and put away, and his last job before slipping down the pub for a pint or two were the saws. Depending on what he had used that week, he would set them out "for a tickle."

There are saw experts who make this really complex, and I don't want to get under their feathers. What we do is just simple sharpening – because it has to be simple to be done regularly. We work only dry hardwood; so when we file, it's straight across. As we do this, we push the back of the file a bit, turning a rip blade into what I am told is a "fleam-cut" blade. The essence is that it's straightforward and at the end of the week you need easy. (Cutting softwood is a different matter.)

Set up the saw in some "saw chops" – two bits of timber carefully made to fit around your saw handle – then use cramps to hold everything still. We have a 4" saw file that fits all our small saws. My eyes are not good enough now to do my 20 tpi dovetail saw, but I still do the others. A bench light shines across the work and tells you where you have been. One stroke per gul-

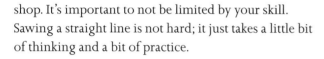

Fig. 14.4. Rip-tooth saw pattern.

let. You can be clever and posh and do every other gullet, then fill in from the other side – but I haven't found this to be worth the effort…but that may just be me.

This process will work for most bench saws. (We have a great saw doctor, Brian Mills, who straightens out our tooth lines and gets our tenon saws back in shape. He's retired now and not well; what we will do without his expert knowledge I do not know.)

I don't know about baseball, but when you go to saw it's like going to bat at cricket. You have this big, beefy guy hurling a ball down the pitch at you – that ball is hard and it hurts. So, stand sideways to give him less of a target. Stance matters a lot.

Set the job in the vice. You are going to rip a line on a bit of 2" x 1" stock. Mark a clear line on the end grain and continue it down to the stop line. Use a pencil or a

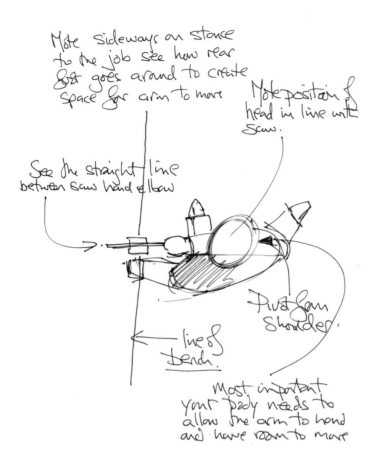

Move sideways on stance to the job see how rear foot goes around to create space for arm to move

Move position of head in line with saw.

See the straight line between saw hand elbow

Pivot from Shoulder.

line of bench.

Most important your body needs to allow the arm to hand and have room to move

Fig. 14.5. Proper sawing stance.

fine pen – it's essential you can see the line.

Now pick up a small carcase saw (not your small dovetail saw – though a tenon saw could do this just as well). Break the complex task into smaller steps. Step 1 is the start. Step 2 is the run. Step 3 is the stop.

Get yourself lined up. Stand with your legs about 3' apart, with your chest pointing 90° degrees to the job. Grasp the saw in your hand with your index finger pointing forward. You should be able to drop the saw down by your side and swing from the shoulder. The action is all from the shoulder – you want a straight line from your shoulder to the tip of the saw. Practice the sawing action in mid-air. Saw to hand, to elbow, to shoulder, all straight and lovely. OK??

You will find your back leg moving around to give you space, your toe pointing away from the job. This is good.

Fig. 14.6. Start the cut.

Then there is the question of "dominant eye." That determines where your head is at any stage of the cut so that you can see the line. Knowing which is your dominant eye is important; it informs the body and the body shifts you into the space you need to occupy to saw straight.

To find out, open both eyes, choose a spot on the wall and put a finger outstretched on that spot. Close one eye, then the other. One eye will jump away from the mark; the other eye is your dominant eye. Knowing is good. This is all about looking hard.

Smooth and lovely sawing is what's next. Step 1, the start. Look at the line across the end grain and put the tip of the saw on the point farthest from you. Line it up with your fingers and aim to saw, leaving half the line still on the job. Now lift the saw. Go on – lift it! You want to just tickle the line. Make tiny little cuts that get bigger as you create a small groove for the saw to sit in. Now lengthen the saw strokes and begin lowering the handle so the cut slowly comes back toward you. And watch that damn line.

Now that you have made the start in the right place and have avoided jumping off line, you are ready for Step 2, the run. This is the line down the job to the stop line. OK…so far, so good. This is about rhythm and focus.

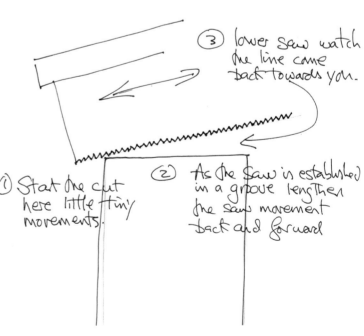

③ lower saw watch the line come back towards you.

① Start the cut here little tiny movements.

② As the saw is established in a groove lengthen the saw movement back and forward

You need to find a nice sawing stroke that uses at least three quarters of the length of the saw. RAH, RAH, RAH. Nice and slow and in control – not fast.

Hands and saws – look at that damn saw handle. Isn't it pretty, with those horns? What do you think they are there for? They are not just decorative; they are there to do a job, to transfer information from the saw to you. And when you are clever enough to sense it, from you to the saw, you will. This is why well-formed saw handles that fit your hand are essential to good sawing. Look at some 19th-century saws, made when hand-sawing was not an option, but the only way. These saw handles are not just beautiful, they work.

Once the saw is moving, back off and hold it lightly – like that of the 4-year-old you are guiding across a busy road – a firm but gentle grip. If you grip the saw hard, you will engage that tooth line far too much. That's much too aggressive and you are not up to controlling that yet (later, maybe, but not now).

Going down that line is very Zen. It's not about correction except by very minor adjustment. Imaging riding a motorbike on a warm summer evening. You have a road that winds left and right ahead. The engine is purring. You are going fast but not too fast; you con-

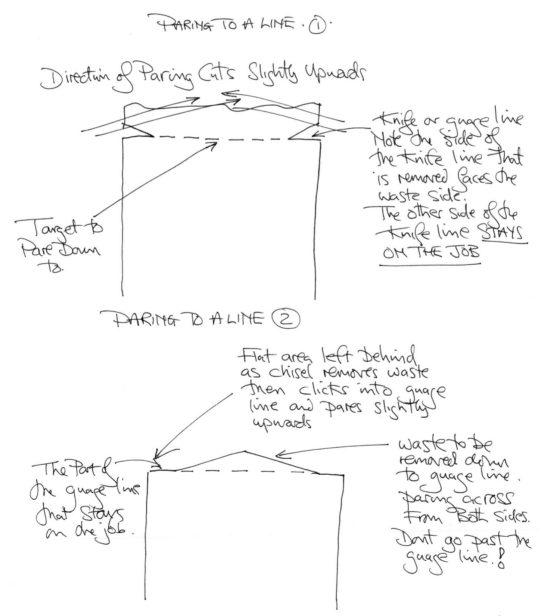

Fig. 14.7. Paring to a line.

Fig. 14.8. A vintage saw handle. Lovely and functional.

Fig. 14.9. This is my old Stanley tenon saw, with a much older pre-WWII Disston tenon saw. Look how toolmakers have diminished the shape of the tool hand to save cost and increase profit.

trol direction by minor shifts of weight in the saddle and minor movements of your head – never with your hands. This is like sawing; your body, that wonderful body, does it for you. But you must focus, focus, focus.

Those of you who go off line (and it will be most of you who are new to this) – do it again and again in an effort to improve. And you will. Your eyes will work better, your hands will not tighten and your back leg will come farther around as your body learns what to do. Don't beat yourself up – it will come right when you are standing correctly and holding the saw right and focusing.

Step 3: Stop on the stop line.

Once you have this under your belt, you will find yourself picking up a handsaw rather than walking to the machine. Sometimes it's just easier, and using a handsaw can be nice work.

Paring & Malleting

Paring is using a chisel by just pushing it – no other force. And you don't use your arms to push (they aren't easily controlled), but the muscles of your chest and thighs. You lean in on a cut. Tuck your elbows in and use your thighs to apply pressure. With a sharp edge, the chisel will cut like a knife in hard cheese, and you must control that cut so that it does not jump away from you.

A paring chisel can be specially prepared because it's not going to be hit with a mallet. Grind the angle at 20° and hone it at 25°. This works with a good, carbon steel blade or a Japanese blade. But no tapping with the mallet, please.

Quite often, the paring technique on end grain goes like this: Mark a clear and deep knife line around the job. Start paring using the corner of your chisel as you get a feel for how much you can pare off.

Pare slightly upward; you want to aim to take a paring to the centre of the job or maybe just past centre, leaving a small raised point in the centre. Work all around the job until you are getting near that knife line. Now drop into the knife line and continue.

What will be left is a clean shoulder of a knife line, all the way around the job. DON'T GO PAST THE DAMN LINE. But the centre will be like a shallow tent in the middle. Sharpen up, then just pare this off back to the line. Job done.

I didn't go near mallets for years. Whenever I did, I would screw up, either by driving my blade past the line, or by breaking out great lumps of wood from the centre of the joint. The truth probably was that my blade was not sharp.

You have to understand the forces at work here. If there is a substantial amount of waste in front of your blade when you whack the tool, the steel wedge of the chisel drives the tool off course, often back behind

Fig. 14.10. Paring chisels. These are my three Japanese long-handled paring chisels. I love them. The long handles fit my stance and give me more control. The blades are super sharp and made of really hard steel that will take an edge at 25°.

Fig. 14.11. Encroaching hollows. Note how the top chisel has the hollow nearly touching the edge. I don't hit the bevel as the Japanese do; I polish the back with #180-grit abrasive then go through the stone grits. It takes only a few minutes. If you think about it, it's a very shallow hollow so it won't take a lot to move it back.

your line. If that happens, you are going too fast, trying to take off too much timber. Bad person. Don't do that. When chopping, you should be approaching that knife line carefully. Chopping is faster than paring, but the risk is you take off too much.

When I watch Daren chopping back to a baseline on a set of dovetails (he would never pare), he sets the blade in the waste close to the edge and gives a tap to locate it, then he moves back so his arms are almost straight. This enables him to sight the blade and keep it at 90° to the work. Tap, tap, tap, and he is halfway into the thickness. He flips it over then comes in from the other side. Tap, tap, tap. Then he moves a little closer to the line. Tap, tap, tap. Flip. Tap, tap, tap.

This is removing waste not brutally, but carefully and quickly. As Daren gets near the knife line, his judgment is this: "Can I get one more cut in before I go in the knife line?" If so, he does. If not, it's go for the knife line.

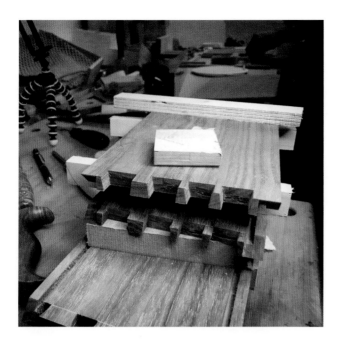

Fig. 14.12. Chunks. A dull chisel tears out rather than cuts the fibres, as demonstrated here by my student, Charles. (He has great technique but his chisels could be a bit sharper.)

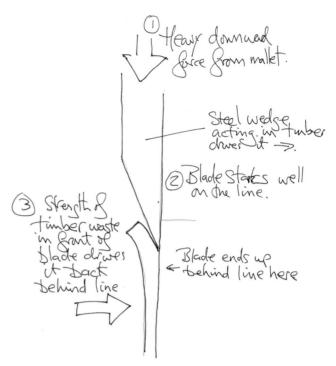

① Heavy downward force from mallet.

Steel wedge acting in timber drives it →.

② Blade starts well on the line.

③ Strength of timber waste in front of blade drives it back behind line

Blade ends up ← behind line here

Fig. 14.13. Mortise chisel use.

Step back. Watch the vertical. Tap, tap, tap.

Just go gentle. We use joiners' mallets rather than a carver's round mallet, as they have a flat face that will drive in only one direction. The weight is important – not too heavy. You are just dropping that weight on the end of the chisel, not hitting it hard.

Happy malleting. Once learned and understood, there are happy times ahead – this method is quick and can be very accurate.

PLANE THINKING

There is no doubt that running a well-set plane over a mild timber board is an experience at which to wonder. Seeing shavings come curling off that board, hissing away, shooting out of the mouth, wrapping about your wrist and filling your floor ankle deep in pleasure. This is why many of us do this; this is where we fell in love.

Yet my first Stanley smoothing plane, the one my dad gave me, didn't do that. It choked and jumped and made me feel inadequate and useless. You need to do a bit of work even on a new plane. A Yorkshireman like me would call it "fettling." Fettling is what any tool needs before you use it. It has to be fettled in order to work, and you should know how to do that.

Well-made modern planes are pretty flat; you should not need to check this. We do it at Rowden out of habit. We have a huge expensive granite slab that is certificated to be within atomic flatness – it is a miracle that we keep carefully wrapped and cosseted. Planes are put on this altar to flatness, and feeler gauges prodded around the sides just to check.

We have seen some (not well-made) modern planes

Fig. 15.1. So true. Creating a flat and shimmering board with a hand-plane can be a joy.

with a very slight hollow in the centre. Check across the sole with a straightedge; try to get a feeler gauge between them. A hollow can be taken out with a little gentle rubbing on fine abrasive, fixed on a glass plate that is supported on a dead-flat surface. You should be fine using #180 grit for this; the hollow will show very fast, as it will at first be untouched by the abrasive. You want your plane sole to be absolutely flat.

Next look at the back of the blade; it should be polished flat in the same way as we described for your chisels. With a chisel the corners matter, here the centre matters much more, as the corners almost never do any work. Grind your plane iron to 25°, but with a slight curve. The corners on my Norris

are about 1/16" back. I know some at Rowden do less than this, but I like a curve that puts my shaving firmly in the centre of the blade. When you hone a slightly curved iron, you flatten the centre making the shaving a tad wider each time you hone. Once my shaving gets wider than two fingers, I think about reestablishing that curve on the blade.

Now look at the back iron; it should sit nice and tight on the back of the blade. We have learned a great deal about back irons from the way Japanese plane-makers value this component and position it in their

Fig. 15.2. Notice the curve on the blade edge and the flat back.

Fig. 15.3. Set the back iron close to the blade edge.

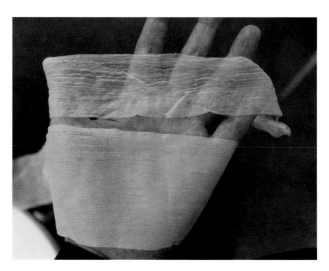

Fig. 15.4. Plane shavings.

planes. First, there should be a very small 70° bevel on the front of the back iron; this can be honed on the #1,000-grit stone (less than 1/32" will do, but it is important to performance). Next, consider its position on the blade. For easy timbers, pull the back iron about 1/16" from the blade's edge; for difficult timbers or for a very fine finishing shaving, pull it back only 1/32" – and when you really want a great surface, keep it within one human hair's thickness from the edge. That will give you performance. The back iron must sit dead flat on the blade and really fit. We have come to understand that this component is key to plane performance; it must be properly fettled and fitted.

Next is the mouth. Most planes come with the mouth cut with a vertical edge. Take a small mill file and file the front of the mouth back. You will be able to get only a certain relief on the edge before you come in danger of touching the back of the mouth – and you don't do that. The angle is not critical, but the relief it gives to the passage of the shaving is important.

Lastly, let's look at the frog. This is the section in your plane that the blade assembly sits on, and it can be moved backward and forward. Again, this is job dependent. For most work you can have a 1/16" mouth in front of your blade; for final smoothing jobs, it might need to be closed up to 1/32". This closing and tightening of all the adjustments makes the passage of the shaving that much more controlled – and it makes the plane harder to push. So, don't do it all the time – just when you really need that performance.

It's a bit like taking a standard Ford and race-tuning it. You now have a bit of a beast to drive that demands more from you – it requires you to understand what's going on with the relationship between the tool in your hands and the board you are working.

Don't be fussed into buying more than one bench plane to start with. Alan Peters only used one: a No. 7. He didn't seem to need any others. (He was mad as hell when he dropped it and broke the casting. Though it was brazed back together, he said it never worked as well again.) I have a No. 6 equivalent with my Norris; it can do most jobs. A small metal smoother will take a bit of setting up to do final shave work, but once set up will be a good tool to have. Don't settle for A2 for this tool; you need a really sharp blade, and that comes only from O1 carbon steel. This is a polishing plane, not a workhorse – go for extra sharp.

I was one of the early Western adopters of Japanese hand tools in the 1980s; more than half of

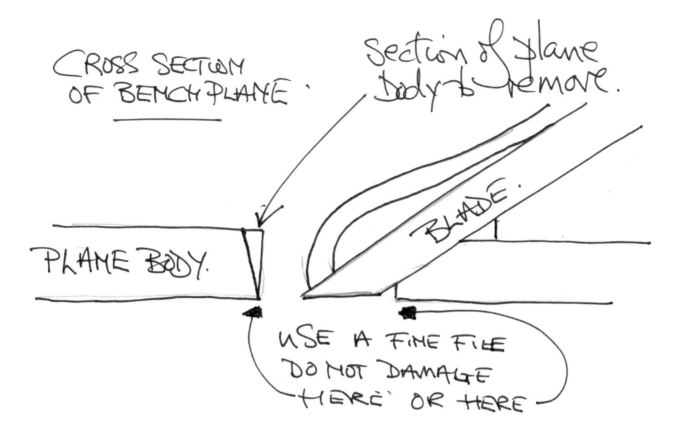

CROSS SECTION
OF BENCH PLANE.

Section of plane
body to remove.

PLANE BODY.

BLADE.

USE A FINE FILE
DO NOT DAMAGE
'HERE' OR HERE

Fig. 15.5. Cross section of a bench plane.

my chisels are Japanese because I love the way they hold a keen edge for ages, and sharpen quickly and easily. They are more heavy than European blades but just as good. What I did not, however, take to until recently was the planes. Now, as my strength lessens with age, I appreciate the light wooden bodies fitted with razor-sharp blades precisely located to give me long ribbons of happiness.

Mind you, these babies are not for the beginner. I never suggest that new students take them up. I would suggest with the greatest respect that you need to have made your bones and really understand what is going on with a metal plane before you start playing about with Japanese planes.

These tools are super-simple and super-sophisticated. Let's quickly look at what we have here – three components, each very developed. There's a block of wood for a body with ramp upon which the blade sits. Cut inside this are two wedge-shaped slots in which the edges of the blade engage. As the blade is driven into the body, it tightens up. That blade is fitted to the body. The cutting edge that projects below the sole is tiny – less than 1/32". The sole of this plane is not like

Fig. 15.6. Japanese plane.

a Western plane; it contacts only just in front of the blade and at the toe of the body. This is a wooden body so it is moving with the weather. In the U.K., I guess as an island we have similar atmospheric moisture to Japan – I certainly have had no problems with plane bodies moving about with the seasons. Users in some places might not be so lucky.

There is no wedge in a Japanese plane, just a steel bar

Fig. 15.7. Body, blade and back iron of a Japanese plane.

that fits across its width. The blade and the back iron fit beneath this bar.

The blade is a hefty lump of steel, highly processed by a skilled blacksmith. This has been hand-forged, laminating two metals together: a hard cutting edge and a softer backing steel. This process brings heat and hammering to the job. These together bring high quality to the cutting edge. Hammering and heat change the structure of the steel. This is what costs the money.

Then consider the wedge shape of the blade. It tapers in thickness toward the cutting edge and tapers slightly in width. As you fit the blade to the body, it is meant to tighten up and get stiffer to fit. This makes the whole plane more solid and less prone to vibration in use.

The back of a Japanese plane iron is hollowed out (like Japanese chisels); this makes flattening the back easier. I remembered my Ward paring chisel every time I do this job. Put this Japanese iron on a good, flat stone and in a few minutes you will have a usable blade.

The front of the blade is ground usually at 30°; my tendency has been to not mess with this but to follow the Japanese practice of honing the entire bevel. Note these blades are not ground to a curve like the Western blade, but honed straight across the width. I find this width of shaving is not a problem because I am using these as finishing planes, and pulling the plane on a skew will create a narrower shaving if necessary.

Honing the blade means holding the whole bevel on the stone. I start with a manufactured #1,000-grit stone, then go to an intermediate natural stone of #2,500 grit, then a second intermediate natural stone of #6,000 grit. I finish polishing with a natural waterstone, which seems to cut at about #10,000 grit. My natural stones are not expensive, but their cutting effect is different from manmade stones, and certainly the longer they are used, the finer they seem to polish. (I have been guided in my purchases of all stones and planes by Tomohito-San at http://japantool-iida.com/inquiry/index.html. His help has been invaluable.)

Now this is where it gets confusing. I used to see a polished edge that gave me a reflection of my left eyeball as the goal, but the natural stones impart a cloudy surface. How could this be better, finer? Then I remembered garnet abrasive paper. It's not used much now since aluminium oxide has swamped the market. Garnet paper is a natural abrasive that breaks down as you

Figs. 15.8. 15.9 & 15.10. The front, back and cutting edge of a Japanese plane blade.

use it. So, #180 grit would turn into #220 grit then #240 grit as the crystal structure sheared off to create new and finer sharp cutting edges. That's what is happening to the natural stones beneath my plane irons. Facets are breaking off to cut and move around beneath the steel, clouding the surface but giving a finer cutting edge. It's counter intuitive, but with natural stones, cloudy is sharper. Look at the edges of samurai swords and you see cloudy.

Last, we have the back iron. In a Western plane this is often mild steel and not well made. In a Japanese plane, this is usually laminated steel of the highest quality, and shaped to fit in the body after the main blade is fitted. The back iron sits snugly on the back of the blade. It has a most important facet right at the cutting edge – a small 1/16" of 70° bevel to drive the shaving up and back on itself. The back iron is also positioned much closer to the cutting edge than is common with Western planes. A back iron fitted within a hair's thickness of the cutting edge is not uncommon on a polishing plane. This is where these tools excel – in creating a surface that is polished straight off the tool. Powerful and sophisticated, these are highly developed handplanes capable of the very best work.

I thought that I could do this research on Japanese planes on the cheap, buying secondhand tools on eBay. I was wrong. It took me some time to work out that I would be better off buying from a reputable maker a good plane that had been set up to work straight away. This would be the course of action I would suggest if you were to take an interest in Japanese planes, and Tomohito-san would be my first point of contact.

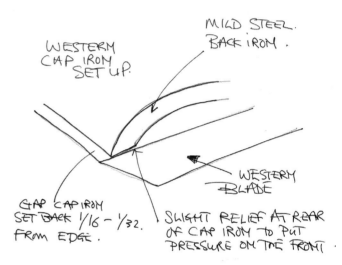

Fig. 15.11. Cap iron setup on a Western plane.

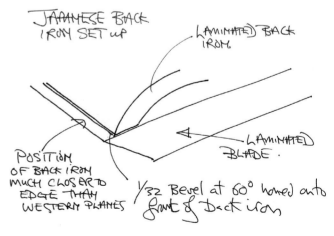

Fig. 15.12. Cap iron setup on a Japanese plane.

Fig. 16.1. At the bench. The upstairs bench room at Rowden.

PHOTO: WR PHOTOGRAPHY

THE TRANSFORMATIVE WEEK

I am jumping now to what a student experiences during the first week at Rowden. I am doing this because it all fits together. Without the doing, the making, the faffing about in the workshop, all the drawing and waking up, there is no context for when you become a designer and a maker.

It's not good enough to sit in a nice clean design office and get your sweaty minions to make for you. Making is what you do. Remember William Morris, and how he was always fiddling with making something or other. Fail to grasp this, and the maker will always be in charge of the dialogue.

"No boss, that won't work – you need three fixings there."

You need sufficient understanding and knowledge to argue. You need to know enough to suggest a different fixing, and to maintain the smooth identity of your design.

So pick up that plane. It's on its side on the benchtop. Wait – maybe first let's have a look at what we have here. There is a proper full-sized cabinetmaker's workbench, about 7' long. It has a newly planed, flat top. The top is beech or maple, and about 3" thick; the undercarriage is similarly heavy. A good bench should be solid, and not gallop about the workshop the moment you put the pedal to the metal.

Look at that benchtop. Many makers may have worked there before you, but it should be in pretty

Fig. 16.2. The Rowden workbench.

good condition – if not unmarked by their work, it should be at least a respectable surface. There have been accidents, yes, that caused the odd bit of damage – but it's a dead-flat surface. We need flat, especially around the end vice, because that is where we work. The flatness of the bench transfers to the job; a hollow near the vice would show up in thin components planed on that bench. The bench has a front vice and an end vice. Working with these vices will be dogs. Whuff, whuff. No – these are pegs that fit in holes in the bench; they are used to secure your work.

The bench is probably the most important tool you will ever encounter as a maker. Later, you will make your bench; it will become the foundation upon which other work will be made. Right now, you'll use one of the Rowden benches. Bench height is important. Stand alongside the bench; let your arm hang and bend your elbow just above the bench surface. Now spread the thumb and index finger of your opposite hand. Add that distance to your elbow. This is your bench height.

It's good to work with a high bench because it protects your back. Much of your work will be done not with your arms and shoulders, but with your trunk – the core muscles – and thighs. This again will protect you from injury. There will be times when you need to get up higher and get on top of a job. Then, use a small "hop-up" – a 3"-high box that you stand upon. This

lives under the bench's bottom rail.

Then there is a bench light. It should be a decent, bright source of light that you can direct into the dark corners of your work. Without a good light you will not be at all times able to see where you are going. A quick maker will be pulling that light around as they move about the job. You need to see the line as you cut.

Then there is a box of hand tools – yours until you can sensibly choose your own. These are prepared tools; all edges have been sharpened by Jon Greenwood to a keen edge. They should all work straight out of the box. All the boxes are different; they hold the same tools but from different suppliers. Spend time trying out different chisels and gauges to help you make informed buying choices. Hand tools have to fit your hands comfortably; different brands offer different solutions at different prices.

With these three – a bench, a light and a box of basic hand tools – you can make a lot of things and need nothing more. Machine work can be done by a local shop; pay them by the hour. You might want some power tools to help out later on, but they are not for now. Most machines are about saving you effort and energy; you want to engage them for those reasons – not because a table saw is more accurate than you are at sawing a straight line.

On the bench, there is a piece of walnut, about 18" by 2" or 3". This is to teach you about wood and tools

Fig. 16.3. Learn to read grain direction.

at the same time. Look at the wood. It has been selected because it is mild and well-mannered. It will have a sawn surface, but you will be able to see the grain of the timber. Think of it as the fur of a cat – which way would rough it up, and which way would lay smooth, if you stroked it? That's the way you plane it, smooth. Place it the right way around between the dogs and tighten the end vice to just nicely hold the job.

This is the bench doing its job in superb fashion. Now you are free to dance about the workshop, waving a No. 6 to your heart's content. You don't have to hold the job – it's fixed in solid position on the bench-top. All actions now are down to you – how you hold and present that edge to the job. This is you, a sharp edge and a piece of timber. Listen. Attend to what that sharp, well-adjusted tool tells you about the surface in front of you.

Is the note the plane makes a nice, high WHUZZ, or is it getting lower, telling you the edge is getting dull? Watch the shaving as it emerges over the frog – is it a clean, full-length shaving or is there a slight hollow just over there? You want information about that surface; the plane is your primary tool of inquisition.

Consider your arms and shoulders during this process. The work should be coming from your trunk and thighs, not your arms. Imagine a piece of string tied around your plane handle and attached to your right nipple. If you push with your arms, it will pull on the string and hurt. Instead, use your core and legs. A long shaving then becomes like a dance step: forward step, forward step, forward step.

Plane a dead-flat surface on one of the 3"-wide faces. This is your "face side." It is important, as this is the side from which all other faces are measured; get this wrong and you are in the poo. From day one, hour one, you are faced with quality. Screw this up, go too fast and slip it in under the bar, and it will come back later to bite you in the bum.

Flat is a terrible monster and can drive a newbie bonkers. But don't let it get you. The sole of your plane is flat – I promise you – so use it. First, let's look at the side-to-side movement of the plane. As you take a shaving, you can get it only about 1" wide from the middle of the mouth of the plane – maybe less. If you

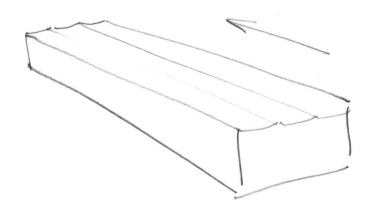

Figs. 16.4 & 16.5. Take overlapping plane passes down the work.

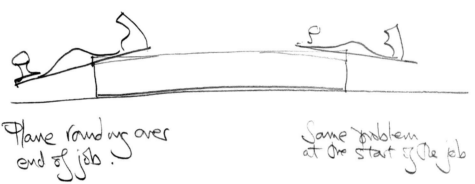

Plane round up over end of job.

Same problem at the start of the job

Fig. 16.6. Adjust your hand pressure on the plane as you come on and off the work.

are observant, you will see that the shaving is slightly thicker in its centre, thinning to nothing at the edge. This is deliberate; you want this.

Run the plane down the job, aiming to get a complete shaving for the whole length – then run another alongside it with a little overlap. If necessary to help you visualise, put a pencil mark across the job and plane it off. Suddenly, this is fun! The plane is working and you are doing the job – you are almost up to your knees in shavings. But the joy of taking long, ribbony strips of fragrant walnut is suddenly ruined by Jon Greenwood coming to your bench with a straightedge.

"Let's see how flat it is." What is usually the case is that you've been planing up onto the job and down off it, creating a crest in the middle. So, you learn to

overcome this by applying more pressure to the plane's toe as you come on to the work, and to the heel as you come off it.

Now check the surface with a straightedge, and hold the job up to the light and see what is going on. (You have a straightedge on the side of your plane; many skilled makers use that, as well as a purpose-made straightedge, for this and other jobs.)

High points can be removed with stopped shavings that address that area. As you approach flat, back the iron off to produce the finest shaving; this will allow the sole of the plane to have more effect. You might find yourself chasing a minor bump. Don't do this; try taking a series of fine stopped shavings to the centre of the job, leaving pencil marks on at either end. Then,

Fig. 16.7. Put winding sticks on your job parallel to one another.

with three full-length passes, go right through, clearing off the pencil marks at both ends. There you are, nearly there.

Now check it for wind (that's pronounced "whined") by using winding sticks – one at each end, and peer across them from one end. Wind is twist. You can have a seemingly flat surface that is actually the shape of a propeller. If the winding sticks are out of parallel, they will visually tell you. This is the last check. You now have a face side to be proud of.

Mark it with a Face Mark, cannily pointing in the direction of grain – the direction the plane or machine must follow. It also points to the Face Edge which is the second surface. This is also a primary surface from which others are measured, so "heads up."

Remember these steps. You may never do them again with a handplane but you will certainly do them with a pile of timber and a machine shop. The steps are identical: Face. Edge. Width. Thickness. End. Length. We use "FEWTEL" as a way to remember the order. You've just finished the first one. Now it's on to the edge.

The objective is straight and flat on the narrower surface of the edge and, this is crucial, square to the face. Use a square to check this. (A good square can keep you safe; a rotten one, one that has been dropped, is a traitor in the camp that will undermine all your work.) Start off by sliding the stock of the square down the face side, and watch how the blade travels down the edge, looking for gaps between the wood and the

Fig. 16.8. A small combination square is ideal for checking that the face edge is square to the face.

blade. Use a bright light behind you to really see what's going on. A square can easily be banged onto the job and tell you lies. Don't let it.

Adjusting an out-of-square edge requires a well-set-up plane and some knowledge.

First, look at the plane. The blade, as you noticed earlier, is just a little curved – not straight across. This is important. This gives you the shavings you have previously enjoyed, with thickness in the centre tapering to nothing on the edges. Now look how that blade is set

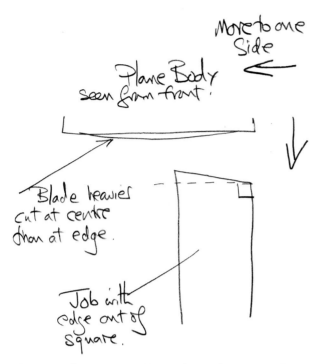

Move to one Side

Plane Body seen from front.

Blade heavier cut at centre than at edge.

Job with edge out of square.

Fig.16.9. Adjust the plane from side to side to make efficient use of the cambered blade.

Fig. 16.10. A wheel gauge is an ideal tool for beginners. Here we're scribing the width on a board.

Fig. 16.12. Use the gauge to mark the thickness all around.

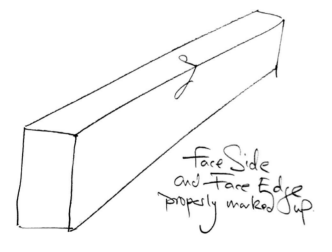

Face Side and Face Edge properly marked up.

Fig. 16.11. Mark the finished edges.

up in the plane body. Look down the sole from the toe, and you will see the thicker, dark shape of the blade in the centre fading out on either side.

This curve gives you the opportunity to adjust an out-of-square edge. Check which way the edge is out of square, then move the plane to the left or the right. What? Yes – look at the way the edge is out of square – it's higher on either the right or the left. The centre of the plane blade takes a thicker shaving than the edge.

So, shift the plane body to the left (or right). Run it down the edge and see a thicker shaving come off that side and nothing come off the other. Without that curved blade, you would not be able to adjust the edge in so accurate a way.

So, engage your brain and eyeballs before engaging the plane. Analyse the situation. Do you need more off here or over there? The square will help – again, register the stock on the finished face and slide the blade down the edge. Use your damn eyes. Hold the job and the square up to the light – don't be lazy.

Once it's square and straight, you have a Face Edge (the second letter of FEWTEL). Put a small "f" on

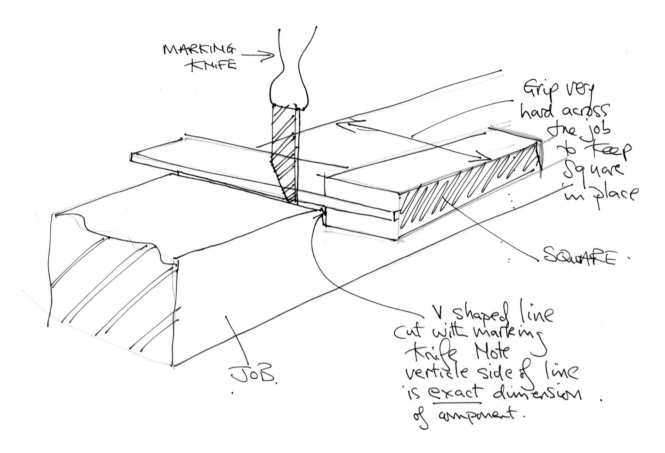

MARKING KNIFE →

Grip very hard across the job to keep square in place

SQUARE.

V shaped line cut with marking knife Note vertical side of line is _exact_ dimension of component.

JOB.

Fig. 16.13. Mark a clean line from corner to corner.

the edge, adjacent to the face mark. You can, if you want, lean it in the direction you want the edge to be worked. Good job. Move on to "W" – width.

This is a surface parallel to your Face Edge, and also must be square and straight. Now you need another tool – a marking gauge. Popular at Rowden are simple wooden gauges that (with a little work) scribe a clean line. However, there is another type, a cutting gauge with a small wheel on the end that I find is simpler for the beginner to use. Both are fine. Toolmakers want us to have both marking gauges and cutting gauges, so that they can sell us more tools. I believe in fewer tools that work better. A single sharp gauge should be able to scribe a sharp line both with and across the grain – but you will need a few gauges because they are often left set up for stages of a job.

Take the job, register the gauge off the Face Edge, and scribe a line as close to the sawn width as you can. Make sure it goes all the way around the job. Keeping

its stock against the Face Edge will be tricky at first; take gentle stokes to avoid digging into the job.

Now, before we go any further, let's have look at that little wheel that made that scribe line (if you're using that type of gauge). Note that it is beveled on one side and flat on the other, and in this case the flat side is facing the stock of the gauge and the bevel facing the outside.

Plane or pare the edge to approach the gauge line. Try to do this evenly all round so there is a little bit of gauge line flapping around all around the surface. Then take one plane pass down to the actual line. Smack on.

Now use your gauge, registered off the flat Face, to mark the thickness all the way around the job. Plane to the line, using the same process as in Step 1. Now you have the T in FEWTEL. Jon will come around with a caliper to check the thickness, to within 0.2 of a millimetre. (It should be 0.1, but we are cutting you bit of slack here.)

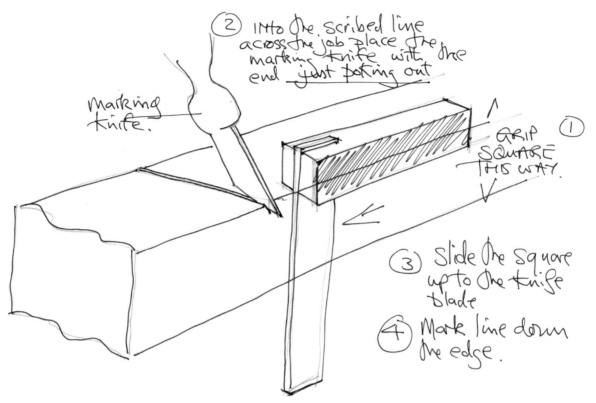

Fig. 16.14. Use the corner of the Face Side line to align the knife for the Face Edge scribe line.

I had a great student named Martin Dransfield, a former Yorkshire miner, who stayed on and worked for me for a while. A student asked Martin, "How do your joints come up so tight and clean?" Martin, being a Yorkshireman, is a man of few words. He paused, rubbed his chin, then said, "Well tha' just cuts to the f-ing line." Which is true. Leave it on and you are effed. Go past it and you are equally effed, but in the other direction.

Thank you, Martin. You are well remembered for your accuracy and your economy of language.

A word on marking-out tools. A cutting gauge, with its bevel on one side of the wheel, is one of a family of marking-out tools that give you a perfect dimension, not an approximate dimension. Mark with pencil and you get approximate. A pencil line has thickness. The marking knife is another tool in that precision family. My personal favourites, made by Blue Spruce Tool-works, are expensive, but you get what you pay for. The blade is long, thin and sensitive. What do I mean by sensitive? Will it take offence if I shout at it, go off in a

huff and roll off the bench? No, I mean it will enable me to click that blade into an existing scribe line and I will feel that click in my fingers. That's what you need from a good marking knife.

Marking with a pencil is fine for some jobs – but not the next one. You're now at the "E" and "L," the End Length, in FEWTEL. Place your square across the Face Side, with the stock on the Face Edge. Hold it firmly between the finger and thumb of your off hand. Pick up your marking knife with the bevel facing the waste and strike a nice firm line against the blade of the square. The line should be clear and clean from corner to corner.

Now you need to transfer that line to the face edge. Secure the job in your vice and put the knife in the existing line right at the edge of the job. Make sure the end of your knife pokes out a little. Now slide the square right up tight to it. When you are up and snug, remove the knife then use it to strike a line across the Face Edge. If you are spot on, the line will be a perfect continuation of the line on the Face Side, and you can carry it on around the work to meet the Face Side line. If it doesn't meet up one of two things have gone wrong: you've mismarked around a corner or the job is not square.

If the marking out is wrong you have no chance of good work. Step back to find out the problem, and start again – either the planing or the marking out, as needed. Engage brain before plane.

I am making this point: Making is an intellectual and creative challenge. It demands that you engage fully with every atom of your being. Your full concentration. Otherwise, you will mess up.

The essence of this is that there are no shortcuts to quality work. There are lots of easier, quicker, lower-quality ways that suit lots of other situations, but if you want to do it right there is no shortcut. We see this penny drop with people; it may take a few days, or a few months. Tom, a student with us now, sat with me recently on a log of Western red cedar and said, "David, I have had a really, really, great life, and this has been the very best year, so far. However, if I had come for a trial week I would have run a mile. It took me weeks to see that there is no shortcut." Thank you, Tom.

This "Doing Thing" isn't easy. You need to listen to the tool in your hand. That blade has an edge engaging with the infinitely variable material before you: timber.

That cutting edge in your hands is the closest you will ever get to understanding this material. The distance between you and it is, at this point, the shortest it will ever get. The information is traveling down that blade into your hand. But do you have the wit to receive it? Our bodies are wonderfully receptive information centres. The body feeds us with information. Do we listen well enough to the sound of the blade in the timber? Do we listen to the note the saw is making, to the feel of the chisel in our hands? Do we weigh the push the tool is requiring and look quizzically at the edge of the chisel? I hope so.

This is why sharpness is so important. With sharpness you have less shove and more sensitivity, control and information. Dull tool/dull maker.

We are asking you to use your eyes in a new and more intense way. This opens the door to learn drawing (more on that to come) for each stage of the process. The ability to draw quick bench notes is an essential skill in making things; it enables us to resolve what's going on inside that joint.

The eight-week hand-tool initiation ritual builds a solid base upon which to learn machines and other processes. This is tiring, ache-inducing, hard-won accuracy. This is accuracy you have never achieved before. That's control. That's you in control. I like that.

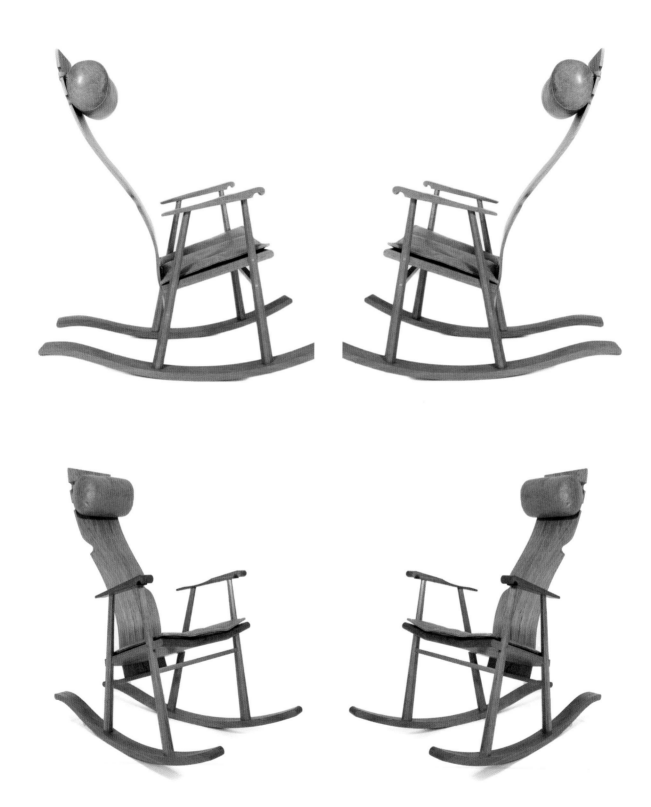

THAT DAMN CHAIR

Before I jump into this burning fire called design, I want to show you a little about the general process we use at Rowden to design a piece of work. This is what determines whether all the following stages are going to be worth the effort. Making is expensive sweat – especially if it's your sweat. We shed sweat and blood on the things we make; we want to get them to the standard of WOW. That cannot be achieved sitting on your bottom and reading. It takes work. To engage in this work, to spend that energy, we need to know that the design is as good as can be. This is the first step – important, and necessary to get right. How do we do this?

I aim to develop a design system that you can modify and apply. I have looked to my own design practice to consider where ideas come from, and how I develop them into sketches, models and prototypes. This is not the only way, but it is a process I have used successfully. Take it, use it, bend it to your shape, apply it to other materials and client bases. Creativity is a process you can plug into and adapt.

Design is complex. It involves uncommon skill and judgment, but these are not talents reserved for the fortunate few. They are acquired with effort. In the following pages we will visit most of them.

First, there is drawing. It's a way to capture visual information, to internalise it and make it yours. Drawing builds your visual vocabulary – a vast library in the back of your head, captured during a lifetime of looking and drawing. Do not think that the digital world will replace this. Yes, it too is a visual library – but it's outside you. Use it, but never rely on it for genuine creative development. All you are doing when you rely on a digital library is adding this tabletop to those legs

Fig. 17.1. A packing blanket resolved one of my problems with the design of this rocking chair.

and hoping nobody notices your sources. They say that originality is the art of concealing your sources, and there is some truth in that, but when everything is online to see, there is no concealing.

Recall – download – images from your subconscious mind, from that visual library in the back of your head. If there is nothing up there to download, all your "ideas" are going to look the same. Later, I write more about "George" – the manager of your subconscious mind. Be careful, treat him with respect and he will chuck you wild ideas the like of which you haven't seen since you were crazy teenager.

Proportion – understanding and using the core divisions of nature – my word, that is important! Why work against the rhythms, structures and growth patterns of nature? With a little understanding and a deal of cunning, you can create proportions within your work that will invite calm – a sense that this piece could only be this way. Change one dimension and it all goes to hell. Whilst at the same time, you can create visual tension and curiosity. "What is going on here? Something's up – I see this and it's right, but it's somehow teasing me. What is going on?"

Presentation – selling these ideas to a customer. Then, development – OK clever clogs, how do we make it? All of this and much more is part of design.

I share a little of my history in effort to explain where all this comes from, for history and context can help explain why – and it's the why that I want to look at as much as the how. Why do we, a relatively small contrarian minority, bother making extraordinary things? Why do we go an extra, uncomfortable and unrewarded mile when the vast, well-fed majority of the developed world would rather sit on their bottoms, eat pizza and watch celebrity TV?

Why are there people who defy this general trend, who work like dogs for modest recognition or reward, but know that they have to do this? I asked the well-loved and respected American furniture designer Thomas Hucker.

"Why do you do it, Tom? Why do you push to develop these great designs that challenge accepted conventions, but that are 'difficult' for people? Designs that effectively prevent your getting a huge audience."

His answer was stunningly simple. "If I didn't do this, I would not know who I was."

First, I want to show an evolutionary process. I have a rocking chair in development that has been with us now for months. No, it's worse than that – years. For me, some designs evolve; they don't drop down fully formed. First, I had a chair, then I put it on rockers – but it was still wrong. What do I mean by wrong? Well, it didn't make me smile. A client once told me that a dining room set I made for her makes her smile every morning as she passes it. That's the way to go.

This chair didn't do that. Often, you don't quite know what's wrong, just that it's not right. So, the chair sat there, rather sullenly gathering dust, hidden from visitors, unloved by anyone for nearly two years. All that time I didn't have an answer – except I felt the back was wrong. But not having an answer doesn't mean the job should be put on the fire or in the dumpster. Allowing the creative brain at the back of your head to think is one of the keys to success. This was a "back burner" problem. This could be left alone to cook slowly. I knew there would come a time when this would become a "front burner" problem, and when that happened I would have an answer.

That confidence comes from having done it time after time. "What do we do about this, David?" Oh, cut it off here. And I am usually right. I have seen this coming and set my unconscious mind to solve it. When Daren comes at me with the question, I have the solution. George and I will have looked at it. (Who is this "George?" Again, you'll have to wait and see.)

Along came Duncan Roberts. He joined Rowden as a maker-tutor, and I needed something to keep him occupied. I sat in the chair and immediately knew that the back was too short, that a rocking chair like this needs a headrest. I got Daren to take a photograph from the side of the existing chair's back. We worked out where the back of my head was naturally positioned. This we printed up to a decent size, and I was able to draw on it to extend the chair back and add a small pillow for head support.

Next, Duncan ripped off (carefully removed) the old chair back and made a mold that extended the curve of the chair back. This component was then made from 2mm-thick oak construction veneer. (This is like normal veneer in that it has sequential leaves of timber, but it is thicker.) The new back was made on the new form in our vacuum bag, then trial-fitted to the old chair.

It creaked a bit when I sat on it, but it was much bet-

Fig. 17.2. This is a hall table by Thomas Hucker . What you cannot quite see is that the surface of the table is made up of thin wires strung betreen the two horizontal members.

ter – especially when we mocked up a headrest with an old packing blanket. Now I could begin to see what this piece would look like.

Suddenly, there was an anthropomorphic form to this chair. Suddenly, she had an identity. She had a head, spine, arms, bum and legs. Edward Barnsley used to say that the best place to judge a new chair was from a three-quarter view from the rear at about 25'. From there, she looked great.

Form following function? Well maybe – but that's not how I go about all designs. What I do is allow the idea the gestate, a period of time to grow.

Next, we worked with the lovely Mary Holland, our upholsterer, on the leather for a seat pad and headrest. What I did not want is the kind of leather in expensive motorcars – surfaced in a protective coating that suits the car environment, but makes the leather feel like plastic. Mary made the leatherwork, then we worked again on the chair back to get it cut to final size, detailed and polished. Mary will be back for the final fit.

If all goes well, we will get to a final image that will sell the piece. I have a feeling this will sell nicely – but no proof that it will sell profitably. There are very few good rocking chairs on the market and we could fill a nice niche. Nursing mothers, presents from grandparents, old folk wanting to sit and snooze – these are comfy little niches for a chair like this.

This chair is an ongoing design, developed over time. However, most of my work is with clients, and it is this design work that I want to share with you now. These potential clients will have seen my work; they will have been on the website and made contact. These are real people with real requirements you can fulfill – if you just damn well turn up on time and listen to them.

To help show you how I work to develop designs to suit client needs, I'll take you through a three-day design process. These are the steps I go through with every client. This is my system that sets me up to do creative work; it's like a warning signal to my body and brain that what's coming is important, and everyone up there better be on their toes. Especially George.

Fig. 18.1. Pay a visit. Meeting your clients in their home will tell you a lot about the commission.

LOADING THE GUN

he phone rings or the email pings – always when I am working on something wet and delicate, and can't stop. Laying a veneer or doing a watercolour wash. Much as I would love to, I do not snarl into the telephone. I answer, "Good Morning; Rowden Workshops. How can …." It is probably a rubbish call, but customers do call and first impressions are lasting impressions. I cannot stress how important this is.

I once had a guy turn up at our exhibition stand in dirty jeans and a T-shirt. And I nearly told him, as he mooched around poking at things, opening drawers, feeling the surfaces, that maybe he couldn't afford our furniture. He turned out to be the manager of Dire Straits, and he wanted a whole room full of my furniture. Oh, would that have been stupid.

I usually arrange a meeting at my client's home. First thing is to turn up, clean and tidy, on time and well prepared. Doing what you promise is key to building this relationship. Arriving on time is the first of these. You will ask them to trust you with a huge lump of cash, based just on your brain cells and a couple of sketches. That requires trust.

In going to the home, you are also able to assess whether or not they can afford your work. A nice Kandinski limited-edition print over the mantelpiece, the new Range Rover in the drive, the covered swimming pool. That should do it. Or not. They may have champagne taste and a beer budget – best to find out soon.

If this is a commercial job for a company it can be more difficult to assess; going to someone's home allows you into their lives in a more intimate way. You can see where the new piece might live and find out how they will use it. People want special, but that need not be a flashy special. It may be a quiet and complex special. I ask open questions and listen. Hard. I want to find out how they see themselves and how they want to be seen by others. Their home can express this. Your work, the pieces you are going to make for them over the years, can do this for them. These people have asked you to solve their problem. They like your work. You may, however, have to go somewhere you had not planned to go just yet.

By that I mean that your way of thinking will not be compromised here – your creativity is yours. But they may want garden furniture and you had never considered making garden furniture. So, roll with it, baby. See what you can do; it may surprise you.

I have to understand the clients and what they want. I take along sample timbers in a nice box. This reinforces the idea that we make really well. If they have found us through an exhibition this is less important; they will have seen that in the pieces on show. But if they've found Rowden through the website, it is important to show how well we make. What we do is exceptional, and we need to remind them of this at every step.

So listening is a huge thing. Most of us hear only a small proportion of what is said. If you've not skipped previous chapters, you know I once stammered, and it still gets me when I am tired. I don't wish that upon anyone, but the upside is that it made me a really good listener. I had no alternative, as I had nothing to say! BBBBBBBB…..

So, ask many questions. "This desk you want – is it light or dark?" "Thin and delicate looking or strong?" "Do you know where it will live?" "How do you use a desk?" "How many drawers?" "Do you want secret drawers or compartments?" "Do you like burr woods?" "Do you have a chair to go with this desk?"

Notice the "upsells" (do you want fries with that?). The chair, the burr wood, the secret compartments all take this job into a different price and content bracket. The client may not go for them, but now they are aware they have these luxury options – options not available on the high street. Always put clear blue water between you and high-street furniture in this way. The basic desk at $10,000 or the "luxury sport model" version with leather, bells, whistles and turbo boost – well, that's got to be $17,000.

Paying attention to people, especially when they want something made, is really important. They like it – for it's rare for people to really pay attention to you.

Having extracted the brief, it's time to reflect it back to the client. The quality of your questions will help get the "real" brief, rather than a superficial one. You may find both partners do not want the same thing. I had a great job once, where the man wanted "a table that I could dance on." His partner wanted something slender and lovely. My job was to (elegantly) point out that I could not do both, and would they please make up their minds. With the brief in mind, quickly write it down. I would leave the clients and drive to a car park and tape my response. I write it up the next day and send it. Doing it fast means you avoid losing the detail, the small stuff that often really matters. This quick response is most important; it signals that you are well organised and efficient.

I write what I heard they wanted. All the detail, green dangly bits with silver bells and, oh yes, the nice dark-wood surfaces. I give a ballpark figure for cost. "No less than $3,000 but no more than $4,000." Sometimes it's necessary to practice this. Stand in front of a mirror and practice saying, "That will be $30,000." And smile. You need to know that you are worth $30,000. Too often, you know the work and you can do it, but this trips you up. A guru of mine calls it "head trash" – it's got to go!

It is important to get to the money pretty early on in the conversation. If you don't, you can waste a lot of everyone's time. When you have a few pieces made, it's a good idea to use that portfolio, without challenging them, to put down some markers during that meeting. "This piece was $20,000" – and watch the reaction. If this draws blood, then you can show them something at $15,000. But don't have your prices written up. I doubled the price of

Fig. 18.2. Avoid head trash. Stand in front of a mirror and practice saying, "That will be $30,000." And smile.

a dining room set from $20,000 to $40,000, just on how enthusiastic my prospective customer was. I looked around and thought they could afford it. Had they flinched, I would show them something cheaper, but they didn't. Some people do not want inexpensive – cheap is not how they see themselves.

It is essential, however, that you do no drawings on this job – even if you think you have a screaming good idea. Give the client two weeks before you start the drawings. Tell them in the letter, "I will not start the drawings for two weeks; please get back to

me before then if I have missed anything, or you wish to amend the brief."

The ball is then in their court. After two weeks of silence you are on. Now do the drawings. Save it up. Hold your fire, baby. Two weeks of thinking time is the best preparation you can have. You have now Loaded the Gun.

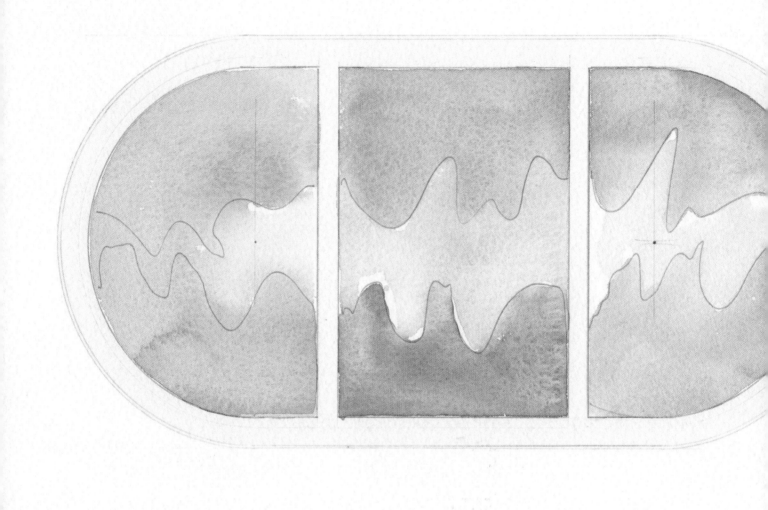

DOWNLOADING FROM CONSCIOUS MIND

Having loaded the gun, set the target and let it cook for 14 days. During those two weeks I will have tried to not think about the brief, and I will certainly have done no drawings. It is essential to allow the subconscious to turn this problem over and look at it – kick it about in the back of the head but do nothing.

Then the stress starts building. This is important. You are a professional; you need to be able to do this creative stuff on a wet Wednesday when the muse is fast asleep in her pretty little bed. The stress is part of turning up the heat to make you work better. We need a little stress now and again. I have given a delivery date to the client. I have told them I will be with them with drawings that do not yet exist. Next week! I must deliver, or I lose all chance of getting the work. I plan for three days of studio work – no phone, no interruptions and no other jobs in that time frame.

My goal, by the end of day one, is to have one set of presentation drawings done and ready to go. That morning, before tea time, is downloading time. I go through a routine – an important routine. (This is mine; you choose your own.) It sets the tone, and it gets my head ready for this special work.

I sharpen five pencils – not six or four, but five nice cedar pencils. I turn off the phone, I make a cup of coffee, I unplug all the digital things that Ping. I put on a playlist of creative music, stuff with no language that I can understand. Opera is good; I don't speak Italian. A nice cup of coffee, the dog sitting quietly under the desk and I am ready to roll. All this is "Othering" – doing anything other than sitting down to do the damn drawing. But it's very valuable, as it signals to a part of

Fig. 19.1. Presentation drawing. What comes after the downloading.

the head that Special Creative Work is coming, and there is a guy back there – I call him George – who needs waking up. Get Ready to Rock n' Roll, George!

So, you sit and doodle (well, that term is rather pejorative; this is a kind of drawing that allows the mind to run free). It's drawing without too much direction. Watch carefully what comes off the end of the pencil. Do not be critical; note it and move on. This is fluid thinking time. Artist Paul Klee famously called it "taking a line for a walk."

When I do this, I tend to use a book with a very fine 5mm grid on the page. I get these from a supermarket that imports them from France, where they are used in French schools. The grid helps me to quickly draw in proportion by counting off the squares. It also helps me keep verticals vertical and horizontals …well, you get it. Sometimes, I use a technical .05mm pen instead of a pencil. Pens are great, as they make you draw very deliberately. I almost never use an eraser at this stage.

Writer and comedian John Cleese, when talking about creativity, described how he wrote the scripts for "Monty Python's Flying Circus." He was surprised he always had more ideas than his fellow writers, but he found he dug deeper past the first idea.

"I would ideally go into a room with no distractions, that is most important, and sit with a pad and paper. Forty minutes would be a good span. The problem, in my case the requirement for next week's script, would be there. It would sit alongside me, not confronting me, but be there with me in the room."

The first ideas that pop out of the pencil are the ones from the front of the head. They are the conscious images, the ideas that you have had before and are reheating for this solution. This is old stuff – and it may be fine. Your client likes you for what you have already done, so a version of that may suit the job in hand. Keep drawing, though – you might get past the obvious first idea to another then another. This is good. Remember, this is non-critical and non-celebratory drawing; just dump the stuff on the damn page. Draw

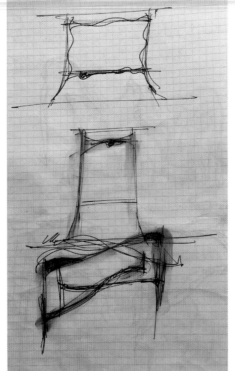

Fig. 19.2. Pen washes.

fast and free. Fill a page with quick scribbly images, download and move on.

After about a half-hour I start to find myself repeating things. This is when it's good to go back, review, find the best sketch and take a break. There is no point going on, breaking yourself over this problem. Note when you are done and stop. This kind of work – this downloading – is exhausting, even to the young and strong.

Downloading demands that there is stuff up there to download! So, what is this stuff? In my case, it is a sketch of rose petals I made when I was 15 years old, a drawing that convinced me I could do this "Art." Essentially, it is any drawing you have done of anything: the shape of a cow's back leg; the articulated form of a seashell; a thistle; the way a leaf fits to a twig. All have interested you at some stage in your life. This is your visual vocabulary. I use those images today; I download images I put back there when I was much younger. If you don't have much stuff up there you will be limited – very limited – in what you can download. But don't worry – just draw and draw and draw. Draw stuff that you like the shape of. Observational, not imaginary. It's called making your bones.

That is why it's called image-ination.

So, get out there and draw. There is no limit to it. The more interesting your visual vocabulary and the wider your visual vocabulary becomes, the better and more challenging your ideas become. The more limited your visual vocabulary, the more restricted you will be when it comes to download time. It does not take a lot of time – it just takes visual curiosity. You want to understand the shape of that shell and the way the leaf sits on that twig. Without visual curiosity – that wanting to really see – you will never do much of interest to anyone.

Originality is within you; your life is one that has been lived by no other person. Your memories – grandma's dining table, the smell of polish on furniture. Your experiences – travel with notebook and

Fig. 19.3. Doodles.

pen, the minarets of Marrakesh. Your understanding of materials and processes – hard won and inside you. All will combine – strands from each tied together – in an evolving response. A response to the original brief.

One of my great heroes is Pablo Picasso. He had this saying about inspiration: "She will come to you as a Muse would come, but she must find you working." So, get out there and draw.

Photos, Pinterest, Instagram – the digital solution is just not good enough. That's the cheap and easy solution, the visual library of pre-digested images. That's great but it's external, fast fun and sublimely superficial. What you need is the internal solution. That is where the integrity of your original response comes from.

Give me five honest lines that describe that exciting form in front of you – not a digital image, this time go analogue and make it yours alone. Having put a drawing of whatever – a child's foot, a shoe, a cup of tea, down on paper – it becomes burnt into your hard-drive memory system. You no longer need the drawing. It's like a stick in the ground, marking the place where this great form is buried. Go looking 20 years from now and you'll find the stick, but the image that comes

off the end of your pencil will be fresh and sweet and startlingly new. This is the power of drawing. This is the power of imagination.

We all can draw. It's not a talent given only to a few. We all can learn to draw well enough to do this. It's no harder to learn than driving a car, and once you know, you know. The Intelligent Hand has another skill, and this will enable her to make more inventive forms with greater cleverness.

This analogue learning is such a primary skill. What I have learnt in my years is to mistrust digital skills. They are wonderful tools, I would not be without them and they have revolutionised our world – but just as the Big Mac is not the answer to nutritional health, digital skills are not as great as they appear.

So, the first idea is there; this is the easy one, but it's good to have. People will probably have seen you doing versions of this idea before. It's part of your style, how you do things. Actually, this is money for old rope. This, in John Cleese's terms, is the Fish Dance all over again. You are not really cooking yet, but tonight and tomorrow you will – believe me, you will. Remember that this is only day one of three. And we have used only the first part of the morning.

Dj 250105 Scale 1:75. D B S

FIRST PRESENTATION DRAWINGS

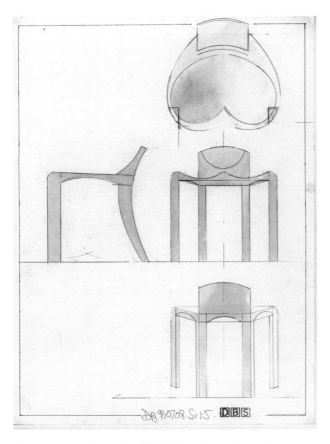

Fig. 20.1. Draw from simplified viewpoints. Front elevation, side and plan view. These are artificial views, but they demand that you focus on the proportions.

Now, after having walked the dog and had a coffee, It's back to work. You have the rest of the day to turn that doodle into a series of presentation drawings. The presentation drawings do two things. First, they develop the idea from a doodle to a tight image. You want an image in which you cannot shift any line without changing the whole damn thing.

The best advice I ever had about making an image was from Geoffrey Rhodes when I was a student at the Ruskin School at the University of Oxford.

"Finishing a drawing is like climbing a mountain; every line has to be right, every space between lines right, add one more line and you stand on top of the world. Add two and you are back at base camp."

You are here, now, to turn this promising bundle of doodle lines into a formal thing – the very best you can do to show what the damn thing will look like when it's made and delivered. So many of my clients say, "Oh, it's just like the drawing!" That is great.

The other important thing these drawings do is become a specification for what the piece will look like when it is made. I now give my drawings to makers who turn them into furniture. That wasn't always the case; I made the damn things myself for many years. So, draw from simplified viewpoints. Front elevation, side and plan view. These are artificial views, but they demand that you focus on the proportions. I will come back to proportions later (they are important), but this is where you apply them.

How high? How wide? Look at the negative space and play with the image. Put your maker's hat on at some stages and say, "How the ____ are we going to do

Fig. 20.2. So, do you need a perspective to sell this idea? This is the judgment call you must now make. Most people don't read technical drawings well. You have to help them see it.

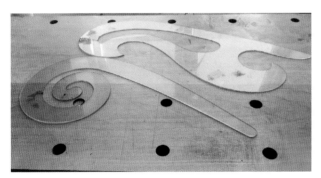

Fig. 20.3. Curve templates.

that?" If you have an answer, fine; go on. At this stage, it's not necessary to go into more detail. If you have no idea of how to make it, then maybe you should stop and ask for help.

Think of it like this. You get an idea: POW! A light comes on that illuminates this wonderful image in your head. You then start to work out what it will look like and how it will be made. As you find out more and more, you realise how complex it will be to resolve this image. The great designs, the great images, are resolved and are efficient in time and materials, and point their way back to the original concept. Most ideas – nine out of 10 of my own ideas – stay at the bottom of the circle. Perhaps they're unresolved, uneconomic or both. These are not bad ideas; they can be recycled. They may point later to another piece of work where you can use all or part of that form.

One of my gurus is Walt Disney. He would put on his artist's hat and look at that damn mouse. Then he would don an animator's hat and work out how to move him. Then a marketing hat, and work out if any one would care if he spent all that energy doing it. You can do the same. If you are going to fail, and creatives fail a lot, fail fast!

So, get that presentation drawing done! A couple of hours, and I usually have something that I can call a drawing. I work on watercolour paper that's about A3 in size (11.7" x 16.5"). I like to be able to hand this stiff, heavy drawing to the client. It feels like a creative has been in charge. Draw to scale using a scale rule and a 0.5mm technical pencil, or better still, a 4H good-quality artist pencil, sharpened up to a fine point.

Years ago I eliminated the draftsman's sliding head and parallel motions on my drawing board as being overly complex. I draw on a very large "double elephant" cedar drawing board with a mahogany T-square. The large board enables me to put vanishing points down if I am doing perspective drawings.

I use two large plastic templates to give me curves. These are brilliant. This is part of the secret sauce of my designs. I made copies of two templates that a great maker and friend, Nick Chandler, had. His father made these by hand when he was at the bench. The hand-made element is important, but clearly Mr. Chandler senior had done a great job of evolving complex radii into two large plastic forms. These templates are like super French curves. (I sell copies to my students at Rowden. If interested, check out our store at: www. finefurnituremaker.com)

The front elevation will probably be the main part of the drawing. Above or below it will be a plan or side elevation. Draw these second images and use the same baseline. Then you can transfer the widths, heights and proportions from the first drawing. It saves time and keeps you accurate.

Scale rules are tools that enable you to draw in a chosen scale. Depending upon the size of the piece, you may use 1:5 or 1:7.5 or 1:10. Choose your scale to get the main image to fill the space nicely. Plan the page

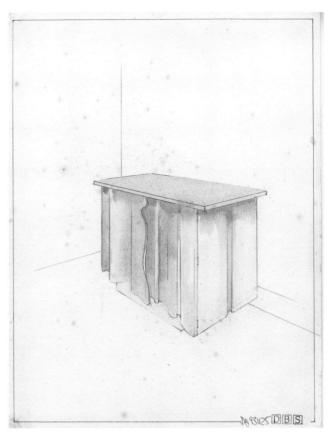

Fig. 20.4. I don't try to make this a great watercolour; I just add a simple wash that helps explain the image to the client.

so you have space for other images above and below if necessary. Whether it's landscape or portrait, that's the first choice. Start with a centreline and a baseline and go from there.

The morning will see you through to a line drawing of your first idea. If you feel this explains itself, then good for you. Most people do not read line drawings well; a touch of colour or a perspective image helps loads to sell that daft idea. This is what we are doing here – selling an idea, an idea that until this morning existed only between your ears.

So, do you need a perspective to sell this idea? This is the judgment call you must now make. Most people don't read technical drawings well. You have to help them see it. You might be working in CAD and the program will just spit the perspective out. If not, you have bit of work to do this afternoon. At the end of day one, aim to have a set of two or three A3 sheets that describe your idea to a total stranger. And, more than that, excite them with the prospect of having that new, unique thing made just for them.

So, I have the huge drawing board. Having done the

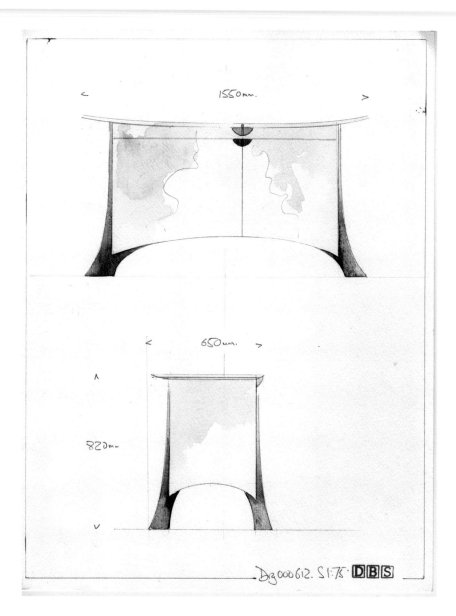

Fig. 20.5. The great designs, the great images, are resolved and are efficient in time and materials, and point their way back to the original concept.

elevation, I will have an impression of the actual piece, its proportions and its presence. I will have a sense of what it will look like when made. Doing a perspective sketch without your front view is asking for trouble. Without this front view, you don't know enough about what you are depicting to get it right.

To do a perspective, you need to plot vanishing points (VPs) on the horizon. Looking up at the prospective piece, your horizon is high on the page. Looking down on the job, your horizon is low. VPs are off to the left and right. If I set up my paper on the left of the big drawing board, I can usually get one VP to the right, reasonably close in. The other VP can be waaaaay out in left field. It's on the same horizon as the right-hand VP. Go to Chapter 34 to see this in the presenta-

tion drawings I did for the desk and chair in this book.

This will leave you with a line drawing or a small pile of line drawings. Each can do with a little colour to help explain what it is. I wait until I have three or four pages before I open the watercolour box.

I don't try to make this a great watercolour; I just add a simple wash that helps explain the image to the client. I find a few browns and yellows will do this; I don't need a full palette. Mix lots of water with a little paint. I use artist's "whole pans" of watercolour, as they give up the colour faster. I don't have time to spare here – I want that colour now. I have a few very good big sable brushes that do the job better than any cheap nylon brush.

Be sure to work on heavy watercolour paper, at least

Fig. 20.6. Watercolour box.

140 lb. (better, 220 lb.). The weight is a measure of the thickness of the paper and is a determination of how well this sheet will take colour without cockling up like a ploughed field. There are "not" and "hot" surfaces; one is bumpy and the other is smooth. Go for the smooth, and try different watercolour papers, as some very smooth papers absorb the colour very fast, which makes it hard to lay on an even wash.

If you draw digitally, you can print out CAD and other digital drawings on heavy paper, then apply watercolour. A pale grey ink works well here, and the watercolour helps cement the idea that there's a creative in charge of the process.

The aim is to lay the wash up to the ruled technical pencil line. At this stage, have the paper untaped and free to turn on the board. Make sure the brush points away from you. A big sable brush acts as a reservoir for the colour. You need to work quickly, so practice is important, but it is a skill easily learned and worth having.

First, paint smoothly along the edge, with the brush pointing away from you. Turn the paper, come down the side, turn again and go along the bottom. Quickly pull the colour into the middle, keeping it all wet, then finish the last side. Practice on scrap paper, laying down larger and larger rectangles of thin, watery colour. Once you can lay one wash, practice two more

techniques. The first is a second wash laid over the first once it is dry. A yellow wash with a thin blue wash over it looks greeny. Play with this. Next, try dropping a second wash onto a damp or wet first wash to see the watery colours blend and merge.

Finally, play with dabbing colour out of the image. Lay a wash and, quickly, before it has dried, take some toilet tissue and dab to remove colour. Play with this – it's back to being a 5-year-old!

When the image is dry, I like to add a red ink border and put the workshop mark in the corner, along with the date and scale of the image. The date is used for reference as the drawing number. If the design is a good one, and liable to be copied, I send a dated drawing in a sealed envelope to my lawyer who puts it with all my others in a drawer with my name on. The date, and the fact the drawing has been held by a lawyer since its inception, helps in copyright issues.

CAD may be very attractive to many of you. It's fast, effective and has the benefit of much higher accuracy. A 2D plan and elevation drawing can be turned with a good programme into 3D. This will enable you to spin the object around to see it from all angles – which is wonderful. The other benefit is that it can transfer forms and dimensions to cutting lists to be used by computer-driven machines. This is the CAM of

Fig. 20.7. Watercolour wash palette.

computer-aided manufacture. CAM is important – and cheap programmes will not offer all the features you might want.

We are now getting into seriously expensive software, but you will want to know how to work with it; it is becoming an important tool. We use Rhino CAD at Rowden, and students get this heavy-duty tool at a huge discount. I am slick with pen and paper, and I don't do well in Rhino – but I know that it's a tool of the present and the future. When it comes to creativity, however, I have some reservations.

I have a great friend who works in the Audi car design studio, and I asked him about computer-aided design.

"Oh, all the very early drawing is done on paper or tablets; this is the fastest way to put down an idea. CAD is great at a later stage to realise and examine what you have just done. It would never be used at the creative start of an idea."

Again, digital does not seem to help in the creative way it promises to help. I see Rhino drawings put onto watercolour paper and "Arted Up" quite nicely, creating the feel of the creative in charge. However, I feel that the fastest, most effective way to download an idea is with the "Ferrari of Mark-making Implements" – a nice cedar 2B pencil in the Intelligent Hand.

Fig. 20.8. If you are going to fail, and creatives fail a lot, fail fast!

WAKING UP GEORGE

Right and dandy, Boo Galloo. You have Day One under your feathers and you are feeling pretty smart – but this is just the start. My wife tells me she knows when I am coming up to a "Three-day Design Event." I am irritable, I snarl at the children and I don't sleep well. So, watch out. Now, having downloaded your best shot, you go to bed knowing that tomorrow you have to do this all over again.

Day Two's goal is a totally new design. The idea is to give your lovely client a choice. Give her one drawing to look at, and she will say "yes" or "no." Give her two, and "no" doesn't come into the conversation. This is another part of the secret sauce. I never, never, never go to a client with just one idea. I go with two good ideas – two solutions, including costs. The first may be closer to what she expects, and the second may only be another version of drawing one. But by digging deeper and harder, you might strike gold. John Cleese found he always had better ideas because he dug deeper; he wasn't satisfied with the first idea – the old stuff.

Let's be frank: The old stuff may sell the job. The client has seen your portfolio and likes your work – that's why you are here. But what if you can show her something she didn't expect?

I go to bed thinking about that damn brief. Almost always, I have a really bad night's sleep and come into Day Two all crabby and tired. But I sharpen five

Fig. 21.1. Let's be frank: The old stuff may sell the job. But what if you can show her something she didn't expect?

DBS — Drg 950415

pencils, turn off the phone, make a cup of coffee and unplug all the digital things that Ping. This is still "Othering" – I do the same things, in the same order, every time I sit down to design. Every time I need creative thinking, I send a clear message to the little filing clerk, George, in the back of my head.

"Wake up George – he's Gone Critical and needs stuff sent up."

That's what Othering does for me.

George has got used to this by now. I do this to him regularly enough for him to see a pattern. He is in charge of my Visual Imagination Library. Fast as light, he flicks through my images. There are tons of stuff, the load of drawings I've uploaded over my life. There are rubbishy old drawings I did at school and at art college, little sketches, doodles, fragments of this and that. (Some of it is deeply pornographic – but we won't go there.)

"Send this up," George says, pulling out a sketch of a lady's bum. And this. And this. And how about that? He has the brief there; I sent it last night, and he saw it yesterday as well – though he didn't do much work yesterday. The Conscious Mind sent stuff up yesterday. George is the Unconscious Mind – and you don't muck about with the Unconscious Mind, with George.

George watched what I did with the stuff he downloads; often he will tease me with images I know about in my Conscious Mind, then sling a really wild image I haven't seen since I was 22. I did that drawing of a beautiful young woman – a young blonde with eyes that could melt steel. It's those eyes again, the shape of them! I can use that!

Sometimes it doesn't work, and you have to think about another version of drawing one, but if you can wake up George and get the lazy bastard to do some work, you get an entirely new idea.

Creativity is about setting yourself up to be creative. It's about allowing the Muse to catch you working. It's about assembling from a whole range of skills, images, understandings and past memories. Then you assemble them into a new personal response to the brief.

Nobody has lived your life; nobody has seen the world through your set of experiences and skills. What you can bring to the job is original by its very nature. Picasso said that we are all born as artists, but as we grow we forget the process of being creative. What is clear to me is that like with most cerebral processes, it

is possible to turn a dormant process back on. You may need to upload a ton of stuff and get in touch with your inner George. But it can be done.

Creativity is a process, and you can set yourself up for success. You can adopt habits, methods and techniques that enable you to swing out more imaginative ideas. So, with the help of George during your process, Day Two gives you another idea, possibly one out of left field, your Unconscious Mind. That's George's department, and as I say, you don't mess with him. You send him lots of images to file away, then gently and politely you wake him up now and again.

With Day Two done, you have Day Three for colouring all your images so they feel like a set, to prepare specification sheets where you describe the options to the client, including the timbers you could use, the delivery schedule and the price. Seeing it written is more solid than verbal.

(This assumes that you had a hit on Day Two. Maybe you didn't, so you have two choices. One, make another version of your best idea from Day One. Go back and look at your sketches and evolve something cool. Or, two, sit down and try to wake up George again. Hell, it only takes a half-hour, so why not sharpen the pencils and turn off the phone and anything that goes Ping?)

You also need timber samples. When I go to the first meeting with the client, I take along a small box of timber samples. (Always make these really well and keep them polished; they signal your ability as a maker.) When I go to the second visit, I go with larger samples. A small board of ash will have figuring and features that my tiny sample would not show. It will also be recently polished; try to avoid taking a sample that is a couple of years old and yellower than the newly polished timber.

It's all about managing expectations and giving great customer service. Sometimes, if I think it is a great job that will make a difference to the workshop, I will go an additional mile. This can be making a demonstration corner of the piece to show the client in 3D what I am thinking. I once made a corner of the table showing how the leg and table meet, plus a silver detail that fit around the edge. The client who wanted a "Million Dollar Table" was holding that sample to his chest during our conversations. That's the extra mile that gets the job.

Quality and customer service are important. Do

it right, and you exceed expectations. And that is rare.

Put all those drawings in a nice portfolio, face down in the right order, with the spec sheet at the bottom. Now sell the idea.

I used to hate being a salesperson. I had that stammer, plus a serious attitude problem. I didn't like rich people. It wasn't until I came to appreciate how good it feels to be sold to, by a really competent salesperson, that I saw the integrity that can (sometimes) reside within the sales process. A great salesperson can take your need for anything from a toothbrush to a motorcar and lead you to the point of deciding which one you want, this or this? They lead you step by careful step down a corridor of choices. Down, down we go, choice after choice, until we reach the door that says, "OK, which one do you want to buy? Would you like blue with silver whistles? No? OK, how about…."

These clients have chosen you for the work you have shown them; your portfolio of work is your identity. In design terms, it is who you are. They like something about that body of work and they like you, so from here on it's not a matter of compromising your delicate design identity. You've listened, responded with your best shot, turned up on time with clean shoes, and shown them the best damn idea you can muster.

Dude, it's been agreed that you are for sale. Now it's just a matter of price.

To get them to part with serious dollars for something that exists only between your ears and on three sheets of A3 paper means that you have to do a lot of things right. You need to explain what is in your mind.

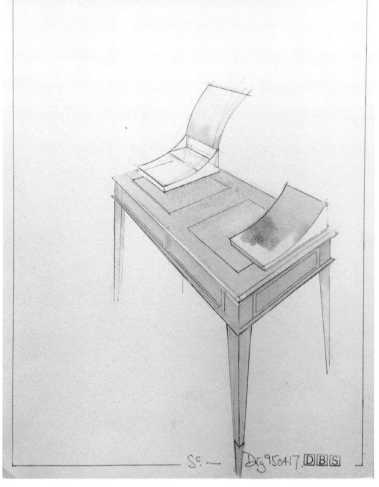

Fig. 21.2. Dude, it's been agreed that you are for sale. Now it's just a matter of price.

Do that well enough, with enough passion to express what you stand for, and someone will trust you enough to put down a deposit large enough to make the piece.

Get this: They are not buying the damn table. They are buying you. Not as a domestic servant, but they are buying something that you stand for – something about quality and individuality that resonates in their hearts, to the degree that they want it in their own home. It is those qualities they need, for they are rare and special. This is what they want, not the damn chairs. Understand this, get this right for them, and they will be back for job after job after job. I have a handful of wonderful customers whom I have worked with for more than 35 years doing just this.

Once they know and trust you, the relationship changes. They gain confidence in commissioning new work. Then a brief can become very open and challenging: "Oh, you know what we want" (which compels the very best of thinking). Or, it goes the other way and they can become both challenging and supportive: "David, you have got the job, but we would like you to have another look at this. I get the idea that we have seen parts of this image before." This is true patronage. This is what a creative person, working with supportive and challenging clients, can become. "You have the job – don't worry; the children will be fed. But we want you to push yourself again into that conversation with George."

And this is what you really want.

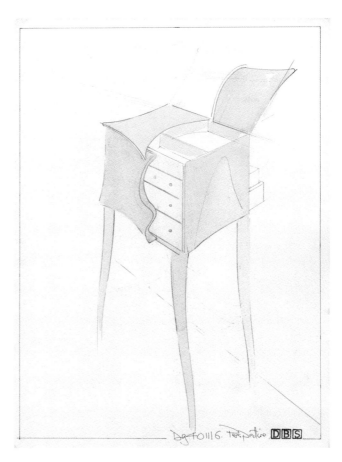

Fig. 22.1. Things that reside in the right brain include drawing, making music and listening to music.

MAGELLANS OF THE MIND

The ages of the past have been of high sea. All sought new worlds by sailing to horizons that were beyond their knowledge. They sought new life, wealth, new worlds and new understanding by looking out as far as they could. Today, we search the skies for distant planets to give us more understanding of who we are and where we came from.

Our age requires that we look not only outward, but inward, to become Magellans of the Mind. We have made greater strides toward understanding what happens between our ears than at any other time in history.

In 1983, Howard Gardiner wrote "Frames of Mind: The Theory of Multiple Intelligences." What Gardiner did in that book was extraordinary; he suggested there are eight different kinds of intelligence. He framed

Fig. 22.2. The left brain knows what a bike looks like, but it doesn't actually see the bike in front of it.

these areas and gave them titles such as "Mathematical and Logical Intelligence," "Spatial Intelligence" and "Linguistic Intelligence." These form the basis of what we regard as "good thinking." When we write or argue a particular point, we now know a special area in the left hemisphere of the brain lights up. When that geeky mathematical kid does her stuff, there is special area, again on the left side of the brain, that lights up. Logical, sequential, rational thought all come from here.

These are the powerhouses that dominate our lives. The decisions that these areas of the brain make are key to our success or failure. Our abilities to write and argue are paramount. To understand number and sequential logic is an essential life skill.

There was once an interesting investigation into the brain of the great Albert Einstein. What might make the brain of Einstein different from mine or yours? After his death, a brain section was taken though the skull. They didn't find what they expected. Einstein's brain was no bigger than yours or mine. What they did find was lots of pale yellow stuff called myelin. What's myelin?

A new thought – PING! – that sets up a synaptic link to the destination of the thought. Access the thought again – PING! – myelin wraps around the synaptic link, making it stronger and faster. Like broadband, invest in a bigger tube, and you get a faster service. Use the synaptic link again – PING! – and it gets bigger, stronger and faster still. That's how that geeky mathematical kid with her pushy parents appears bright. She uses that neural pathway, and each time she does, it gets better. Her maths gets easier and she looks more impressive, as if she were more intelligent. She is more intelligent, in the sense of use it or lose it. But this was developed by using her mind, not by birth. That's why pushy parents are so important. Pablo Picasso was blessed with one of the best art teachers of a generation, his father. He managed, bless him, not to put Pablo off drawing,

but to encourage and excite him. Mozart similarly was blessed with the possession of a piano from birth, and a deeply talented piano teacher as a father. Like Picasso, Mozart had the wit to enable and encourage the young lad without putting him off the piano. What parenting, eh!

As well as lots of myelin, Einstein's brain showed a robust connection between the two hemispheres – which is a little puzzling. For it is in the right brain that the so-called "less useful" intelligences reside, yet Einstein seemed to need to use them pretty often. Right-brain "Kinetic Intelligence" will come as a welcome justification to our sports men and women. We had an English football captain who could barely string a sentence together, but he could bend a ball over a wall of players into the top left of the goal, and he could do it time and again. Since he was young boy, he'd practiced with a tennis ball against a wall: synaptic memory, determination, repeat, myelin, result.

I am mad as hell at Gardiner for his right-brain "Spatial Intelligence" moniker – it should have been "Visual Intelligence." I will just have to live with it.

I knew a young man, Barney, who has exceptional spatial intelligence. He played a high level of rugby with my son, Alex. Barney could see the game around himself; he knew where all his nearby team members were even without looking for them. He would get the ball, draw the opponent, take the tackle and pass without looking; pretty near every time he made a good pass – 360° spatial awareness. Barney should have been the star player at fly half, where he could have dominated the game. But as is the way of these things, that place was reserved for the coach's son and heir, and Barney only got to shine when he was away.

To say that the right brain is underused by our lopsided society would be an understatement, but it's pretty clear to me that it is a particularly important resource for what we could do. Things that reside in the right brain include drawing, making music and listening to music. Plus sitting and thinking – finding a meditative place where you can get at a part of the mind in which intuition and instinct play with one another.

So, let's see what happens when we start using the whole of this wonderful resource between our ears. Let's look at what happens when we want to start drawing. OOOOh …that sends the left brain into control-mode overdrive.

"Why do you want to bother with that?" "You know you won't be any good at it." "There is just no point."

All of this comes from a part of the left brain that stores images – usually images and symbols learned when we were children. This is where all those childish images come from when we try to draw without direction. These left-brain images are there as a quick reference: this is what a bike looks like; don't bother looking at it. BAM!

The drawing class can be one of great intensity – no talking, just looking. visual judgment based on observed reality.

I had a group of students in the drawing studio arranged around a still life, a bike placed against a support. Still life is great – true to its name, it remains still. Because the class was quite large, we arranged everyone around the subject. Most had a good view, but two on either side could not see the frame, having a view only of an edge of the tyres. They couldn't see the entire wheels; this upset me, as this was one of the things I wanted to see well observed. But one of those students who couldn't see much did a drawing just like the one at left. BAM!

"But you can't see that frame can you?" I asked. "No." "And those wheels are not circles, are they?" I said. "Oh. No. They are not." That's the controlling left brain banging out an image to save time – a bike. BAM! I made that student look again, and to draw what was actually in front of him (which he did with great success).

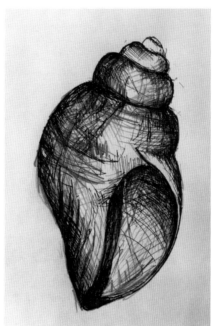

Fig. 22.3. Drawing is active meditation.

When we ask you to take up paper and pencil, we want you to use your eyes to see what is there. The left brain gets flustered, but if you persist it will go to sleep.

Listening to what is going on between your ears is critical. You need to be aware of the negative effect of left-brain thinking. Our advice is the leave the negative thinking at the studio door. We want only visual thinking. "Is this line too long? Is this one too short?"

I will pause a moment to say a huge Thank You to Betty Edwards, who wrote "Drawing on the Right Side of the Brain." Her book has helped us develop and extend a sound, basic premise into a system. Our system enables anyone (who is prepared to engage and look) to learn to draw very quickly. Drawing, when developed as a skill, is like active meditation. You will see yourself working hard, struggling to get the best set of lines. It makes you tired, yes, but you have a calm feeling of goodwill.

Drawing can be like a mind-enhancing drug. Come out of the studio after an intense two-hour session and drive home. The light is going down over the fields, the colours are intense, the outlines are clear and hard. That's enhanced looking; your eyes and brain have just come from an intensive session and they don't stop functioning in that way as you leave the studio. Do this, and you just see better.

So why do we have this lopsided educational system where teaching favours dominant intelligences? Well, maybe that's why they are the dominant intelligences! More and more we are seeing our schools failing to effectively teach even the most basic literacy and numeracy – yet the focus seems to be even more tightly structured around these skills. Why can't someone use another intelligence at school and receive credit and reward? Dance. Music. Art. Sport.

We desperately need more creative people in our new world; this narrowing of the curriculum to logical-thought maths and English is a tragedy. We need to learn to think not just in a straight line but in concentric circles. The left brain, your left brain, combined with the right brain, will enable new thought and new ideas.

Fig. 23.1. You can make a pretty serviceable bench in a few days, but this is a cabinetmaker's bench built to suit the maker.

THE STONE BENEATH ALL OTHER STONES

A workbench is the first major project. It's a big but simple joinery project done to furniture making standards. We have been teaching it for more than 30 years, and we have not found a better project than this to give people skill and confidence.

We have had a few clever clogs who say, "No, I will buy a bench and get on with furniture." Down the line, they are never as good as those who make the bench and do it properly.

I know you can make a pretty serviceable bench in a few days, but this is a cabinetmaker's bench, built to suit the maker's height, with a tool well, a front metal vice and a tail vice. The construction challenge gets more difficult as we progress to the tail vice; it's a demanding moving structure that can take all of two weeks. The entire bench can be built to Rowden standards in about eight to 10 weeks. It is the foundation stone on which all your other work will be made. Do your very best – it won't be perfect, but it will be as good as you can do now. The next job will be better, and the next better still.

Fig. 23.2. The bench is just a giant, flat holding device that allows you to get into the correct position to do the work properly. You are then free to concentrate on balance and being in control.
PHOTO: WR PHOTOGRAPHY

Fig. 23.3. The indispensable tail vice.

Fig. 23.4. The face vice with replaceable jaws.

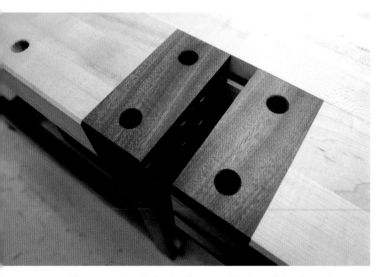

Fig. 23.5. Dog holes in the movable jaw of the face vice.

The most important thing the bench does for you is hold a job whilst you work on it. (I remember my early days without a bench, struggling to hold work with one hand whilst cutting with the other. I am amazed I came out without more damage to my digits. The opportunity to saw off part or all of my hand was a daily event.) The bench is just a giant, flat holding device that allows you to get into the correct position to do the work properly. You are then free to concentrate on balance and being in control. That's what matters – control.

There are a few things a cabinetmaker's bench has to be. It has to be heavy. You will be exerting horizontal and vertical forces on it, and you don't want it moving around – so spend some money on timber and make it heavy.

Make your bench to suit your height. This is critical. Many benches I see are very low. The bench height we suggest has rewarded us with strong, undamaged backs. It's a high bench surface set up for general planing. To determine the right height for you, stand alongside a bench. Bend your elbow. Extend the forefinger and thumb of your left hand. Touch your thumb to your elbow. The point of the forefinger is where your benchtop should be. This will do for almost all work. In case you do need to get on top of a job, keep a small "hop-up box" stored beneath the front rail.

The bench has to have tool well. This is the place to gather the tools in use for a given project. The working surface of the bench should be kept as clear as possible at all times. The benchtop is for the job at hand –nothing else. We know that this game is about skill with speed, and speed is about organisation and picking up and putting down tools fast. Thinking ahead, not being slowed down by a lost chisel in a pile of shavings, is key. We go nuts about such professional practice at Rowden. At the end of day, we put tools away sharp. I know you are tired, but sharpen your tools, sweep the benchtop, sweep the floor – then go home.

Benchtops need to be swept down regularly to keep them free of dust and shavings. Christopher Schwarz sent me this brush as a memento of our visit to Shaker Village at Pleasant Hill. Just look at the design and workmanship! The ends of the bristles thin down to fine strands, and at the bottom they form not a straight line but a gentle arc. Perfect for this job. Look at the binding wrapping elegantly in groups of three, then a

Fig. 23.6. Kentucky turkey-wing bench brush.

Fig. 23.7. A clean, well-lighted place.

Fig. 23.8. This is Lowrie's bench, set up to use as a drawing table.

gap, gathering more with the movement of each group of three down the handle. At the base, the full handle is bound with an inexplicable hanging hook, coming from the centre of the binding. How did they do that? This, Chris calls a Turkey Wing, I call it the best bench brush ever to have been made.

You can go a long way with great bench, a bag of good, sharp hand tools and good bench light. As my eyes have dimmed, the number of bench lights I need has increased – but you will likely need only one, a good one that can be moved around all over the place.

The tool well collects everything from shavings to dust, tea mugs to half-eaten sandwiches. That's what it's for. The bench surface is golden territory – keep it clear and clean; do it no damage. When making this surface, you will respond to the timber that you actually have available. But don't be tempted to make the bench surface too wide. You need to keep this surface flat, and if it's very wide, you will need very long arms to flatten it…and the task will be tiresome and not done as regularly as it should. There will come times,

usually when developing third-scale prototypes, that you use this bench surface as a datum reference surface – so it's important to keep it spot on. Our practice is that at the end of every big job, the surface is dressed lightly with a bench plane. Just a shaving all over gets it clean, flat and new – ready for the next job.

The timber choice is important. Naturally, everyone wants to work with highly figured timber – but this would be foolish. The stock is ideally 4" thick for

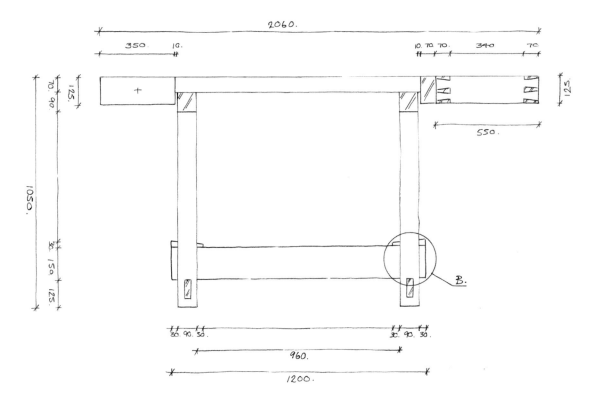

Fig. 23.9. Workbench elevation.

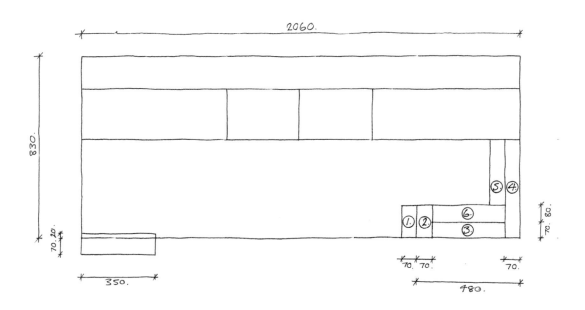

Fig. 23.10. Workbench plan.

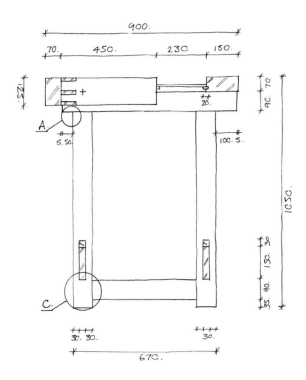

Fig. 23.11. Workbench profile.

Fig. 23.12. This is Miklos looking at the timber just arrived off the lorry. He has long clean boards of Sapele that he has to organise and turn into components – what comes out of what?

Fig. 23.13. Slab of native white oak .

the frame and 3" thick for the benchtop. Good, thick stuff is not easily obtainable; the challenge with thick timber is the moisture content – a board can be dry on the outside and wet as a pear in the middle if it's not been kilned well. For this reason, we advise students to use sapele for the base. This is a reddish wood from Africa, and it's often used in conservatory construction (popular house additions in England), so large dimensions are in common use and available. It usually comes S2S (surfaced two sides), with the bark and sapwood removed, and there are very few knots or defects. It's as near to "really easy" timber as we can get, and that's what we want our students to be using.

But there is always one outlaw who wants to use native oak. This time it's Steve, who has been to our local and reliable timberyard where he bought one massive plank of 3"-thick oak.

That one piece will make his whole bench. It's a quite stunning piece of timber, but though it had been air-drying for five years, it still needed time in our slow dehumidification chamber.

We got some metre readings at 27- percent mois-

ture – pretty good air-dry at the start. The "kiln" at Rowden is a very small room with insulated walls and door, and a domestic dehumidifier. We built it under some low eaves – otherwise unusable space. We turn the dehumidifier on low and keep watch, emptying the water-collection tank and checking the wood every day with a pinless moisture meter. (The old way was to drop your trousers and sit on the board; if it felt damp it needed more drying. Students got fed up with my doing that.) A good session will see this timber dry down to 15 percent or 16 percent in a couple of weeks. We don't crank the dehumidifier to "high" – you want slow and gentle moisture removal.

Benchtops tend to be made of maple, as people like its hard surface. While it's an expensive choice, 3"-thick maple is available. Beech used to be the bench timber of choice; this is what I used when I made my wobbly old bench 40 years ago. I am quite ashamed of my early efforts now when I see the benches everyone makes here. I was young and silly and followed a Scandinavian plan that gave me a narrow-based bench at the tail-vice end, and that wobbled badly. Bad design. (Still, I made a lot of furniture on that bench so it can't be that bad.)

This is a bench cutting list. You need this to work out how much timber you need to buy. It's what we use to work out the exact sizes and the number of each of the components. You have two choices. You can take your cutting list and timber-requirements diagram to a timberyard and pick out the best, most economical boards. This is what I did at the start; my time was cheap and my pennies were few, so I saved money

Fig. 23.14. Checking the stock with a moisture meter.

CUTTING LIST   26/8/94

	DESCRIPTION	CLIENT				JOB NO		CRAFTSMAN
	WORKBENCH							
NO	COMPONENT	MATERIALS	QTY	L in mm	W in mm	T in mm		NOTES
1	TOP.	MAPLE	1.	2060	150	70		
			2	1920	150	70		
			1.	1510	150	70		
2.	TOOL WELL	BIRCH PLY	2.	687.	230	9.		
			2.	343.	230	9.		
	WELL SPLINES	" "	2.	2060	20	9.		
3.	VICE JAWS.	MAPLE	1.	350	125	70.		
			1.	350	125	20.		
4.	VICE SPACER	"	1.	250	150	40.		
6.	LEGS.	SAPELE	4.	945	90	90.		
7	TOP RAILS	"	2.	820	90.	90.		
8.	BOTTOM RAILS	"	2.	670	90	90.		
9.	STRETCHERS	"	2.	1200	150	90.		
10.	WEDGES	MAPLE	4.	150	32.	30.		

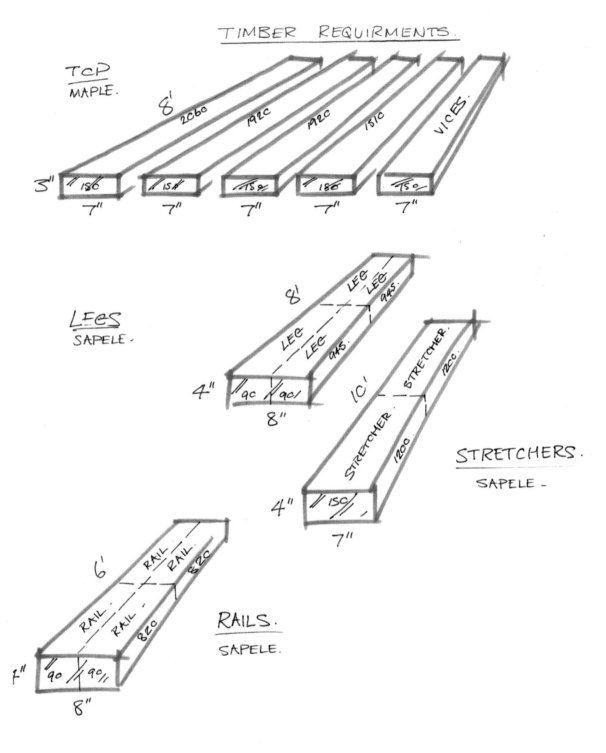

TIMBER REQUIRMENTS.

TOP
MAPLE.

LEGS
SAPELE.

STRETCHERS.
SAPELE -

RAILS.
SAPELE.

MAPLE — 5 BOARDS @ 8' X 7" X 3"

SAPELE — 1 BOARD @ 8' X 8" X 4"

1 BOARD @ 10' X 7" X 4"

1 BOARD @ 6' X 8" X 4"

this way. Or, you do it on the phone. Steve went to the yard and bought oak; the other students in his group did a group purchase from one yard. This can work well, as you can argue for a quantity discount. You need to give the yard workers rough dimensions of the boards you want. They go to the yard, look at specific stock and come back to you with a price. Usually, they will add more than you don't need, so a bit of arguing needs to be done. Remember – timber salespeople are like secondhand car salesmen; they are selling a constantly varying material. The yards we use have learned to treat our students with care, as they give quite large orders. If they skin our students once, we take them off the list for a year. "Mr. Savage, why are you not buying from us this year?" "Well, your yardman, Mr X., added a 50-percent wastage factor to one of our orders last year, and I won't have it!"

The orientation of components tells you how they sit in the job in relation to one another. Notice how the face sides all face the front. That's why they are called face sides. And face edges are on the top of the components. These are your best faces, so when you are selecting this rail from the big board keep this in mind. All that FEWTEL stuff now gets used with the machines. Face. Edge. Width. Thickness. End. Length. Do it always in that order.

When the timber lorry arrives, you find out who are "the soldiers" and who are not. Usually, we get a great turn out; small workshops need "soldiers" – people with a team attitude who will hold the other end of that big board whilst you cut it, and who will expect you to do the same for them.

Lay the boards out on trestles (with ours, the more weight you put on them, the better they get). Give each board a really good look, take a piece of chalk and mark defects. A check at the end of the board that stops 2" in? Mark it an inch farther in –the split may well carry on. Turn the board over and do it again. Use. Your. Eyes.

Now begin thinking about what component will come from where. When you've decided, mark out

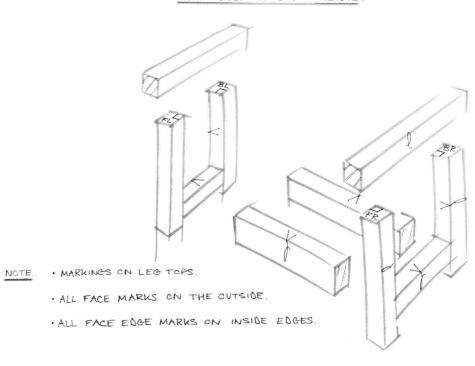

Fig. 23.15. Orientation of bench components.

the components. At this stage, go oversize by 1/2" in width and 1" in length. Use a chalk line to mark clear, straight lines. Blue chalk lines stand out nicely for the band saw to follow.

The first cut will be across the board to help you with handling it. We use a great DeWalt heavy-duty radial arm saw for this. I've just had the motor rewound at huge cost, but this is my first problem with this wonderful saw in 25 years. (Mind you, we use it for rough crosscutting and little else; more accurate crosscut work is done on the table saw.) Down the line a bit, we'll want accuracy from our machining, so that they need only one or two strokes of a sharp handplane to get them ready for assembly. But for now, machine one face side and one face edge on each component. Pay attention to the grain direction. Like most timber, sapele machines well…unless you stuff it in the wrong way. Mark it up with face and face edge marks.

You can now thickness to within 1/8" of overall width and thickness.

Now return to the bench shop and run a good, sharp handplane over that face side. You should know the grain direction – your face mark tells you that. The surface is flat but has machine marks; take those out with parallel strokes of a your finely set plane. Six to 10 stokes per side should do it. Having done the face side, do the face edge as well. If you are taking off more than the machine marks, you are doing way too much.

If you are unlucky, you may have some wild grain and a scraper will be needed. We are not wild about scraper planes at Rowden. I do almost all of my scraping just with a card scraper, working into the figured area and trying not to create a hollow. But we have had fun with the old Stanley No. 80 – this is basically a card scraper in a small body, and you can work it in all directions once you know how to set it up.

In Praise of the No. 80

OK – I will digress here, but only because the No. 80 is such a wonderful simple tool – way better than the more expensive scraper planes we have seen. See on the image below the slightly blue area on the sole of the scraper? This is where it cuts. Note the knob on the front; it can be tightened to curve the blade so it only cuts in the centre.

Sharpening is key – we prep the two long edges at 25° straight off the grinder, then turn a burr with a good burnisher. To be safe, hold it in the vice and stroke the burnisher at 25°, then roll it down to 35°. You should be able to feel a nice little hook. (You should be able to turn three burrs before you need to regrind, as with most scrapers.) Put the blade in the body and snugged down onto the bench. Some makers slide a sheet of paper between the body and bench to set a small blade projection, but I prefer to bend the blade.

I do that by twisting the central screw on the front until the centre of the blade just pokes out. This gives you a fine scraping. The bed of the plane is small, so needs to be checked for flat. It's an inexpensive and very useful plane.

Fig. 23.16. Lay the boards out on trestles (with ours, the more weight you put on them, the better they get). Give each board a really good look, take a piece of chalk and mark defects.

Fig. 23.17. The Stanley No. 80.

Fig. 23.18. The sole of the No. 80.

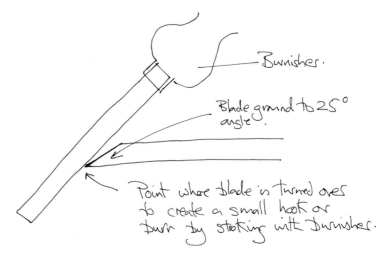

Fig. 23.19. How to turn the hook on the cabinet scraper.

Fig. 24.1. Basically, a mortice is a hole. With hand tools, you can chop it out with mortice chisels or drill out the waste and pare to the lines. But we use a morticing machine.

JOINTING THE STONE

Joinery – that's what this is about. Joints that hold components together. In this case, versions of one joint, the mortice and tenon. There are on this bench frame three different versions: stub mortices and tenons; through-wedged mortices and tenons; and through dry-tusk-wedged mortices and tenons. So that you can take this structure apart to move it, the tusk wedges are just friction fit, but the bench is solid as a rock when assembled.

To gain strength, we use wedges in two of the three joints. In the knockdown joint, the top of the mortice is angled – a wedge is driven in above it to hold the structure. But this is getting too complex too soon – let's look at the simple through-wedged mortice-and-tenon joint.

Basically, a mortice is a hole. With hand tools, you can chop it out with mortice chisels or drill out the waste and pare to the lines. But we use a morticing machine, which saves lots of work. This is basically a drill bit that cuts slightly ahead of a square cutter that chops out the corners.

First let's get into marking-out mode. This diagram

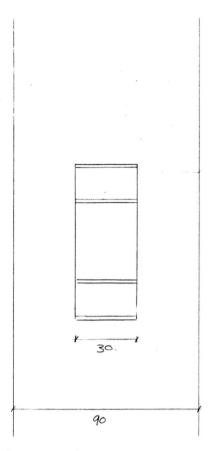

Fig. 24.2. Exterior of the joint.

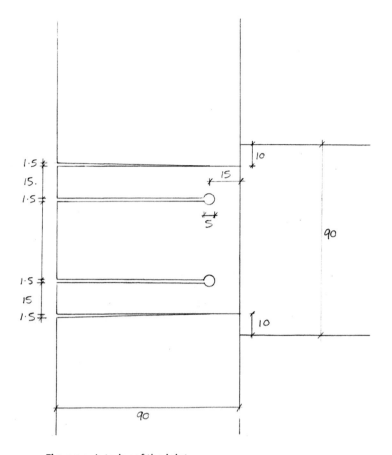

Fig. 24.3. Interior of the joint.

gives you the idea. Mark distinctly both the component position and the mortice position. Mark the mortice with a mortice gauge, with the knives set 30mm apart. As always, mark from the face side of each component.

This is the type of drawing (above) that I like to see every student make before making a joint – it helps one to think about what is being done, and to think about the mechanics of this joint. This is not just a peg in a hole with glue; it's a mechanically effective joint that would hold up without any glue. The two small wedges turn the tenon into a dovetail, splayed wider at the outside than the inside. It's as tough as old boots.

Fig. 24.4. The completed mortices.

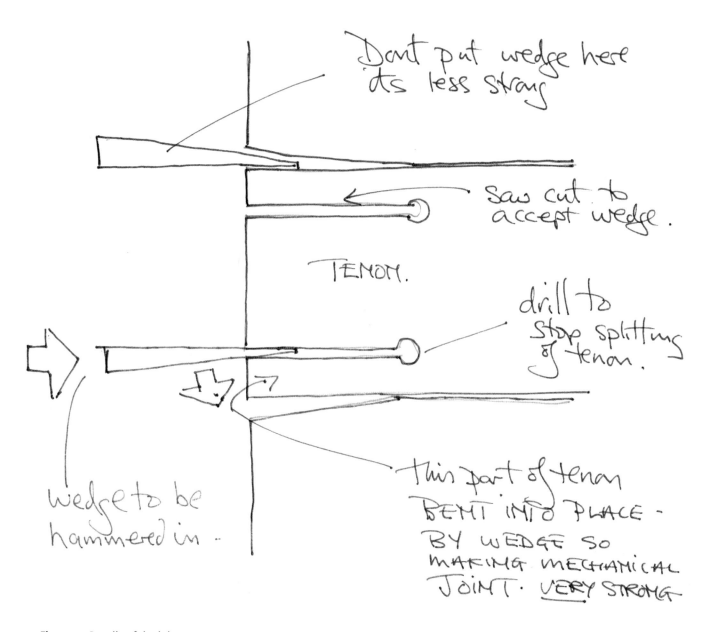

Don't put wedge here as less strong

Saw cut to accept wedge.

TENON.

drill to stop splitting of tenon.

wedge to be hammered in —

this part of tenon BENT INTO PLACE — BY WEDGE SO MAKING MECHANICAL JOINT. VERY STRONG

Fig. 24.5. Details of the joint.

First make the hole (the mortice) then the plug (the tenon) to fill it. Our morticer cuts pretty cleanly; I like and use machines that save me time and do a better job than I could. Chopping out a mortice by hand is nice and sweaty work – and some of you will be happy doing it.

The tenon gets marked out with the same mortice-gauge setup (30mm, marked from the face edge). We use a setup on the band saw to cut those tenon cheeks to exactly the right size. Because this joint gets cut a lot, a dedicated setup for it makes good sense.

Have a careful look at the drawing above right,

noting the stop and spacer at the bottom of the page. This stop is simply a block of wood cramped to the band saw table. Next to it is 31.5mm-wide spacer against the fence. The fence has a stop at the end to prevent you from going too deep past the shoulders. The idea is this: After the first cut, you need to move the fence 31.5mm to make the second cut and get a 30mm tenon. Try it out with some scrap. Cut one tenon cheek, take the spacer out, move the fence then cut the second shoulder. Does this give you the tenon you want? If not, cut a new

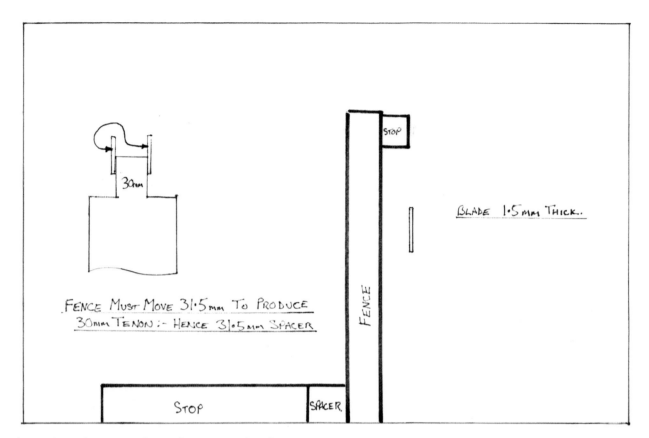

Fig. 24.6. Band saw setup for cutting tenons, plan view.

spacer, thicker or thinner, as needed.

Make sure your blade is good and sharp and that you run slowly into the blade. Chunka, chunka, chunka....

We cut the tenon shoulders at the table saw. The blade height will be the same for all; the shoulder position will be measured for all and a stop set up probably off the end length. Tenon lengths will be different for the different kinds of joints.

2060.

830.

70.20.

350.

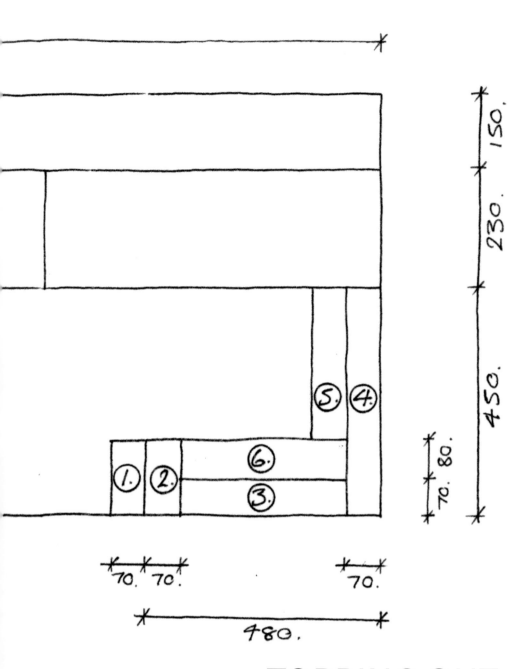

150.

230.

450.

80.
70.

⑤. ④.

⑥.

①. ②.

③.

70. 70.   70.

480.

TOPPING OUT

The benchtops here are usually maple. We can get 3"-thick, kiln-dried maple pretty easily, and it's nearly always good quality. It arrives S2S, with two straight sides – so no mucking about with sapwood and waney edges. We don't want students wrestling with timber that is twisting or has checks and knots. (There's plenty of time for that later.) The two straight sides mean we can specify width when ordering.

The benchtop plan shows a shorter front board, allowing for the later installation of a cabinetmaker's end vice at the right end (if you are left-handed, it goes on the left end). Be careful here – do not make this front board too wide – the end vice will have to be made the same width, and a wide end vice tends to sag over time and cause problems. I would not go wider than 5"; my old beech end vice is that wide and has run well for more than 40 years.

Students here tend to get carried away with bench width. The boards sometimes arrive a bit wider than specified, so they make a wider benchtop with a mean tool well. Don't do that. Unless you have really long

Fig. 25.1. The timber shown here is sapele (right) and maple (left) – nice, clean S2S (sawn on two sides to remove the waney edges) boards for Miklos to break down and machine up.

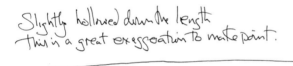

Slightly hollowed down the length
this is a great exaggeration to make point.

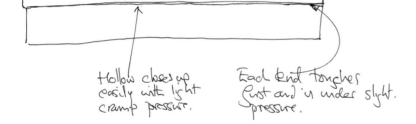

Hollow closes up easily with light cramp pressure.

Each end touches first and is under slight pressure.

Fig. 25.2. We are looking for a long, straight edge that is very slightly hollowed down its length. Having a long board and a short planer (what you in North America call a jointer) will achieve this naturally; it's one reason we don't need a long planer.

and strong arms like Popeye, it's difficult to reach across a wide benchtop. And the tool well is important territory – where else can you keep your cups of tea and half-eaten sandwiches?

So, machine your maple to dimension. Choose that front board carefully; you will be spending a long time in close association with it. Make sure that board has a nice, clean square end that will form one side of the end-vice jaws. I would use the table saw for that cut. Everything else is overlong. We are going to concentrate on the long-grain joints that make up this top. There will be probably be three of them, each 7' long and 3" thick. That's a big glue-up and lots can

go wrong. Our aim is for invisible glue lines the full length of the bench on the top and bottom. Not just one invisible glue line – all three.

If you can do this demanding task on such a large component you can do it anywhere. It's not hard; it's all down to good, careful machining and good hand-tool technique.

Carefully plane and thickness your timber, paying special attention to getting a straight edge off the jointer that is also square to the face side. If it's not bang on, take another pass – a fine trimming cut at the jointer, like you would with a handplane. Good workmanship depends on sensitive use of well-tuned machines that

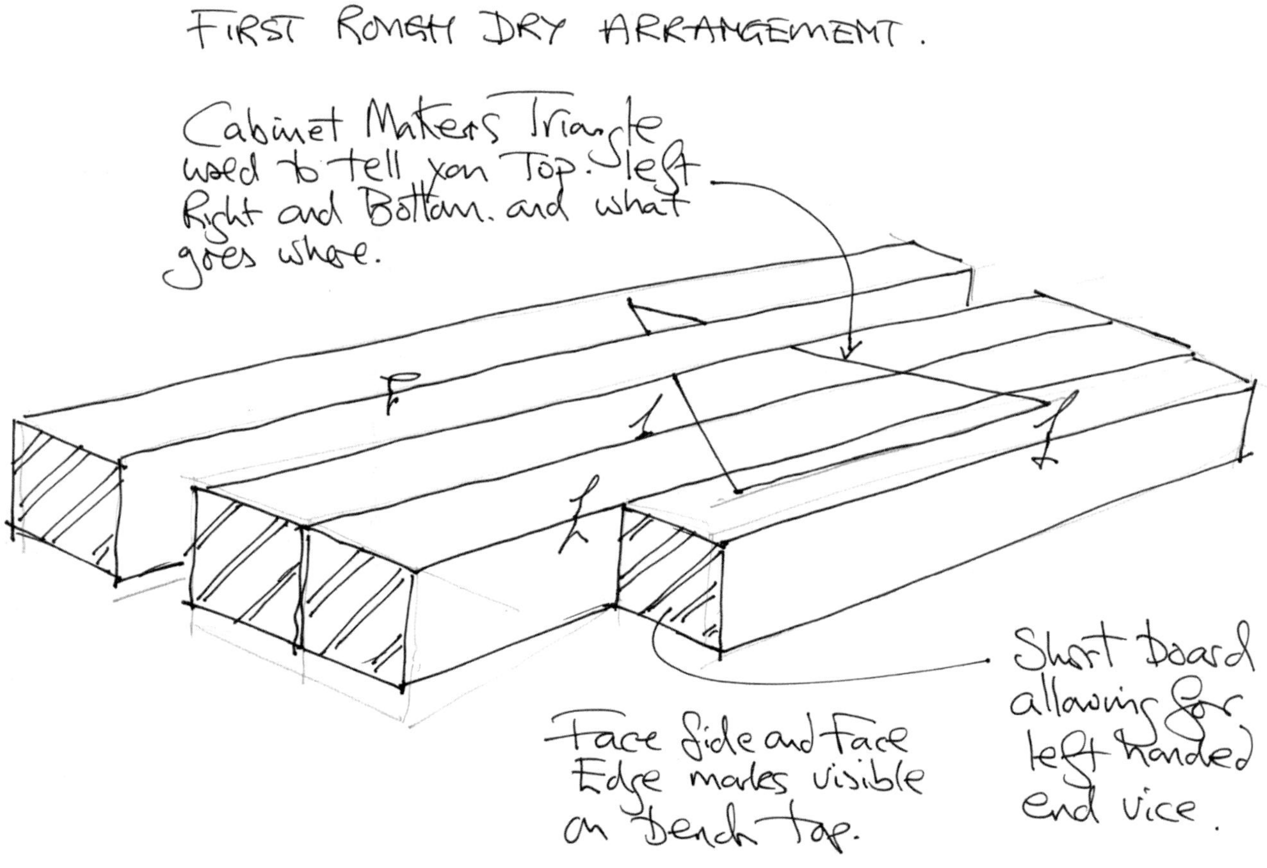

FIRST ROUGH DRY ARRANGEMENT.

Cabinet Makers Triangle
used to tell you Top. Sleft
Right and Bottom. and what
goes where.

Short board
allowing for
left handed
end vice.

Face Side and Face
Edge marks visible
on Bench top.

Fig. 25.3. Arrange the boards in the way you want (remember to put the best-looking edge at the front, because it will also show) then mark them with a cabinetmaker's triangle. It tells you top, front, back, left and right.

are set up correctly. That means you must be sensitive to the machine's needs. Are those blades in need of honing? (Yes, we hone planer irons between grindings, just like a handplane's iron.) The goal is to get the dimensions and surfaces bang on from the machines; then, they need just a tickle with handplane to really, really fit.

We are looking for a long, straight edge that is very slightly hollowed down its length. Having a long board and a short planer (what you in North America call a jointer) will achieve this naturally; it's one reason we don't need a long planer. Our Sedgwick is about 5' long, which is pretty standard for a good machine of this size. We get less than a 1/16" hollow over a long board from this setup.

In this glue-up, the stress is at the end of the joint. All the changes of temperature and moisture will attack there first. The hollow puts pressure first on the two

ends of the joint as the cramps are applied. Get the ends good then take a well-earned bow to the assembled and admiring audience.

Let's now arrange the boards as they will be glued up. Your face sides will all be show surfaces; they will be on the top. Arrange the boards in the way you want (remember to put the best-looking edge at the front, because it will also show) then mark them with a cabinetmaker's triangle. It tells you top, front, back, left and right – so even when you take these to the machine shop and mix them up, you always know which board goes where. The triangle also helps if you have to go back to machining; it tells you clearly which is the top – the side that rides against the carefully set-up planer fence.

A cabinetmaker's triangle is a wonderful thing to use whenever three or more boards are grouped together.

Now get into super-critical mode and really look at

Fig. 25.4. When assembling pieces like this, it's lovely when it's dry, but the moment glue goes on you are wrestling with a wet, slimy monster that has a mind of its own.

those face edges. Are they square from end to end? Do you have a smooth, straight hollow? Some will pass the test; one or two will have to go back to the machine shop. Hey, you are only human.

Having got the machining done, set up a good bench plane. Rowden students don't usually have a smoother at this stage, so they use a No. 6 or a No. 5-1/2. Make sure it's nice and sharp, and set it for fine shaving. Skew the body of the plane on the job to reduce the effective length of the plane.

Here's a trick. When you are bringing together two 7' long x 3" surfaces for a perfect fit, you have a real job on. That is a huge amount of surface to match up. So, cheat – don't even attempt it. Plane a slight hollow in the edge that curves along the board's thickness, just

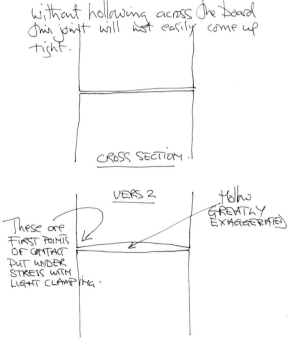

Fig. 25.5. Plane a slight hollow in the edge that curves along the board's thickness, just a few shavings.

Fig. 25.6. If you find yourself bending the cramp handle to pull a joint tight, something is wrong. Step back, engage your wonderful brain and work it out.

a few shavings. If your bench plane is taking a shaving as wide as two fingers, then three passes will do it: one down the centre first; then one shaving as near as you dare to the bottom; then the last and trickiest – one just at the top, without touching the very edge. Hurrah!

Like the hollow along the length, this hollow transfers cramp pressure to the bottom and top edges, where we want them bang-up tight. This is how you achieve an impeccable, invisible glue line between two thick maple boards along a 7' length. Pretty cool, huh?

I must stress this is achieved by probably no more than three long shavings – more than that, and you start damaging the machined surface rather than improving it. You get the idea: nice, tidy hand-tool skills used to improve really good machine work.

Now let's look at what stands between us and assembly. We need to rout a groove in the second board.

The tail vice will run in it, so it is important that the groove be straight and parallel to the benchtop – so rout carefully.

When assembling pieces like this, it's lovely when it's dry, but the moment glue goes on you are wrestling with a wet, slimy monster that has a mind of its own. We badly want that benchtop surface to be what we call "in register"; that is, the surfaces should line up very closely. Without that, we are in for a shed full of handplaning to get a dead-flat surface.

So, we insert a few biscuits along the face edges to help with registration. Biscuits are wonderful; the biscuit joiner has been a favourite machine at Rowden forever. Set it up to cut a slot 1/2" from the top surface, then mark the two components with

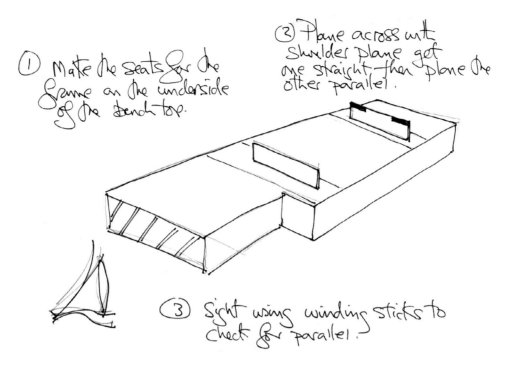

① Make the seats for the frame on the underside of the bench top.

② Plane across with shoulder plane get one straight, then plane the other parallel.

③ Sight using winding sticks to check for parallel.

Fig. 25.7. Get a good, long straightedge and check out the benchtop. Look for high spots and mark them.

a pencil across the joint. Register the biscuit joiner on that mark, cut a slot in both pieces, then insert a dry biscuit. The biscuits are compressed beech; when glue hits them, they expand and make a really tight joint. We suggest you don't paint glue on the biscuits as you insert them; they are just there for location purposes. With glue on them, you have to be blazing fast with your glue-up and, with respect, you are not quite there yet.

We are approaching glue-up time. Our procedure for a simple glue-up is the same as for a more complex one: first, do a dry-assembly. This demands that you gather all the cramps you need, that you make or borrow cramping blocks and check very carefully how the surfaces pull up. The rule is "two nicely made surfaces, a little bit of glue, a little bit of pressure." If you find yourself bending the cramp handle to pull a joint tight, something is wrong. Step back, engage your wonderful brain and work it out.

Another rule is to have a glue-up buddy, someone who can remain calm and pass you that missing cramp whilst you are climbing around the ceiling. OK, you are set up. It has gone together dry, you and your buddy have glue brushes at hand and you have hot water and rags to clean up the squeeze-out. And it's not Friday afternoon. Go for it. With PVA (yellow glue), you have 10 minutes of open time. This is the critical time – you and your buddy want the job cramped inside of 10 minutes.

I love glue-ups in the shop; it's a time of stress and adrenaline, a time to gently tease and support. We manage at Rowden to bring almost all glue-ups to a successful conclusion because of our system. When we design a piece of work, we design for glue-up by breaking a huge, high-stress project glue-up into two or three smaller sub-assemblies that are more easily managed.

The Friday Syndrome

I used to ban all Friday afternoon glue-ups. It was Dobbo's fault. A young man who was keen as mustard, Dobbo had a small cabinet with dovetailed corners, with two drawer rails to go in the front – nothing complex. Dobbo was banging away at his cabinet hoping to get the joints glued on a Friday afternoon.

He was worried about his dovetails. But after he glued up, he came away with a grin on his face.

"All OK" I asked?

"Yep, all OK," he said.

I wandered over to his bench. "Dobbo, what are these two drawer rails doing on the bench?" Silence. Then, "AAAAAGH!!!!"

It's natural to want to get the project together, then go home for the weekend with a warm, fuzzy feeling of a job well done. But rushing a glue-up is stupid. You may have weeks of work at stake – components with carefully cut joints, carefully made surfaces. Don't risk it.

Flattening the Top

With the glue dry, it's tempting to take a bench plane to the benchtop. You can, but I would wait until it is fixed on the frame. Get it cut to length and plane the front and back edges. Then plane up the backboard of the tool well.

You now need to cut grooves in the benchtop for splines that support the tool well. These splines are just three pieces of MDF, and they need to be loose because you will want to slide them about to poke cramps up through the tool well every now and again.

Now cut a mortise in the benchtop to house the face vice on the left end (or right end for lefties). We use Record 63-1/2 vices here; they have a quick-release function that can dump your job on your toes once every 10 years, but we put up with this as an endearing foible rather than a reason to go elsewhere. A good metal vice with serious wooden jaws is what we want here. You will find that the end vice will get more general use, but this is still a key tool.

Set the benchtop on the frame. Does it sit flat on the two rails, or is one corner high? You can plane the whole surface, but I would plane just two areas on the benchtop where the rails sit. Make them dead flat and parallel. Use winding sticks to check them. Now fit the top to the frame. Affix the backboard behind the tool well now, too. You want your flat surface to include that backboard. Why? Well, there will be times when you use this surface as an engineer's surface plate. Developing models, making small-scale prototypes – all will be done on the bench. If you draw a 79° angle on the

Fig. 25.8. It's flat and lovely, and you are feeling pleased with yourself – and rightly so. Now resolve to keep it in good order and not damage it too much.

benchtop, you need to know the benchtop is really flat so that the 79° angle is actually 79°.

Get a good, long straightedge, and check out the benchtop. Look for high spots and mark them. Following Daren's lead, set a plane with a quite heavily rounded iron to work, planing diagonally. Then go the other way, so your second passes cross the first at right angles. Then change planes to a regular No. 6 with a more typical iron and go down the length. Finally, take thin wispy, shavings as you get near to flat. I have watched Daren doing this on his own bench – usually after a big job or at the end of the year. It sets his bench to right.

So, there you are: It's flat and lovely, and you are feeling pleased with yourself – and rightly so. Now resolve to keep it in good order and not damage it too much.

Oh, I did have a student who was so proud and anal about his benchtop that he couldn't bear to work on it. The solution was me, much encouragement, a large hammer and a cheering crowd to get him past that one.

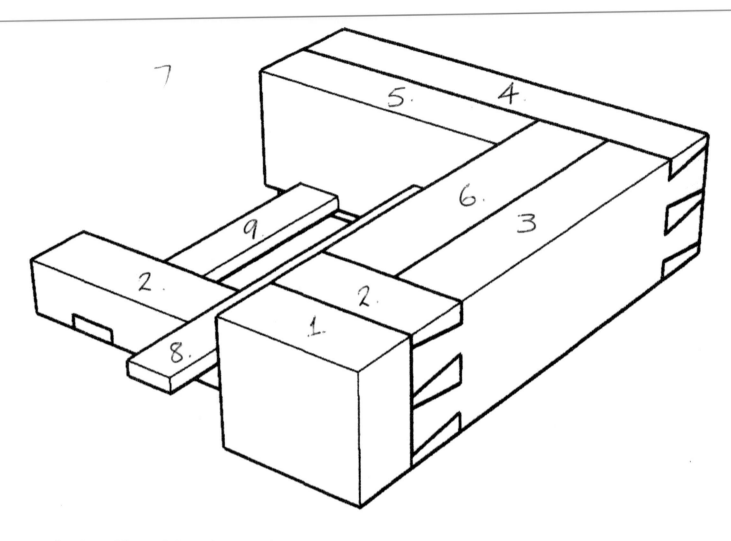

Fig. 26.1. Building a tail vice such as this is difficult. And that's a good thing.

THE END GAME

The tail vice is the one you will use more than any other. You will use it with dogs in holes up and down the benchtop, and without. It is, unlike the metal face vice at the other end, an unrestricted way to hold a job. The jaws will be leather lined to avoid marking your work, and it will become your buddy – the tool that holds the job flat and lovely.

It's true: This is deliberately difficult and hard to make. And this is exactly why you should make it, rather than buying a metal end vice. There's nothing wrong with many commercial solutions – it's just that

making this in wood, the old way, is good for you. Once you have, and complete the bench, you can stand back and proudly say, "I did that!"

Let's start with the drawings – always a good place to start. Fortunately, we have a few.

Have a good look at these three on the facing page and see what they tell us. First, the main components are labeled 2, 3 and 4. They are joined together with huge dovetails (I said this would be fun!). Those three components come together to make the moving part of the vice. Components 1 and 5 are fixed to the benchtop. Component 8 is a rail, fixed to the underside

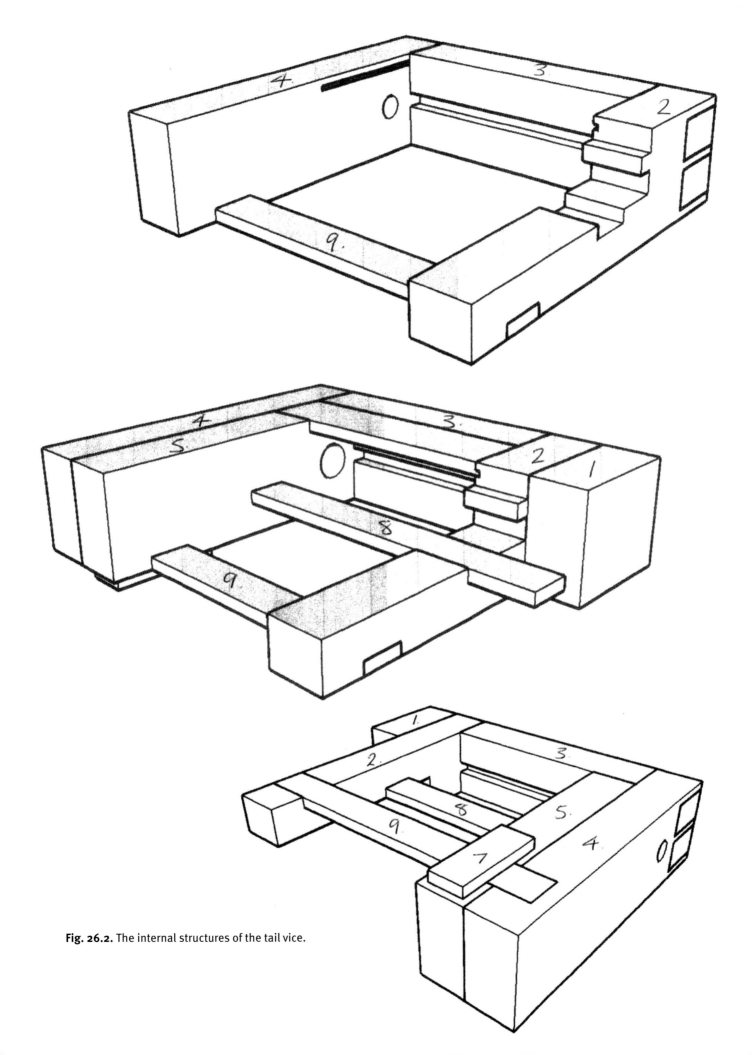

Fig. 26.2. The internal structures of the tail vice.

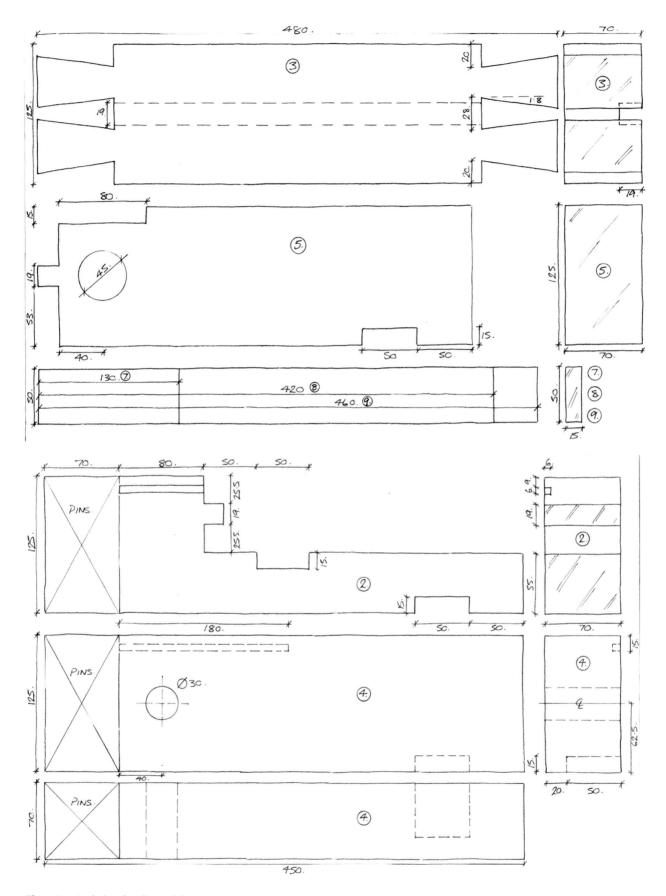

Fig. 26.3. End vice details and dimensions.

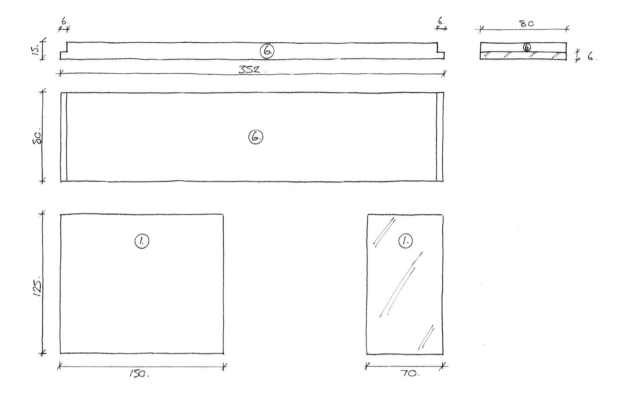

Fig. 26.4. End vice details and dimensions (continued).

of the bench, and 9 is a strut to help keep everything nice and square.

By now you should be a dab hand at making up a cutting list, going out and selecting the stuff, cutting it up using the FEWTEL mnemonic, and bringing it back to the bench shop.

This is Alex's bench – at this point, she's finished the base and top, has selected and milled the end-vice material. She's ready to build and install it.

Now this is fun – you are about to cut big dovetails and learn to use a band saw with the same kind of accuracy you want from a dovetail saw. Your band saw has to be running nicely to do this. You cannot condemn that poor saw just to roughing out and cutting curves! Get a nice blade, set the guides up and get the table at right angles – that's about all there is to getting a band saw to run OK. (Well, maybe a bit more magic with a black cloak and a club hammer.)

Let's first understand what is going on here. Component 3 is cut first, then used as a template to mark the position of the pins on components 2 and 4.

To get this to work what do we need? We need a jig! A nice simple 1:8 jig that looks a bit like the drawings on the next spread. This is a simple guide that holds your job and runs against the fence. You cut line 1, then flip the job and cut line 2. You then turn the component and cut line 3, then flip it to do line 4. All you have to do is saw down those lines and stop at the back line. Easy peasey. Reset for the half-pins and do lines 5, 6, 7 and 8 in the same way.

Next cut all the rubbish, clearing to the back line. You can get pretty near with a band saw, but chisels and mallets finish the job.

We pretty well always cut the tails first then use them to mark out your pins. And that's what we do here – not with a blunt pencil but with a nice, sharp knife.

Set up to transfer your lines and mark a nice, clear knife line. Then, we use another band saw jig (well we would, wouldn't we). This is a cradle that holds your job but at the 1:8 angle for cutting the pins. You snug your job against the jig and move the fence until the band saw is set to make a cut that barely leaves the knife

Fig. 26.5. Alex's bench.

Fig. 26.6. Dovetails cut.

Fig. 26.7. Tails cut; pins marked.

line – not miles away because this would leave you with loads of paring. If you leave just a hair's breadth on each side, you will get a fit straight off the saw.

Right – this is where it gets complex. This is where students sit on the floor for a half-hour just looking at the underside of a neighbour's bench, trying to work out what the heck is going on.

You have the major parts: the benchtop; the vice made of three components dovetailed together beauti-

fully; and a few more bits and bobs. Let's look at the drawings shown earlier. There are two basic guidance systems on which the vice moves. Look at component 5, which gets fixed to the end of the benchtop. Notice that at the left end it has a small tongue that mates with a groove in component 3 (same drawings, upper right). This is the main guide. Now look at component 2. There is that tenon again – only this time the groove is in the benchtop. Be sure to make these tenons nice and snug fits in the grooves.

The other guides are flat rails, components 8 and 9. Component 8 is fixed to the underside of the benchtop and component 2 has a groove that fits around it to slide up and down. Component 9 is in mid-air; it's fixed to components 2 and 4, and there is a rebate in component 5 that 9 slides in, with a cap piece that holds it in place – the cap is one of the last pieces of the jigsaw puzzle.

The key to doing this, and to recognise the reference surfaces (from which you mark), is a full-size drawing of all the vice components. It sounds a faff, and most of our students get around it with revising their components to an old full-size rod (what some people call "the print" or "the plans").

First comes Component 2 – make sure the tongue matches the groove in which it has to run. The other factor is setting the top of the vice just above the benchtop by half a millimetre.

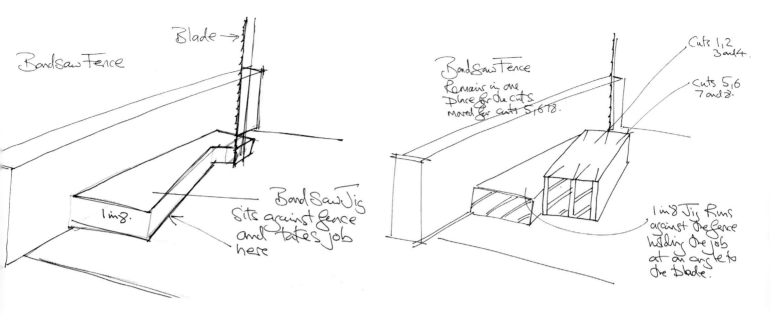

Fig. 26.8. Band saw jig for cutting the dovetails (left) and in use (right).

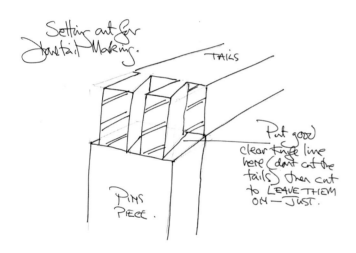

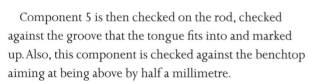

Fig. 26.9. Tail transfer setup.

Fig. 26.10. Tails complete on component No. 2.

Component 5 is then checked on the rod, checked against the groove that the tongue fits into and marked up. Also, this component is checked against the benchtop aiming at being above by half a millimetre.

Cramp together components 4, 5 and 2, making sure they're in the correct orientation and flush at the front and top, then scribe the dado locations across all three parts. These dados capture Component 9.

Mark and rout a small groove in components 4 and 2 to accept the panel (which isn't numbered) that covers the metal screw and also forms part of the vice top – it's

Fig. 26.11. Components Nos. 4 and 5.

Fig. 26.12. Alex at work on the tail vice components.

Fig. 26.13. Alex checking for square/flat.

not structural, but it's an important part as it's where your plane sits waiting to get used.

Once you've marked them out, cut close to your lines with either a band saw or handsaw. Then pare the tenons carefully to fit the grooves, making sure all the shoulders are clean and square. It's all good, solid and straightforward making – it's just that you need to be careful and accurate to get this baby to slide. Which it will.

Components 1 and 5 are fitted to the benchtop. When I made my bench, component 5 was attached with a couple of long coach bolts. Now we recommend biscuits and long screws – lots of them.

When assembling the vice, it's critical to keep everything square and true. Look how well Alex has kept her vice true to the squareness of the benchtop. It fits up close. And where it didn't this morning it does this

Fig. 26.14. The completed vice.

afternoon (after a few shavings with a plane).

Once you've fit it, plane it flush with the bench-top then drill for dog holes in the vice and in the benchtop. Then turn a vice handle, and you are done. Well done, my dear.

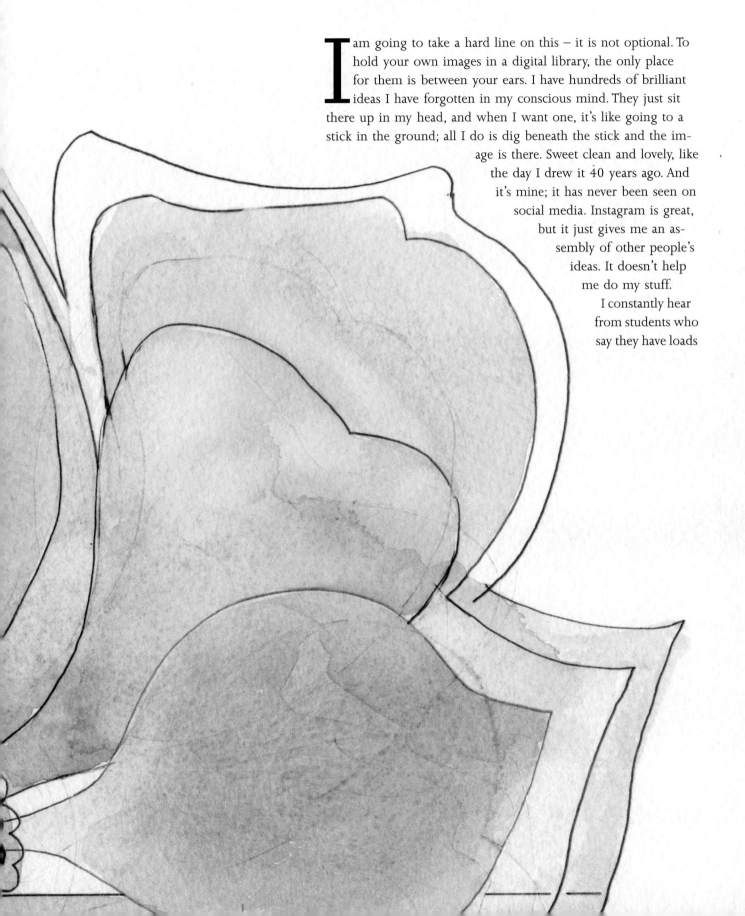

THE NOW CURIOUS EYE

I am going to take a hard line on this – it is not optional. To hold your own images in a digital library, the only place for them is between your ears. I have hundreds of brilliant ideas I have forgotten in my conscious mind. They just sit there up in my head, and when I want one, it's like going to a stick in the ground; all I do is dig beneath the stick and the image is there. Sweet clean and lovely, like the day I drew it 40 years ago. And it's mine; it has never been seen on social media. Instagram is great, but it just gives me an assembly of other people's ideas. It doesn't help me do my stuff.

I constantly hear from students who say they have loads

Fig. 27.1. We start with still life, which is what is says on the tin. Still life doesn't move. We simplify this to white cubes, cones, rectangles and cylinders.

of ideas but just can't put them down. Well here is how you do that – you learn to draw. Drawing is the means for you to express your visual ideas. It need not be a great drawing, as long as you can read it.

I have never been one for sitting quietly, watching a candle and minding my breathing. Meditation always struck me as inactive. The drawing class is, however, the closest I get to meditation whilst being active, whilst doing something, whilst making something. The atmosphere is intense. It should be. We are all concentrating very hard. I go into a drawing class grumpy and preoccupied; I come out drained but energised, exhausted but centred, calm and focused. I have just used a part of my head that seldom gets used, a part of the brain central to our existence.

To draw, we need to use the right half of our brain – this is where music, visual intelligence and that holistic instinct comes from. To use the right brain, we need to be aware that the dominant left brain is always dominant. It will always want to interfere. "Why bother doing that?!" it says, looking at you drawing a bicycle. "Here's a great symbol for that." That is why so many early attempts to draw can get pushed aside – we make childish drawings that really are not what is in front of us, that are not true.

We begin to teach you to draw by removing all complications – movement, colour, curves, light and dark

– anything that may jump up and bite you. We start with still life, which is what is says on the tin. Still life doesn't move. We simplify this to white cubes, cones, rectangles and cylinders. There are some curves there for the clever amongst you, but mostly this is straight-line stuff. We set this up on a white paper background and tell it to sit still.

Now we tell you to sit still. And we mean it. Your head must remain in one place when you are drawing. You can't waltz around the studio being arty and creative; your job is to sit quietly and look damn hard. Set your board up vertically on an easel. Now tape the paper on the board. Are you looking to the left or right of the board? Is the right your dominant eye and you are looking right of the board? OK – that's the goal. Spend a little time moving your easel in toward the still life and out to get the image to fill your paper. This is critical: You are going to draw the same size as the still life. Not bigger. Not smaller. The same size exactly on your paper as you see the object to the side of your drawing board.

Place the board at the end of your arm. What? Extend your arm from where you are sitting, head in one place, with a nice, straight arm. The paper should be just there at the end of your reach, so you can mark a line on it easily. Please don't whine about your arm getting tired and wanting to bring

Figs. 27.2 & 27.3. We need to train the eye and the hand at the same time. So far, we have quite free, long movements of the hand to make those straight lines. Practice, practice, practice; move, move, move.

the board nearer to you.

Paul Cézanne, when painting Mont Sainte-Victoire in Provence, said, "I have three paintings from here, one if I move my head to the left another in the middle and a third to my right." He wasn't joking. So, keep your head in one place, sit on a chair and once set up, mark on the floor where the chair is. Don't move it.

Now start looking. Pretty soon, the left brain will start getting stroppy, but let him go quiet. Only let thoughts into the drawing studio that are about drawing. Is this too high? Is that line too long? Is that line the correct angle? Any other thoughts, such as, "You are no good at this," and "It's waste of time," leave at the studio door.

Start with the nearest point. All I want from this are about 10 well-observed lines – the edges or corners of the white stuff in front of you. It will take you a good hour, and you will be knackered at the end. But you will have 10 well-looked-at lines. Use your arm and a good, long pencil. Choose an edge of a component near you – say it's the side of the cube, and it's at about the middle of your page. Take your arm and move it up and down, with the pencil near but not on the page. You are practicing, moving your arm and the tip of the pencil where it needs to go, but the lead of the pencil is not touching the page. What if I lowered that pencil and it touched the paper, but I still kept my arm moving? Oh! It's a nice line. Right. Good job. Let's build from that.

Arm outstretched, head still, let's find the top of that line on the still life. Put your pencil horizontally on the exact top of the line on the still life. Now move your arm across to your drawing and see how it intersects with your pencil line. That's where the line ends. Make a small mark, then repeat the process to check that mark is right. Now do the same for the bottom of the line. Now my arty friend, we have One Well-observed Line. A line in the right place that stops and starts where it should. Phew! Nine more to go.

This process is called sighting. It's an ancient technique to measure visual distances accurately. There is little artiness in this; we are just looking damn hard and putting down what we see. To transfer an angle, put the pencil on the angled edge and move it across. Soon, you are building up a group of lines and you can look at the gaps between. Is this higher than that? Is this longer than that? Repeat this a few times, and it will make more and more sense. Drawing at the start is just looking very hard.

We need to train the eye and the hand at the same time. So far, we have quite free, long movements of the hand to make those straight lines. Practice, practice, practice; move, move, move; dab the line in there. Keep it free and loose.

But drawing is lots of different kinds of lines; lots of different hand, arm and finger movements all need practice. Start with stirring a cup of tea round and round, and soon we get this.

The essence is not to stop and get tense, but to look at the form to be expressed and then draw, see what

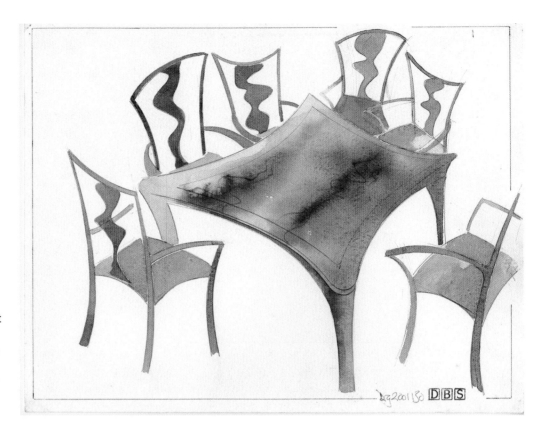

Fig. 27.4. Ignore that man in the front of your head who says, "You can't do this! Who the bloody hell do you think you are?"

happens on the page, be surprised. Try to avoid being too controlling; what you want is the back of your head in control, not the front.

My advice to students is to look hard and draw like this four times a week for maybe 20 minutes. That will get you looking pretty well after only a few weeks.

The difficult thing is just doing it. You will want to do it, but you must make it important and must make time for it. Most of us are silly and just find something more important to do – like sanding. You must not do that. Drawing is the most important thing you can learn.

Draw anything near at hand – a teacup, the handle of a mug. The mundane should not stop you. You will find visual depth in the way a handle fixes on to a mug. Just draw, dammit – and don't stop drawing. The more you draw the better you get, and the sharper your eyes get. Do you know most of us only use 20 percent of our visual ability? The ability to see more is within you – just draw.

Pretty soon, as the "see more" kicks in, you will be coming home from walks with a bunch of nettles or a seashell – things that caught your now-curious eye.

This new object is something to look at really hard, something to feed your imagination, to fill in new shapes, to put down new forms you like to play with. But first draw and understand; without understanding, there is no knowledge, just impression.

To put down images with not knowing why…we do lots of stuff in this drawing game without knowing why. We put down doodles and sketches because it feels right, not because we have reason. We are close now to our instinctive side – using our intuition and listening to what she tells us. Pay good attention to her. Learn to listen and do what she says, even if it makes no sense; she is the best guide you have.

Ignore that man in the front of your head who says, "You can't do this! Who the bloody hell do you think you are?" Ignore him. But that quiet voice from the back of the head, in a softer, more gentle tone that says, "David, are you quite sure about that?" To this woman, I have learned to listen.

Fig. 27.5. We are close now to our instinctive side – using our intuition and listening to what she tells us.

Sc 1:75. Drg 180723 DBS

Fig. 28.1. What we have are skeletons of what were once great buildings. These temples, for that is what they were, were the home of a god.

PROPORTION: IT'S ALL GREEK TO ME

This is a good one. Please do not think, just because I went to two of the best art schools there are, that I was taught this stuff. Christopher Ruscombe-King, a lecturer at the Ruskin, once did a very bored and disinterested sketch of the Fibonacci series on the side of my drawing, but that was it. I saw the nautilus shell and wondered what it was all about.

I first stumbled across this proportion thing while on holiday in Europe. It was the summer of 1971, and I was driving around in an old and rattly open-top Morgan with a young, beautiful blonde Jan Savage. We were traveling from campsite to campsite in Greece, heading for the islands. John Fowles' novel "The Magus" had just been published, and the mystic nonsense of that was attractive. I saw a road sign to Delphi that rattled my memory systems. "Something happened there; I think it was an Oracle or something; shall we go see?"

I am not one for looking at piles of old stones in the hot sweaty sun, but two things at Delphi grabbed me by the throat: the first was in the museum, the second was the ampitheatre.

In the museum are many wonderful things, but the stunner is a bronze statue. This is a life-size image made in honour of a Sicilian charioteer who won an important race eons ago.

What remains for us is the driver with the threads of the reins in his hands; what we can imagine is the whole chariot with horses. The eloquence of the charioteer is stunning. This depicts the moment of victory when he presents his horses and chariot to the crowd. It celebrates his prowess as an athlete, for athleticism was celebrated, but it also shows his control and humility.

Look a little harder; the astounding feat is the technical casting of this bronze. Done in 480 BCE, it was as clean and complex a bit of casting as you will ever see. I was sharing a house at that time with a sculptor, so I had some understanding of the process. The reins, those floppy bits of bronze, the delicate eyelashes. All the little fiddly bits you might expect to have been poured in separate castings and affixed later. No – this

Fig. 28.2. Look a little harder; the astounding feat is the technical casting of this bronze. Done in 480 BCE, it was as clean and complex a bit of casting as you will ever see.

Fig. 28.3. Oratory and poetry were of great importance to the ancient Greeks, so they made amphitheatres with perfect acoustics.

PHOTO: ANDREA SCHAFFER

was one casting! It was poured and cast – in 480 BCE –with hot metal at one go. I doubt if we could do this now. And we think we are clever.

We left the museum to stagger out into the stunning heat of the day, and went to sit at the top of a well-preserved ampitheatre. The place was empty – empty that is, except for a Dutch couple talking waaaaay down at the bottom. They were about 300' away, but we could hear their conversation as if they were next to us (which is how I knew they were Dutch). "What's with this place! This is weird," I thought.

I learnt what was going on by sharing this many years later with a student who had been a musician.

"Ah," he said. "They were standing near the sounding stone."

Oratory and poetry were of great importance to the ancient Greeks, so they made amphitheatres with perfect acoustics. One place toward the back of the circular stage, near where the modern-day path cuts across, gave perfect acoustics. This was the sounding stone, where you would stand to give perfect oration to the whole audience.

How the Greeks achieved this I do not know. But the following all play a part: the stone, which bounces sound pretty well; the circular lay and arc shape of the seating; and the amphitheatre's circular shape (the circle is a particularly important form in classical architecture).

Whatever. I immediately became a Classicist. Let's understand, shall we, what the term means. It refers to a period of Greek history around 400 BCE. When I am talking about "Classic," I don't mean last year's Mercedes, or an old style of brogue shoes. Advertising has corrupted the usage so allow me, in this case, be pedantic.

I'll put it in a primal manner. The measurement of proportion: How big is it? How high, how long, how wide? How far away is it? Will it eat me, or will I eat it? These are life-saving proportions and essential measures. And they have nothing to do with numbers. These are visual proportions measured with the eye.

My discovery of Classical proportion has been a 40-year journey, during which I learned that Classicism has been rediscovered at least three times in European cultural history: First by the Romans, in about 100 BCE; then in the Renaissance in Florence in 1400 (the very word, renaissance, means rebirth, a rebirth of Neo Platonic values, or all stuff to do with Plato); then with architect William Adam, we have Neo Classicism in the early 18th century. All had to do with rediscovering the values and civilization of the ancient Greeks.

Let me take you now to Segesta, in Sicily. This was another holiday with Jan, this time in a lovely open-topped yellow Citroen Dyane Six. This yellow tin can pulled us reliably and lovingly to another Greek mind-blowing experience. The Italians are rather better at keeping Greek stones intact. The Greeks, despite their protestations, have in the past tended to knock down and reuse Classic buildings for material, which explains why some of the best Greek sites are, in fact, in Italy.

Fig. 28.4. The Greeks regarded architecture as a low and miserable art form – nothing compared to mathematics or poetry.

What we have are skeletons of what were once great buildings. These temples, for that is what they were, were the home of a god. They were constructed in special locations worthy of their inhabitants.

Segesta is on the top of a cliff, overlooking the sea. We camped nearby, and I made sure we got up early to be the first on the site when it opened in the morning. Having a few minutes alone in a place like this can be intoxicating. The sun was coming up over the sea; it was just stunning.

I have to say here that looking at photographs doesn't really do it for me. They remind me of what it was like to be there, but they do not take me there. Go stand in front of these stones and slowly, if you can, gather in what they mean. That is the way to do it.

The Greeks regarded architecture as a low and miserable art form – nothing compared to mathematics or poetry. The word *poesis* in Greek means "where before there was nothing." This is a familiar term to any creative; we are used to pulling stuff out of nowhere. Yet the temples are places of great presence. Each temple would have within it a single statue of the god whose home it was. These were places of high theatre. What we see is a stone skeleton of dusty remains.

Within that stone frame was a painted wooden structure that has not survived and within that, the god. Surrounded by flickering lamps, extending before the god, would be a shallow pool that often reached to the edges of the room, and it was often filled with olive oil. The god would be a large wooden image, frequently ivory-clad, 20' or 30' high. Just imagine, if you will, her image reflected dramatically in the pool. You, a poor supplicant, were allowed to approach the god – though she was of course jealously protected by the acolytes. This was your experience – just a glimpse of a real god.

But just looking at the stone bones now left to us, what do we find? Well, it's hard to explain, but it feels like very complex simplicity. On first view, there is not a lot to look at: an entablature or floor, with steps up to it; a whole load of columns; a pediment on top of the columns. That's it. Three elements – what the heck is the fuss about?

It is the simplicity and the complexity shown through each of those elements. It's as if the maker wanted to give us something simple, then tweak it to make the eye look again. The entablature is as flat as pancake but domed in the centre, very slightly extending a curve down the building and across. The dome is almost not there – but it is there.

The columns are not parallel sided, as that would be far too easy to make. They are a complex construction, and belly slightly out on each to be subtly curved – a feature called "entasis." While not a feature at Segesta,

Fig. 28.5. The columns are not parallel sided, as that would be far too easy to make. They are a complex construction, and belly slightly out on each to be subtly curved.

PHOTO: PEDRO HERNANDEZ

many columns were also fluted, a technique used to break up the harsh sunlight to define and reduce this heavy form into delightful thin lines of light and shade. Another complexity is that the columns are not vertical; they lean in slightly. This could be good building practice in a land where earthquakes are common. Or it is another tease for the eye. Or both.

Then we come to the intervals between the verticals and horizontals; mathematicians go bonkers about this. I suggest, however, that it is not about measure and number but about visual relationships.

The Parthenon is, of course, at the centre of ancient Greece. It is magnificent. Its architect, Phidias, is a marvel of the ancient world. But modern restrictions and restoration work on the site stop your getting too near it. So as great as the Parthenon is, if you only can get to a couple of places, go to Sicily to see Selinunte and Segesta.

Failing that, go and stand in front of a good Classical building. There are lots in Washington, D.C., so go and look at what is going on. Take your dividers and measure with your eyes. Find squares and circles. Find

relationships of low-integer numbers – 1:1, 1:2, 3:2. These are what you are looking for. These are the applications of Classical proportions you need to know. You need to know because you need to know how to hide them in your own work.

When, much later, I married Carol, we went on honeymoon to Turkey. Not far away was Ephesus, one of the centres of the ancient world, so we took a trip. It's a big place with old stones everywhere, hard to understand. But Carol found me as I sat staring at the wonderful reconstructed facade of The Library of Celsus. I had a pad and pencil and was waving my arm about measuring heights and widths.

"What you doing?" she asked.

"Oh, well, I am just looking at this building."

"How long are you going to be?"

"About half an hour! This one is more complex than I thought!" I think she must have wondered what kind of idiot she had married.

This building is a Roman example of the complex use of Classical proportions in a facade. How many squares can you see? Take it from this side of the

Fig. 28.6. The Parthenon is, of course, at the centre of ancient Greece. It is magnificent. Its architect, Phidias, is a marvel of the ancient world. But modern restrictions and restoration work on the site stop your getting too near it.

column to the outside of that column. Go from the big pediment to the floor. Then that empty space – is that a golden section rectangle? Now you are looking! So far, we have introduced two forms, the circle and the square. As we develop this, we will see how those simple forms recur and evolve to fit with other proportional schemes.

You have come to Classical architecture and have examined, at least superficially, an element of the most advanced European culture. You have seen the way simple forms, steps, columns and a pediment can be arranged with wit and sophistication. They can also be arranged with banality and dullness. So, look for the good ones. I will show you what to look for, then when you get there, sit down, draw it, measure it up, see what's going. Use digital to record as an aide memoire – but don't trust digital to give you the juice.

Fig. 28.7. The Library of Celsus is a Roman example of the complex use of classical proportions in a facade. How many squares can you see?

PHOTO: CAROLE RADDATO

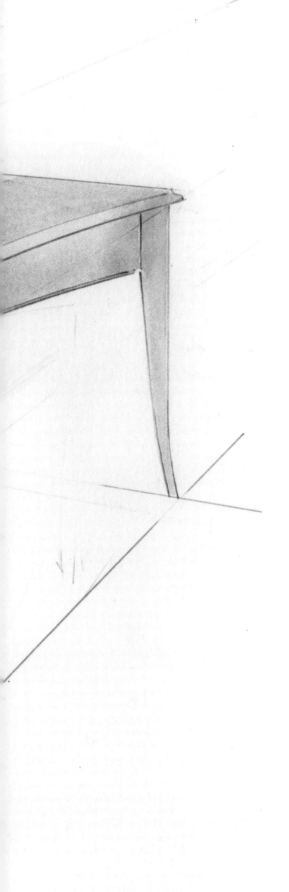

EUCLID, VITRUVIUS, FIBONACCI & ED'S SAXOPHONE

I suggest that the best way into proportions is to look at flat façades of great buildings and draw them. Now, I want to link mathematics with the core building blocks of nature and suggest to you that, by using these mathematical elements whilst you are designing, you are working with nature– not against nature.

We must now go to Ptolemy's library and university at Alexandria, where he invited scholars – including Euclid – to assist him. Euclid wrote "The Elements of Geometry," which became the basis of a best-selling maths textbook for the next 2,250 years. I hated maths, but I do wonder what happened to Euclid's royalties.

One of the enduring proofs that Euclid developed was the squaring of the circle. (See those circles and squares again?) This is what he did: Take a line of any length, a few inches or a few miles; it matters not. Somewhere near the middle, mark a point we will call centre. It need not be the exact centre, just a mark somewhere near. Then scribe a semi-circle; it can be of any radius less than the length of the line. Then draw a square – the largest square you can inside that semi-circle. The relationship along the baseline this gives us in all cases is 1:1.618. It's rather curious, this, for the relationship also works for the whole distance of the line touched by the semi-circle. That's the largest part to the furthest point where the square touches the baseline: 1:1.618.

Fig. 29.1. The desk for Carol begins to take shape on paper.

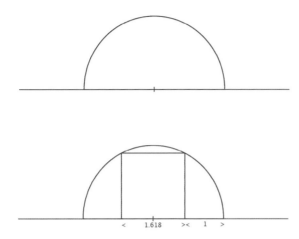

Fig. 29.2. Ptolemy's "squaring of the circle."

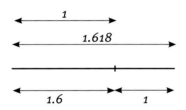

Fig. 29.3. The relationship along the baseline this gives us in all cases is 1:1.618 as per the constructions above.

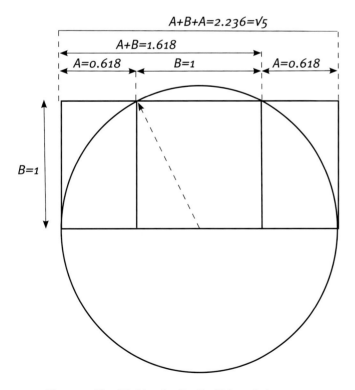

Fig. 29.4. The "Golden Section" within a circle.

It's funny stuff, this, and it gets a bit more spooky the more we get into it – but bear with me, please. This is called by mathematicians "Phi," and remembered by furniture makers as "One to One and a Half – and a Bit."

This "one to one and a half – and a bit" gives us the relationships of the Golden Section or Golden Mean: 3:5, 5:8, 8:13, 13:21. Each of those relationships are "one to one and a half – and a bit." Or they can equally be created by adding each together to get the next in the series. I am now jumping about 1,000 years to the Renaissance and Fibonacci of Pisa – but why not!

This pretty much is the drawing that Ruscombe-King drew with great indifference on the side of my drawing when I was at art school. What he neglected to tell me was what it was all about. Even a young numpty like me could see the elegance of the nautilus shell that emerged like magic from an unexplained construction. But what is going on here? Well, it's another way of looking at the Golden Section – but instead of using 1:1.618, let's just add it up.

Start with two squares. That's unit one. Then add a square based on two. Then add two and one to create a square of three. Going on to squares of five and eight in the same way. Now create the "nautilus." Using a compass point on the inside corner, scribe an arc in each square. It spirals down to nothing.

This is the way maths link with the building blocks of nature. The nautilus shell creates new, larger cells to allow for growth of the animal within and, as I was told by a former naturalist student, "to create buoyancy." The form is a natural response to its requirements to live.

The spiral and its mathematical purity (for it is very simple and pure) was developed in the early Renaissance by Leonardo of Pisa, better known by his nickname, Fibonacci. The series of 1:1, 1:2, 2:3, 3:5, 5:8 and so on has become known as "the Fibonacci Series."

The same proportional relationships can be seen in shells of all kinds, a few of which are illustrated here. It can also be seen within the centre of a sunflower, or daisy or fish. Look also at another great mathematician of the Classical age, Pythagoras, and remember his triangles: a right-angle base and relationships of 3:4:5. They occur naturally in so many things – just look at the fish on the following pages.

The sunflower has a heart-melting centre of warmth,

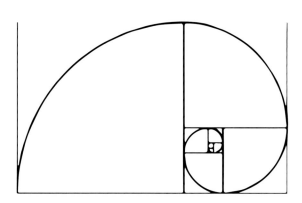
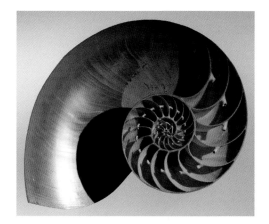

Figs. 29.5. Even a young numpty like me could see the elegance of the nautilus shell that emerged like magic from an unexplained construction. But what is going on here?

PHOTO: FERRAN PESTAÑA

with memories of fields of yellow heads, each following the sun during the day. Look into that centre and see the spiral growth pattern.

I will not go on and on with this – I am not a botanist or a naturalist – but what I will do is ask you to consider is what mathematician Sir Edmund Whittaker said about Euclid:

"It is not expected that a single mathematical system such as Euclid's should furnish relations covering the whole extensional aspect of physical reality. However, Euclidian geometry undoubtedly describes with close approximation a large class of properties of the actual world and embodies our most fundamental notions of it."

As a diversion from dry mathematics, let's see how one of the greatest artists in the world used these proportional divisions in the creation of one of the great works of the Renaissance: Leonardo da Vinci's "The Annunciation," now in Florence's Uffizi Gallery.

As with many great buildings, you can work out what the structure might be beneath a great painting – you may be wrong, or there may not be any structure there, but let's see. (I had the pleasure of sitting in the Uffizi with all the idiot youths of the world snapping selfies of themselves with Lenny.)

My belief is that "The Annunciation" is a clever arrangement of horizontals and verticals, constructed so that they cannot be any other way. You move one, and they all have to change.

So here is the first construction division: a vertical

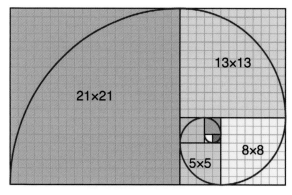

Fig. 29.6. The squares behind the rectangles behind the shell.

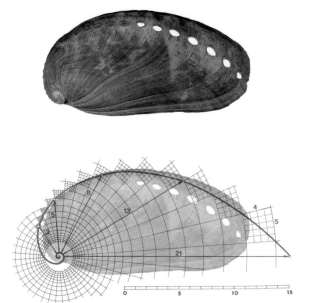

Fig. 29.7. An old shell game.

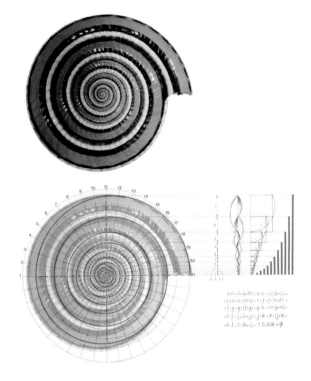

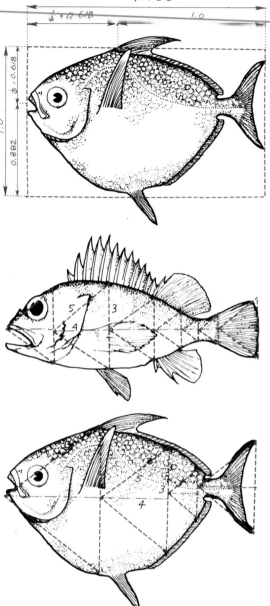

Fig. 29.8. This is the way maths link with the building blocks of nature.

line creating a square to the right, and a Golden Section rectangle to the left. Note that Leonardo doesn't show that division as a hard line; he hints at it with the gossamer fabric falling from the bookstand.

Next is the division spotted on the back of the angel's eye that goes down to the crook of the arm. Draw this, and we create two equal rectangles. Those have potential to have squares and golden section rectangles above, but only if we create a horizontal here – curiously, right on the line of the wall behind the angel and just touching the tips of her outstretched fingers as she gestures toward Mary.

Now this may be a crock of effluent, but I do not believe that Leonardo was unaware of those divisions within his canvas as he laid out that composition. What is clear, though, is that they are not up front and shouting at you. Leonardo is a magician of visual deception; he likes to hide his thinking, to conceal his structures. He waves his hand over here to stop you looking over there. Whoo hoo – over here!

Working in Florence, just before "The Annunciation" was painted, was Leon Battista Alberti, one of the great architects of the Renaissance. Let's stop to look

Fig. 29.9. Remember the triangles: a right-angle base and relationships of 3:4:5. They occur naturally in so many things.

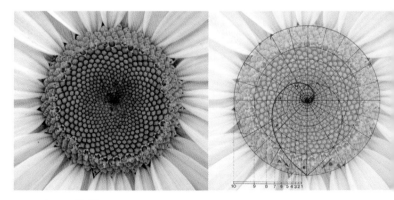

Fig. 29.10. Look into that centre and see the spiral growth pattern.

Fig. 29.11. Leonardo da Vinci's "The Annunciation."

Fig. 29.12. Santa Maria Novella. Look at the way these elements are structured. See how it builds it up, layer on layer of decorative element. Some areas are in relief, but generally, this is a flat facade broken up with colour and detail.

for a moment at one of his greatest achievements: the marble façade of Santa Maria Novella, one of the most important churches in Florence. First let's just enjoy his beautiful façade – a balanced and complex image that pulls the eye from left to right as if engaged in a visual tango. Rata Tata Ta Ta Ta. Now look harder; look at the way these elements are structured. See how it builds it up, layer upon layer of decorative element. Some areas are in relief, but generally, this is a flat façade broken up with colour and detail.

But let's look at a little of what Alberti himself has to say about architecture. "We shall therefore borrow all our Rules for the furnishing of our proportions from the Musicians who are the masters of this sort of number and from those things where Nature shows herself more excellent and complete."

Music, huh? I love to see this done at Rowden each year. Ed Wild, one of our tutors, plays the saxophone; he comes in to show on a single-stringed instrument (basically a primitive guitar) how sounds are related to distance – to the length of the string.

Moving the finger down the neck creates harmony and discord at points closely related to Phi, or Fibonacci's series of great numbers.

I'll wrap up this section with look at one of the most enduring images of the Renaisssance – a drawing not much larger than this page, made in about 1490 by Leonardo da Vinci. This is a drawing of a man with arms extended inside a square and a circle: "The Vitru-

vian Man." It's named after the great Roman architect Vitruvius, who is responsible for recovering in about 100 BCE classic Greek proportions that had disappeared. It was Vitruvius who first posed this problem, but it was down to Leonardo and his incisive mind to solve it. The issue that drove Leonardo – and others, as it was one of the great Renaissance philosophical underpinnings – was this: to express humanity at the centre of all things.

Many attempted. But all, until Leonardo, failed to comfortably fit the human being within both a square and circle. He managed it by creating two centres: the groin (as centre of the square) and the navel as centre of the circle). He also showed that there are no rules that cannot be broken – only assumptions that restrict us. When tested with a living model, these proportions work as well today as when Leonardo made this powerful and enduring image.

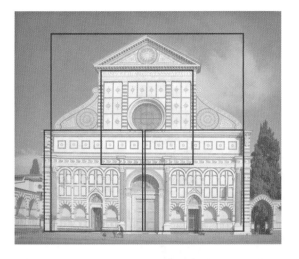
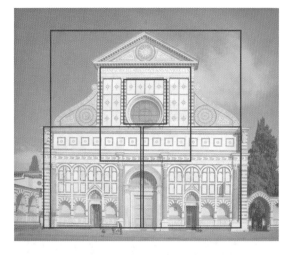
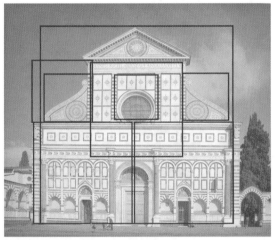
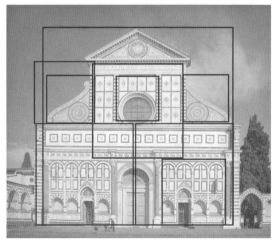

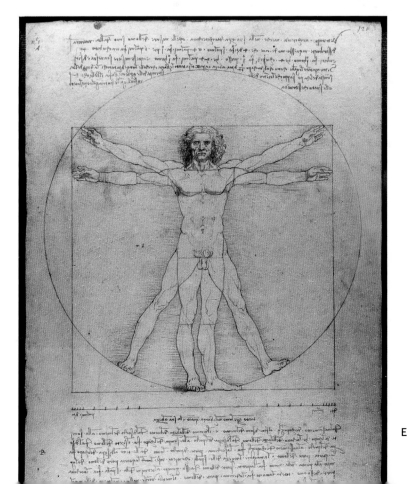

Fig. 29.13. All, until Leonardo, failed to comfortably fit the human being within both a square and circle. He managed it by creating two centres: the groin (as centre of the square) and the navel as centre of the circle).

ALBERTI & PALLADIO

When you were born, the first thing that you could see, a thing of enormous significance to your suckling, dependent, vulnerable mind, was a circle. Slowly it came in to focus, and you came to attend it and see the love of your mother. The circle of the eye is the one thing as we grow old that does not change. The circle is a symbol of that humanity.

Circles and squares are a base – unarguable forms that we Classicists have used in our work since 400 BCE. The essence is to stick to low-integer numbers – whole numbers, if you can. I know – one and a half and a bit – but that's what happens when you let mathematicians in.

The essence of this is not mathematical, it is visual. Just you and your dividers. Do you think the great masons who built Notre Dame did so with stick, rope and dividers, or with a slide rule and a calculator? Artisans' intelligent hands throughout history have used visual measure, marking out with dividers proportions that made sense to them. Eight of these that way; five of these this way.

Before I round this section up and discuss how we can use classical proportion, I must give you a few more variants on this theme. We have been playing with it for 2,500 years, so there is a bit more to tell.

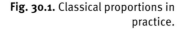

Fig. 30.1. Classical proportions in practice.

Dg 170308 Sc 1:5. ⬚D⬚B⬚S

I want to return to two of the greatest proponents of classical proportions in Renaissance Italy: Leon Battista Alberti and Andrea Palladio.

I will be brief as I know this can get tedious. However, this is a reference section to revisit when you have a piece of work that doesn't fit conventions.

This is the diagonal of the square, a ratio of 1:1.414 – a powerful form first outlined to us by Alberti.

Next comes a simple whole-number variation, a square plus one third: 3:4. Then comes another simple whole-number variant, a square plus one-half: 2:3. Finally, we have a square, again solid and reliable, plus two-thirds of a square: 3:5.

These are the systems Alberti and people such as me, have used all our working lives. Palladio, however, went on to develop this further.

There is a wonderful road going inland from Venice to Verona that is punctuated by a series of magnificent Villas by Palladio. The first on this road is Villa La Rotonda, built with more squares and circles than you can shake a stick at. Then comes Palazzo Chiericati.

Palladio's designs incorporated not two but three proportions encompassing a space. The first is "The Arithmetical Mean." Take the length, add to it the width and divide the total in half to give you a height.

Next is "The Geometric Mean." Multiply the lesser extreme (4) by the greater extreme (9) to get 36; take the square root to get 6 and use this for the height.

And the third is the "Harmonic Mean," which gives you a relationship of 12:6 with a height of 8. I have never bothered with it in 40 years of fiddling with shapes – but you may want to Google it. Palladio was no fool.

Palladio's work formed the basis of inspiration for later architects including Inigo Jones and Robert Adam, who later in the 17th and 18th centuries went on to develop "Neo Classicism" – the form of the English country house. Those of you in the United States – can you see in these the forms and relationships between these and your nation's great public buildings in Washington, D.C.?

So, this is your toolkit – a set of ways other builders have used proportion to create a harmonic whole that is in tune with the natural divisions within nature. The difficult thing is that these tricks have been used by designers and makers for 2,500 years, and your fickle, all-seeing Mark One Eyeball has seen all this stuff; it

Fig. 30.2. These are the systems Leon Battista Alberti, and people such as me, have used all our working lives.

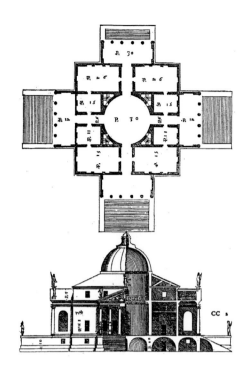

Fig. 30.3. The first is Villa La Rotonda (top left), built with more squares and circles than you can shake a stick at. Palladio's plan for La Rotonda is above right. Then Palazzo Chiericati at below left.

IMAGES: GRAEME CHURCHARD (LA ROTONDA); FRANCISCO ANZOLA (PALAZZO CHIERICATI)

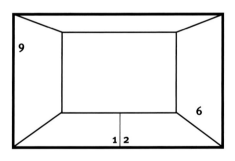

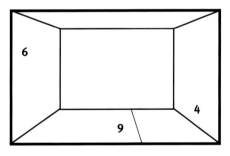

Fig. 30.4. Andreas Palladio took this all a stage further involving not two but three proportions encompassing a space. The first is "The Arithmetical Mean." Take the length, add to it the width, and divide the total in half to give you a height. Next is "The Geometric Mean." Multiply the lesser extreme (4) by the greater extreme (9) to get 36 take the square root to get 6 use this for the height.

bores her into a torpid sleep.

"Oh Darling, this is all so last season."

(What's the Mark One Eyeball? I use the term to describe the critical visual process. The eye has seen it all, has experienced all the visual tricks that designers and artists use. She knows it all and is desperate for something new, something that amuses and challenges her. The issue is to be amusing and new without being silly, without putting square wheels on a car. Most of the designer/maker frivolities of the late 20th century will end up in the Dumpster of History. The challenge is to amuse the Muse but avoid the Dumpster.)

The answer to the Mark One Eyeball is low, wicked

Fig. 30.5. Most of my furniture has curves, and for a damn good reason. Having curves allows me to put the edge of a curve on a Golden Section and a foot just tickling the other side.

cunning, deception and guile. You'll recall that I described Leonardo as a cunning magician who distracts with a wave of an elegant glove. It took me about two hours to work out those simple proportions – he was so good at sending you the wrong way. You must do the same.

Never start with a proportional system. Start with a sketch, a drawing that you can feel good about. The relationships should be something you really like.

Then draw it again, coming up to scale, enlarging the image and tightening all the relationships. This is the time to test your drawing's relationships with 8:13 or whatever. If it nearly fits. Hurrah! Now tighten your design so it fits exactly. If nothing fits, and you have been though everything including Palladio's Harmonic Mean, have a really hard look at your divisions. Are they really as good as you think? Feeling they are OK is great – but are they really right?

This is where I listen to that tiny voice in the back of my head. It's very different in tone and volume from the negative voice in my left brain. He says in a big voice, "You are Prat." "You never could do this; why, for God's sake, aren't you selling insurance to feed the kids?"

This guy, I can ignore. I know his tone. It's her tone I want to hear. "David," she says very quietly, "might you want to think about this again, darling?" That's the silent killer; she is always right. The more I follow her words the better I get. So, get clever at hiding this proportional stuff.

For example, I have just seen a student's table elevation. He had wide, lovely cabriole legs on a low table. If he placed a proportional relationship on the outside of the knees, the extreme outside dimension where there are no verticals, that is being a cunning, sneaky woo.

The last thing you want to do is bang up a box with 8" by 13" as the outer dimensions. Your eye will not forgive you. It might look OK, but ultimately will be consigned to the "also ran" Dumpster of History. Hitting the numbers dead on and obviously doesn't often work.

Most of my furniture has curves, and for a damn good reason. Having curves allows me to put the edge of a curve on a Golden Section and a foot just tickling the other side. Sneaky Woo. You be one too, or that miserable bitch will consign your stuff to the "dumpster."

Dig N. 401112 Perspective DBS

Fig. 31.1. Do the usual thing when you see a really good building like this – sit down and look. What is it that tells you it's a really good building, not just another dog? Well, what is your response to it?

$$0.618 \quad I \quad 0.618$$

$$1.382 \qquad 0.382$$

$$A$$

$$2.236 = \sqrt{5}$$

$$1.382 : 2.236 = 0.618$$

JAPAN & EUCLID

I t was with some surprise that when I traveled to Japan, I found a very similar system of proportions working in ancient Japanese structures and Zen gardens. I was being shown the woodworking treasures of Japan by kind representatives of my "Furniture with Soul" publisher, Kodansha. For a week of travel I was not allowed to put my hand in my pocket to pay for anything. It was like traveling with dad again.

I would like to tell you about two of the many wonderful sights I saw in Japan. The first is relatively straightforward so you can easily see what I am wittering on about; the second is more surprising.

First, let me take you to the Katsura Imperial Villa. Do the usual thing when you see a really good building like this – sit down and look. What is it that tells you it's a really good building, not just another dog? Well, what is your response to it? Great art is out there, transmitting all the time. You may not have your receiver switched on – like the young woman I saw in the Florence, taking a selfie of herself with her finger up the bum of Michelangelo's "David." No point transmitting to her. But you are using your eyes, building your visual sensitivity, drawing, looking and, at last, seeing

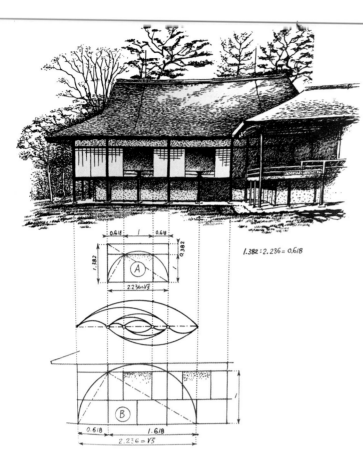

Fig. 31.2. This drawing shows two central screens drawn back, and the diagram in red below looks as if Euclid had been squaring his circle here in the 17th century when this was built.

VILLA DRAWINGS FROM "THE POWER OF LIMITS," BY GYÖRGY DOCZI (SHAMBALA, 1981)

stuff. It doesn't come all at once, and it shouldn't be easy. Nothing worth having is easy.

The two drawings in this chapter show the beginnings of the relationship of the inside and the outside – relationships that are at the core of Japanese architecture. The way rooms, the interior spaces, are set up, positions them to experience the outside. The drawing shows two central screens drawn back, and the diagram in red below it looks as if Euclid had been squaring his circle here in the 17th century when this was built.

I have not done the red drawing calculation here; someone with a more mathematical turn of mind than I did. But I subscribe to it, for it explains to me why some things are dead right and some are not. This one is pretty dead right.

The next is more difficult because I think it is more surprising. The context is this: the Zen garden, a place of supreme peace, tranquility and mindfulness. Raked gravel, a few stones and…well, that's it, dude, raked gravel and stones; nothing else to look at. Except that is the exact opposite of my own experience.

I was taken to Ryoan-ji (my hosts thought this was the best Zen garden in Japan). It is a walled garden with a viewing platform where you are meant to sit and look. That is the idea; you come here to think, or to empty your mind. You come here to look and experience the visual treat before you. As I sat amongst the small crowd, a light rain came down that changed the colours and textures. The stones that had seemed dull now sparkled with colour – intricate moss patterns and stone striations. As you moved around the viewing platform, the stones took up different relationships to one another.

To say this was a special place would be an understatement. A huge understatement. Again, it's superficial simplicity with a depth of complexity for those who have the eyes to see. As I left, I saw the way wooden tiles were shaped around a curved roofline. There must have been easier ways to do that, but "Wow!" (spoken quietly).

But why? Why does this work? Well, I offer a solution that my red-penned friend would suggest explains why we find those stones in those places to be exactly right: Nowhere else would quite do. I do not believe that Zen Buddhist monks knew one whit about Euclid. However, they did know about nature and its relation-

Fig. 31.3. A Zen rock garden.

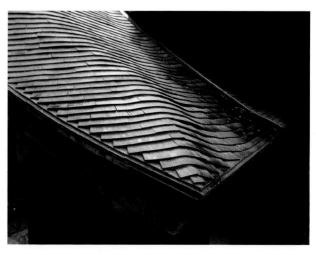

Fig. 31.4. As I left, I saw the way wooden tiles were shaped around a curved roofline. There must have been easier ways to do that, but "Wow!"

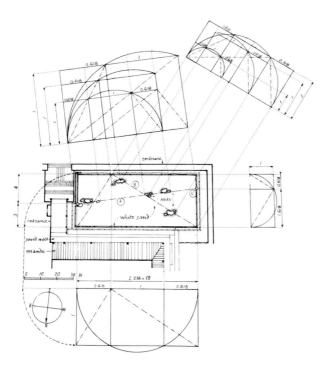

Fig. 31.5. The idea at a Zen garden is that you come here to think, or to empty your mind. You come here to look and experience the visual treat before you.

Fig. 31.6. This piece of calligraphy is one of my few treasured possessions. I look at it like I look at my Picasso print of the "Dove of Peace" and I wonder: "How did he do that?"

ship to form. They did know how to reduce and refine with complexity and simplicity, to comply with a natural rule of doing. Of making well.

I have on my studio wall a piece of calligraphy from Ryoan-ji; it is one of my few treasured possessions. I look at it like I look at my Picasso print of the "Dove of Peace" and I wonder: "How did he do that?"

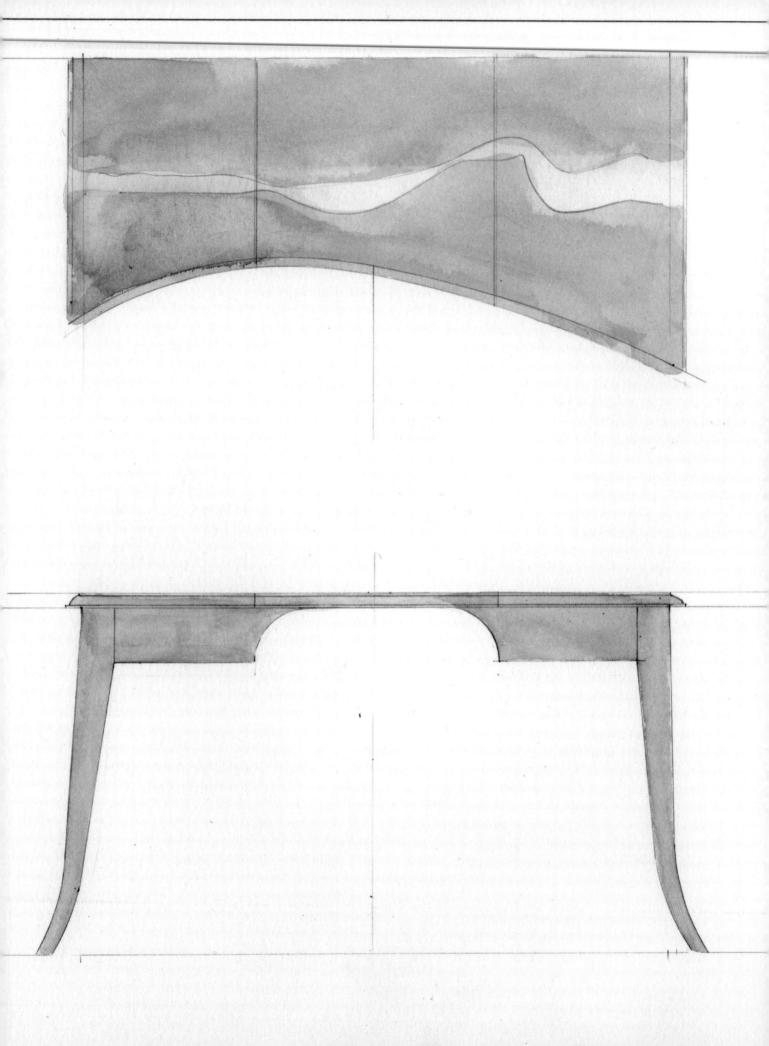

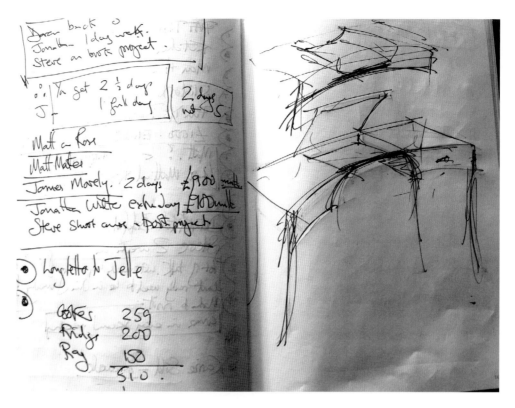

Fig. 32.1. You want to make a special piece, but you are facing the probability that it won't actually be that special…and you don't want that.

DESK & CHAIR SKETCH DRAWINGS

"OK, smart arse. You do this for a living. You have been doing it for 40 years. But today, I don't think you can get it up. You are rubbish."

That's what I listen to when I think of doing these drawings. That's how, for most of us, it feels every time we go to the drawing board. That is the terror of the white sheet of paper, so perfect and clean; all that clumsy old you can do is to make it worse.

Earlier in the book I shared a process, one I have used to help get over this nightmare – a process that will help a professional get a decent drawing done on a wet, gloomy Wednesday. But this wasn't going like that. I was be-

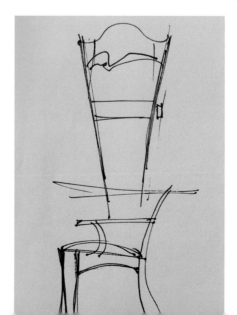

having like an amateur again and subject to all the fears and doubts that go with that status.

Writing this book had moved along quickly to get to this point where I really needed to be creative. I had to have drawings done before we could make the two serious pieces included. And then, as they were being made, write about them being made. So, no pressure there.

Christmas came and went. The kids came back from university, then came a wet and rainy January. We were also opening new studios and a brand new and lovely drawing studio, so that was a serious distraction. My illness was making me more tired, and I was having to use my time with greater care and precision. In the back of my head

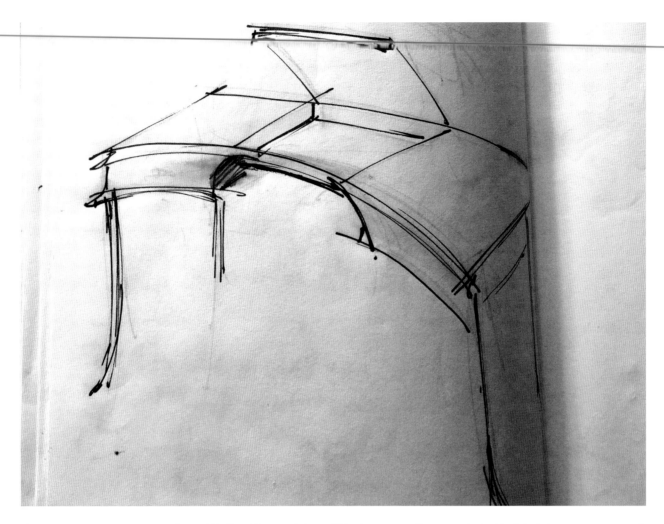

Fig. 32.2. You can tell people of your blinding ideas and they will look at you as if you needed a kind, helping nurse. Poor sad old devil; can't get it up any more.

were these drawings.

That was the problem – they were in my head and not down on paper where I could show them to Daren and Steve and get the damn things made. The more I thought about it, the more I realised this is how most people feel when faced with doing a new design. Scared. Scared big time. You want to make a special piece, but you are facing the probability that it won't actually be that special…and you don't want that. This was to be a lovely writing table for my beautiful wife, Carol, and with it a special chair. We have made lots of chairs through the years, and I have built a reputation for it. I wanted a chair that would sum this up in one piece. I wanted it to be elegant but not overly complex, to be the most difficult piece in the book, but makeable for the careful amateur maker.

If you are like me, you carry images in your head of the pieces you want to make. They may not be in clear focus or show the whole piece of work. But they show

us bits of it – a leg, or a detail for a flashing moment of clarity on the drive to work, or whilst soaking in the bath. But nobody else can see it there between your ears. You can tell people of your blinding ideas and they will look at you as if you needed a kind, helping nurse. Poor sad old devil; can't get it up any more.

So, you go to downloading. This is the process of getting it down somewhere in sketchy notes. Three or four lines in ink on a Post-It Note can do the job. Which was all I had at the start of the chair.

When I came to the desk, I banged an image down as I was talking to Steve, the guy I had in mind to make it. This is what it might look like, Steve. I could never do that with a client; it would make it look too easy. But I did get an image down.

As you can see in the photo on the previous page, it's in my everyday notebook, with job lists and notes to talk about with Steve, and costings to improve the student kitchen. The two images show the thin centre

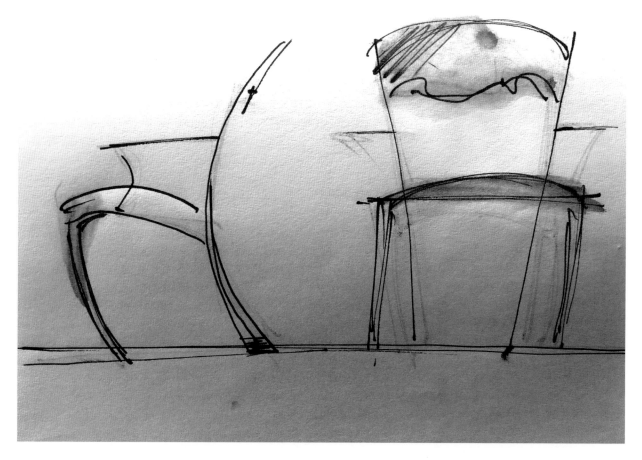

Fig. 32.3. This is what I wanted for the side view – a chair ready to leap forward and bite your leg off.

section for the tabletop but in the lower drawing, it's turned upside down. Much better.

Then do the second drawing. Here is a great tip: the drawing that you have just executed shows slightly through the back side of the paper, especially if you used ink. Then, it's easier to make another version – but cleaner and sharper – guided by version one. Which is what I did.

You don't start from nowhere when you do this. There are requirements, especially with my wife. I knew this desk or table was to go in front of a window and be between two display cabinets that were about 1.8 metres apart. This suggested the length of the piece would be about 1.5 metres. Height is a clear 75cm; almost all worktables are between 70cm and 75cm, though the relationship between table and chair is the big issue here. A low chair needs a low table.

So, I had major dimensions that made some sense. I knew that Carol wanted a delicate, slender piece that had a feminine quality. She told me "curvy legs." I knew that the main surface needed to hold a laptop

computer and store it away when not in use. There needed to be two drawers that had storage for paper and other office stuff, but other than that, a clear surface – no cubby holes or secret compartments. And no locks on the drawers.

(When I was beginning this journey many years ago, I went to a furniture auction that featured a lovely Queen Anne bureau – walnut inlays and marquetry at its best. However, the top drawer had been levered open with a large screwdriver and the lock was broken. It seems granny had died, the keys were lost and the family was searching for the jewelry. The furniture just got in the way. This prompted me to avoid locks if I could.)

The chair was another matter. Above is the first drawing, again in pen on smooth paper in my notebook. These are small drawings so the arch of your wrist can make a nice, energy-filled curve. This is what I wanted for the side view – a chair ready to leap forward and bite your leg off.

Then I turned the page and used the bleed-through of that one to guide the second drawing as I refined it.

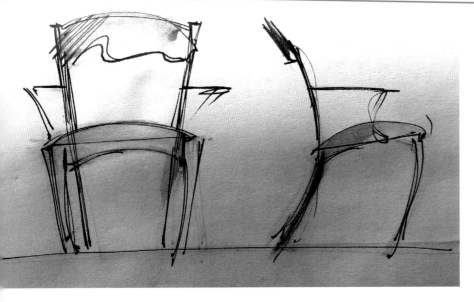

important to the character of the chair.

The width of the seat tells a lot; a 60cm-wide (approximately 24") seat says this is a large and comfortable chair, even for a person of generous proportion. You need to consider this, especially if your chair has arms. A small chair with arms means that persons of generous proportion can get their bums stuck in your chair. They get up and the arms grip them by the hips. The chairs stays attached to them. It's not a pretty sight.

Because the ink is water-soluble (most pens are) it's possible to add a little tone by licking the end of a third finger and quickly wiping down the back leg. This dissolves the ink and creates a tone that can add a little to the drawing.

Be aware of using too many curves. You do need some straight lines in the design for the curves to work against, to push against. Adding a straight front rail to the chair seat is a good example of this.

When you are developing an idea like this, it's important to not do it in perspective. Doing the drawing in front elevation and side elevation, as shown here, is an artificial view — rarely do we look from a few inches above the ground, face-on to the job. However, it gives us a constant viewpoint — which is essential. Get the shapes right in the front and side

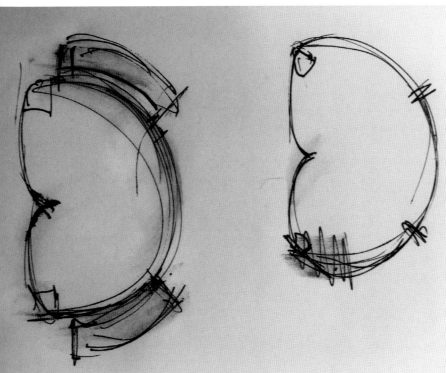

Figs. 32.4 & 32.5. The second sketch of the chair (above) and a plan view of the seat.

elevations.

When you are drawing, look hard at what the negative space is like. The gaps between the legs really matter. You should be looking at the direction and relationships of each component. This is a structure that has to be light, strong and beautiful from all around.

I don't let construction get hold of the idea too soon, but at some stage I take off my designer hat and put on my maker hat. How would this be made? If I can say, "Yes, I have a way of making this," I go back to designing. If not, I stop and have a good think about making.

Note how the curved back legs are used to affect the front elevation. They are twisted so that from the front they "open out." They are also angled, narrow at the bottom and wider at the top, so that the feet are quite close together whilst the back splat of the chair is open and welcoming. The positioning of the back leg is quite

There is no point in developing spiffy designs if they cannot be made efficiently.

I expect that these back legs will be laminated; I want the stiffness and strength this provides. I plan to have the top of the leg really thin and flexible, so the strength of the lamination here is critical. I have a chair already in production with a laminated back leg, so I may well use those molds to give me this shape. These are the kind of things I consider.

Having done the front and side elevations, it's time for a plan view. This is the view from above. The plan of the seat is critical as it determines the joinery you use. I am pretty sure I want a curvaceous seat, so I am going to adapt a construction used in some pretty visually complex chairs – a stacked plywood seat. This will be a lamination of four or five layers of 20mm-thick plywood. That would be very heavy, except we are going to cut out the centre to keep the chair nice and light. This construction enables me to curve the sides, and the edges can be sculpted. Legs can be joined to the seat easily, then the ply gets covered in webbing and upholstered in leather. Leather is good as it can be pulled to a shape both ways, with the warp and with the weft, unlike fabric which pulls only one way.

The photo at right is an example of this construction used on "Perseus," a chair I made about five years ago.

The goal is a smooth, sculptural shape. To avoid the undercloth (the fabric that conceals the webbing) being visible, it has to be upholstered on the bottom as well as the top.

Having determined that there are virtually no limits to the shape I can use for the seat, I set to drawing it up.

(This is essentially the shape of a human bottom, a shape I've been incorporating in chair seats for years. When I made a male and female pair of love chairs some years ago, it was suggested that the male chair have a shallow bowl in front centre of the seat in which to cup the user's testicles. We toyed with the idea but didn't do it. It is one of my very few regrets.)

So that's the developmental sketches downloaded. I now have basic shapes to work up into a set of presentation drawings. Developmental sketches are private;

Fig. 32.6. The seat of the Perseus chair served as a jumping off place for the new design.

presentation drawings go public. They refine and present the idea to the client and to the maker.

You will probably be the maker. I know if I were making, it wouldn't go as well as if Steve or Daren made it. I used to be a pretty good maker, but not now – but that isn't the problem. I know if I were making this chair I would be much more careful with my time and much less inclined to take the risks that are sometimes needed.

If Steve or Daren is making this, I can come in, see the job afresh and say, "Can we take 6" off at the knees?" If I had been making it, I would have felt the problem but be too scared of the solution. I would have just taken an inch, then another, then another. When they are making for me, all I am risking is the money it costs me to waste their time – I never want to risk wasting my own.

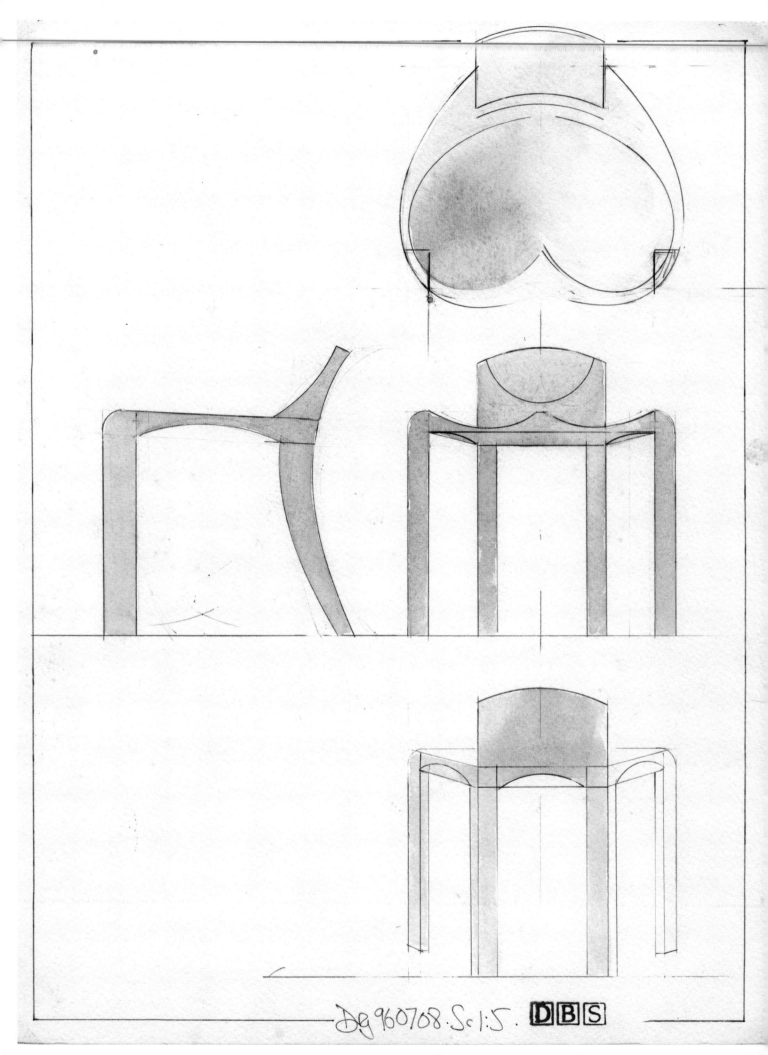

Dg 960708. Sc 1:5 . DBS

PRESENTATION DRAWINGS

If I were learning to create presentation drawings now, I would probably not be learning analogue skills, but instead go straight to computer-aided design (CAD). A good-quality program that will link properly to computer-aided manufacture (CAM) program would be the tool here – not a cheap 2D version, but one that will show you the job, turning it around to show it from all angles. I am reliably told that a good two years should see you fluent in CAD. We teach the possibilities of CAD at Rowden, using Rhino, but getting fluent takes time; it's a complex program.

However this is for Lost Art Press – and doing decent watercolour presentation drawings is getting to be archaic. This is a shame, as good watercolours send a clear message to the prospect that we have "a creative" in charge here. That's a good thing.

Have a look at nearby printing facilities. Heavy watercolour paper is like thin card stock – it's so thick. If you can find a printer to accept this thick paper, you can print from CAD using a fine grey outline that can be gone over with pencil and watercolour to a similar effect.

I wrote earlier about the tools and what you are attempting to achieve. Now I will be specific about how these drawings came about.

First the chair. I had the sketches; I would never go straight to watercolour without a sketch to work

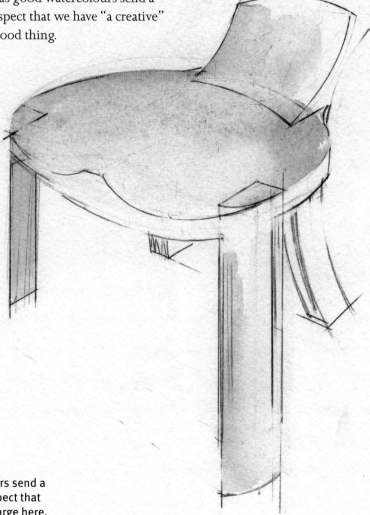

Fig. 33.1. Good watercolours send a clear message to the prospect that we have "a creative" in charge here. That's a good thing.

Dag 160709. DBS

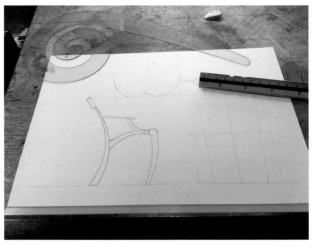

Figs. 33.2 & 33.3. an old American-made Windsor chair (left) in the studio that I keep as a chair totem. I look at it and take measurements from it when questions come up. Above, I'm working on the plan view of the seat.

from. I want to improve upon it here, while sticking with what I've downloaded to keep the proportions and the idea nice and clear.

The side elevation was first; this was a matter of choosing a scale to draw with. I knew my paper was going to be in landscape orientation, as I want the side elevation with the front elevation alongside so I could transfer dimensions from the first drawing to the second. If need be, I work a plan drawing in there somewhere. The layout of the page is critical. So, I chose a scale of 1:5 to nicely fill the page.

I use what is called a scale rule – a triangular cross-sectional rule with several scales; 1:10, 1:7.5 and 1:5 are the three I use most. The paper is A3 (11.7" x 16.5") 140 lb. watercolour hot-pressed paper – really heavy and super smooth. I fix it to my cedar double-elephant-sized drawing board on the left in the bottom quarter, fixing on all four corners with translucent drafting tape. Over the years a mound of this tape has built up in this section of the board – a witness to the hundreds of drawings I've done on it.

I put the paper on the left to be near the ebony edge of the cedar board on which the T-square slides. I got rid of parallel motions and clever architects' drawing aids years ago in an effort to have only simple tools that

would always be accurate if I held them correctly.

Double elephant – huh?! Well, yes – it's not a measure often heard now, but it was a size of paper when paper was not measured in A-whatever or inches. In the old days we had elephants as a way to measure the size of a sheet of paper. This is the biggest drawing board I could find; it's about 42" x 31". You need a big drawing board and a block of wood to support it at an angle on your bench. It's got to be big to do perspective drawings – but that's for later.

The first line on the page is the floor. I look at how large the chair might be, how high and how wide, then work out where the side elevation should sit on the paper at 1:5. A line for the height of the seat goes in next; here, it's 14-1/2"; if the seat is to compress when you sit on it, I put this line slightly below the top of the seat.

Now I put two lines down for the back leg and the seat. I look hard at the sketch and how that seat slopes and how the back leg leans way back. Here, I use one of my two big French curves mentioned earlier, the one that is a big spiral, with the radius opening out as you go around it. I used this tool repeatedly on this drawing, as I wanted a family of shapes that would have the same feel, the same DNA.

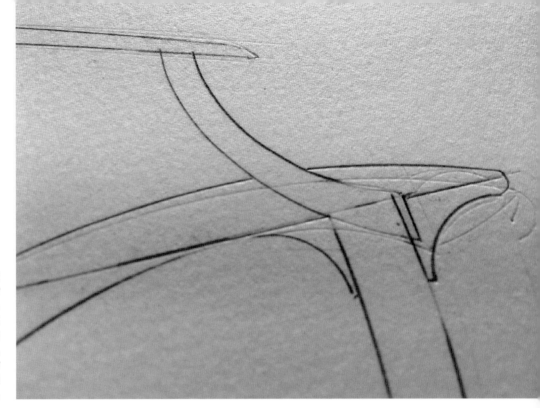

Fig. 33.4. I cut a sharp edge on my eraser so I can use it really accurately – just that line. Then, with a really sharp 3H pencil, I set about making the change. It's always a tussle, and you can see some of my old lines compressed in the paper.

I do this a lot on chairs when I've designed a curved back leg shape – using the curves to develop the front leg and arms, while trying at the same time to use it differently to create different shapes with the same origin.

Having put down the side elevation to the best of my ability, I think about the front elevation and the plan. Chairs are very three-dimensional; they have to look good from all around. This means thinking in three dimensions, accepting that this side elevation has a consequence on the front and plan elevation. You find yourself chasing around the image. Top. Bottom. Side. Side. Top. Bottom. It's a subtle form of madness.

Bang in the first lines for the front elevation – the baseline or floor. Do this as an extension of the line on which the side elevation sits. Next, put down a centre line at 90°; this places the front elevation there. The front legs are next. I have an old American-made Windsor chair in the studio that I keep as a chair totem. I look at it and take measurements from it when questions come up such as: How wide should a chair be? How high should a seat be? This old chair is strong, light, comfy and good-looking all around. All I have to do is that – but totally differently.

So, the front and back leg positions are added. The front legs are 550mm apart overall, and the back legs lean out, opening the chair back up. I put lines in from the side el-

evation across to the front to show the top of the crest rail and the bottom back of the seat. OOOooo…this makes a nice square – or it will when I tighten it up. This is what I am doing at this point – tightening up the proportions, hiding squares and rectangles, making shapes I like, then checking them against Euclid.

You can see the seat plan view (at left) going in above the side elevation. Once I positioned the top of a leg on it at a 550mm width, I saw a problem. If that leg is to stay there, the side elevation must change; the leg must come further back. Grrrrr….

When this happens, you need look at what you have already done and accept that it can be better. On the paper, it's easy to erase lines. I cut a sharp edge on my eraser so I can use it really accurately – just that line. Then, with a really sharp 3H pencil, I set about making the change. It's always a tussle, and you can see some of my old lines compressed in the paper.

My drawings are nothing like it, but if you look at great drawings such as Leonardo's "Vitruvian Man," you'll see they often have an air of having been carved in the paper – with many corrections and amendments.

PRESSING THE LUDICROUS BUTTON

A student came to Rowden this week in a Tesla sports car. It had a button marked "Ludicrous." She wouldn't show us what it did, but she said it required dry tarmac and a long, straight, wide road.

I have wanted to press the "Ludicrous" button all my life (I have given it a shove a good few times). Do not become, as Thoedore Roosevelt said, one of "those cold and timid souls who neither know victory nor defeat."

The following projects, Carol's desk and chair, have an element of the "ludicrous" – for what is the point of life without a little controlled danger?

So, bear with me. These pieces may look unusual to you at first sight, but I hope they will grow on you. If I am wrong, then they will be consigned to the great dumpster of history as designer decadence, and Alan Peters will stop revolving in his grave. If I am right, we will move the boundaries of desk construction and chairmaking an inch or two – which is our job. When Edward Barnsley was asked what contribution he thought he had made to furniture design in his long and productive life, his answer was, "I may have

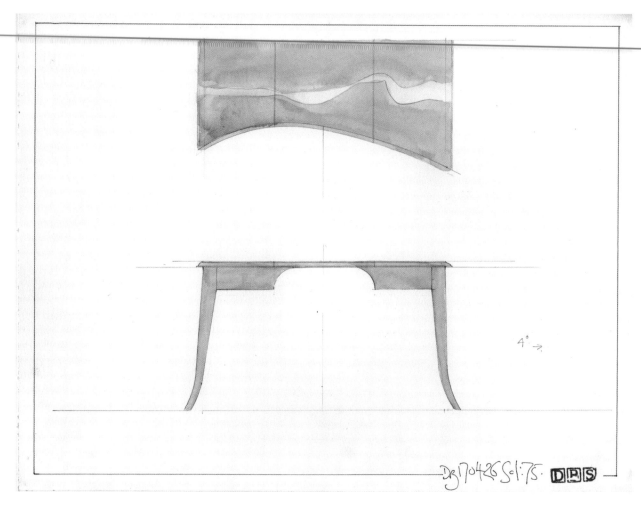

Fig. 34.1. The thinness of the top is a major feature of the design. It's what gets you looking, and it gets you to look again, to see what's going on.

encouraged people to make cabinet components a little thinner." True modesty and honesty.

Let's talk about the desk first. It is not straightforward, but it's very makeable when you follow the process here and in the following chapters. As well as classic cabinetmaking techniques, we will consider the use of modern materials, such carbon fiber, to give us the stiffness needed for the work area. The thinness of the top is a major feature of the design. It's what gets you looking, and it gets you to look again, to see what's going on. This is what good designers have to do: evolve forms and shapes that make us look again and say, "Yes, that's right." It also gives us all the daftest furniture design. (You know, the stuff that can only be cured by a jolly good fire; the stuff Alan would be most cross and disappointed by.)

Earlier I introduced the subject of presentation drawings. Now I am going to show you drawings specific to the chair and desk, and explain a little more about how they were done.

In the image at right, you can see two yellow post sheets with "VP1" and "VP2" written on them. The circles and crosshairs indicate vanishing points, which you'll need in order to do perspective drawing. Notice how one VP is on the drawing board and VP2 is way off left field. That's OK – and it's why you need this elephant of a board.

You also need a sharp, fine-pointed 4H pencil, a good bench knife and an eraser. Cut the eraser so it has a clean, pointed edge that enables you to erase with precision just that one line, not the whole sheet.

(Again, use really good watercolour paper. It will be expensive, but thick and heavy, like fine card. A good paper will allow you to "work the image," putting in and erasing lines until its right.)

The objective in this case is four drawings: two of the desk and two of the chair. If these were for a client, they would be made and presented as a set, so the colours should suggest they were done as group.

As I stressed earlier, work first on elevation and side

Figs. 34.2 & 34.3. At the drawing board (left). You also need a sharp, fine-pointed 4H pencil, a good bench knife and an eraser (above). Cut the eraser so it has a clean, pointed edge that enables you to erase with precision just that one line.

elevation drawings; then, if necessary, a plan. Doing this is a way of refining and defining the sketch idea, of putting it down exactly to scale.

First the desk. I set out the paper in landscape format with the aim of putting down a front elevation, then a plan of the desktop directly above it. This allows me to transfer dimensions from one drawing to the other. The sketch had given me the idea of a thin centre section that opens to store a laptop. I've made desks like this, but never with this thinness. I knew we would have a deep back rail. That will stabilise the back – but what about the front? Here, two options came to mind: laminations of very thin plywood or carbon fibre laminations with veneered surfaces. Both are stiff and can be made very thin.

As the designer, I just need to make sure it is "do-able." I will leave the construction details to Daren Millman; his knowledge of structural materials and techniques is more complete than mine. However, be certain that as the designer you know enough about making, about Daren's job, to not put him in a difficult situation.

"I want that thin middle."

"No, David, it's too thin. It's going to bend and there is going to be racking."

The essence is to push the boundary but not step over the functional edge; don't make a pretty desk that's impossible to work at.

Whilst drawing this up, I was able to make sure that two squares were built into the elevation, which make a nice proportion, and two drawers would fit into the front. Having enjoyed bedside cabinets with piston-fit drawers, I wanted these drawers to open in the same way. I lean out of bed in the morning and can open a drawer using its very corner. The room is then scented with cedar, as are my socks. Opening a drawer on its corner is nice, and those curved corners gave me a perfect place for a drawer handle.

Handles are important; it's where you engage with the piece of work. Plan these early and make them nice to feel and touch.

The plan of the desk was developed second. I know where this piece will live, and I know Carol will approach it from the left, always. So, the flow of the surface can enable and encourage that. As I divided the tabletop and worked out what would open and what would not, I saw there was an opportunity for pen trays on either side of the well for the laptop.

As I know that charging laptops is a pain, involving wires and cables dangling everywhere, I guess

Figs. 34.4 & 34.5. The yellow pages (at left) show the vanishing points for the drawing (below left).

there will be some cable management and a socket within the laptop storage area. (This will date the piece to 2018, as next year this will all disappear as laptop technology moves ahead to wireless charging. Or something.)

Next was a perspective drawing. See those lines by the feet of the desk? They come from the vanishing points VP1 and VP2; you saw them on the image on the previous page, but here is another view.

The vanishing points are placed after first sketching out the position of the desk. You can see the faint outlines on the paper. This shows you how the image will occupy that sheet of paper. This is you placing the image here on the page.

Then, take a long rule or T-square and select two vanishing points, one to the left and one to the right. Use the sketch as a guide to the direction of where the VP is. They will be on the same horizon, level with your eyes. Here you are looking down on the top of the table, so the horizon line will be above the tabletop. One VP will help position the second. Here we have one VP close in on the right and the other way out on the left. It's dull to have both the same.

Using the VPs is easy; they help you position things such as table legs more accurately. For example, draw the front leg in and estimate its length, then take lines to the left and right vanishing points to determine the lengths of the other three legs. They now all look too long – cut them down a bit. Use the VPs again.

Next came the chair. It's the same process – take the

Figs. 34.6 & 34.7. The rough sketch of the chair (at left) and the result (right).

sketch and develop it. Look hard at the negative spaces – the gaps between the legs – and the shape of the seat. Ahh, yes – the shape of the seat. This is a reasonably complex chair, but the seat is straightforward and allows all sorts of chair seat shapes to be used. Designer joy! It's plywood stacked up to the thickness needed, then cut out in the middle and shaped. Where the legs attach it can be left thicker.

In the drawing above you can see the VP lines coming in from the left and right to create a box within which I could begin developing the shape of the chair seat. The seat is not parallel to the ground. It has to slope back a bit, so I drew that in first, then developed the curved seat shape.

Then the legs went onto the seat. This is where I cheat and use a big plastic template – an unwinding circle with arcs that get larger as the template opens up. I used it all over this chair. (I love these two templates; we all have them at Rowden to help with getting clean curves.) The templates do more than just give me a clean line; they enable me to generate a family of shapes that associate well together and look like they belong.

When Beethoven wrote "Symphony No. 5," he began with a loud Fanfare of Ba, Bah, BAH… BAH. Then he took the same four notes and turned them around and on and on right though the middle of the symphony. I know, I know, my keyboard and words do a poor job of sounding like the Vienna Philharmonic, but you get what I mean. They are the same family of forms,

Fig. 34.8. Templates result in clean lines and fair curves.

just turned around and reassembled. Beethoven stayed clear of introducing new forms, and new and different groups of notes within the piece; he just pumped these four notes for all they are worth. At the end of the symphony he returned to the opening notes – simple and very complex.

And that's what my templates do. They restrict me to a connected family of curves – forms that live well together, that are developed from one another and that look good together.

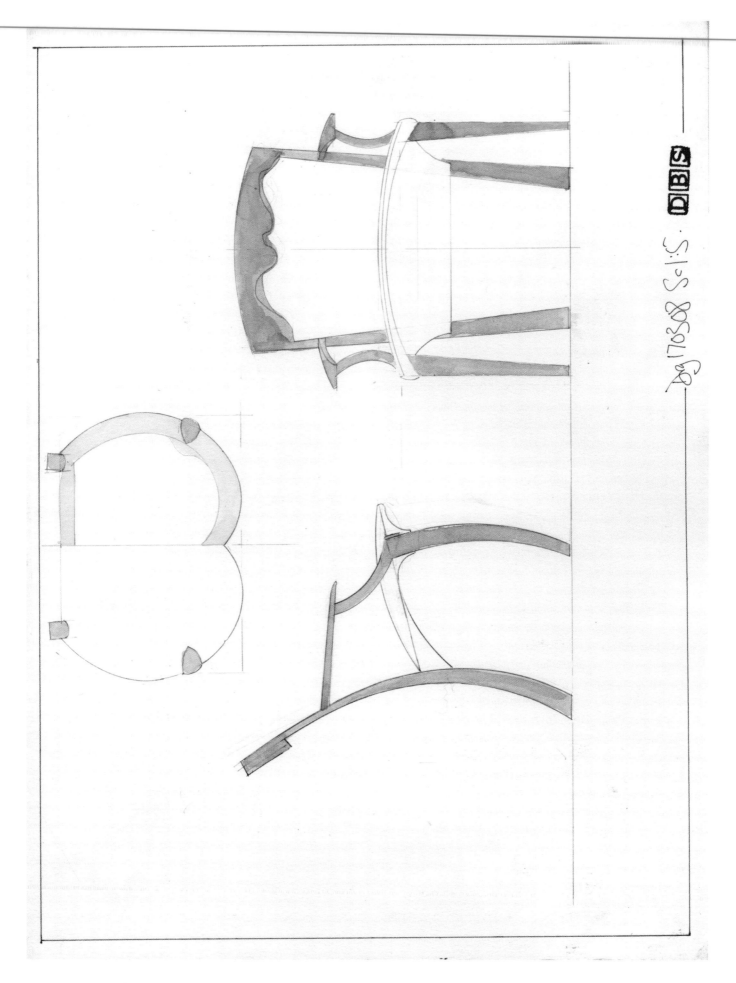

Dwg 170308 S-1:5 · DBS

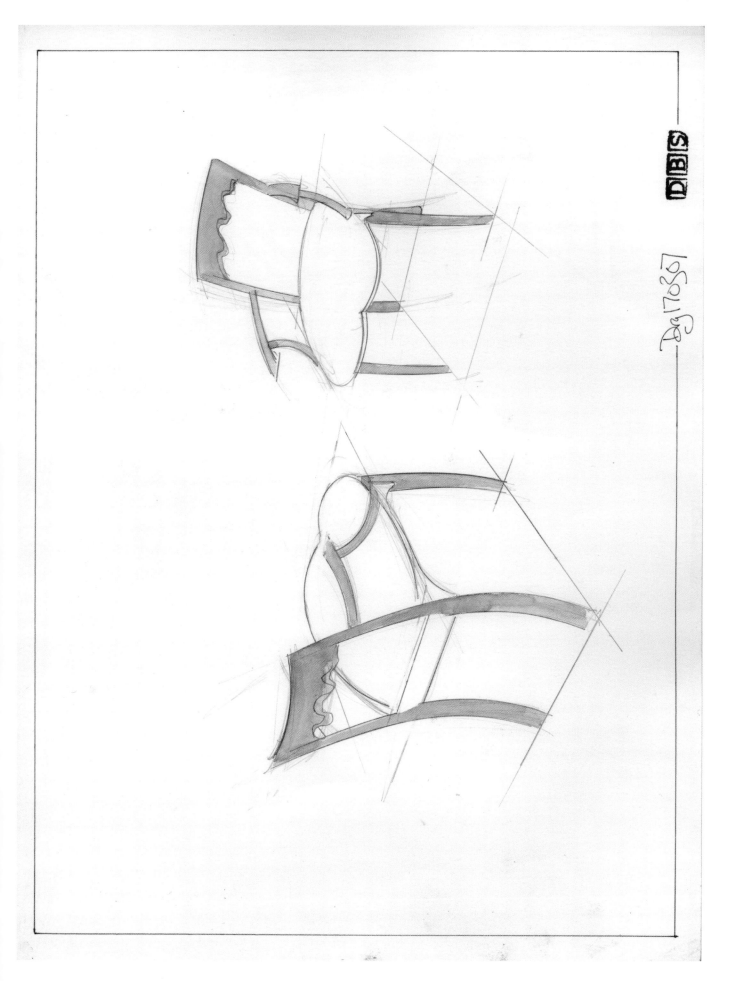

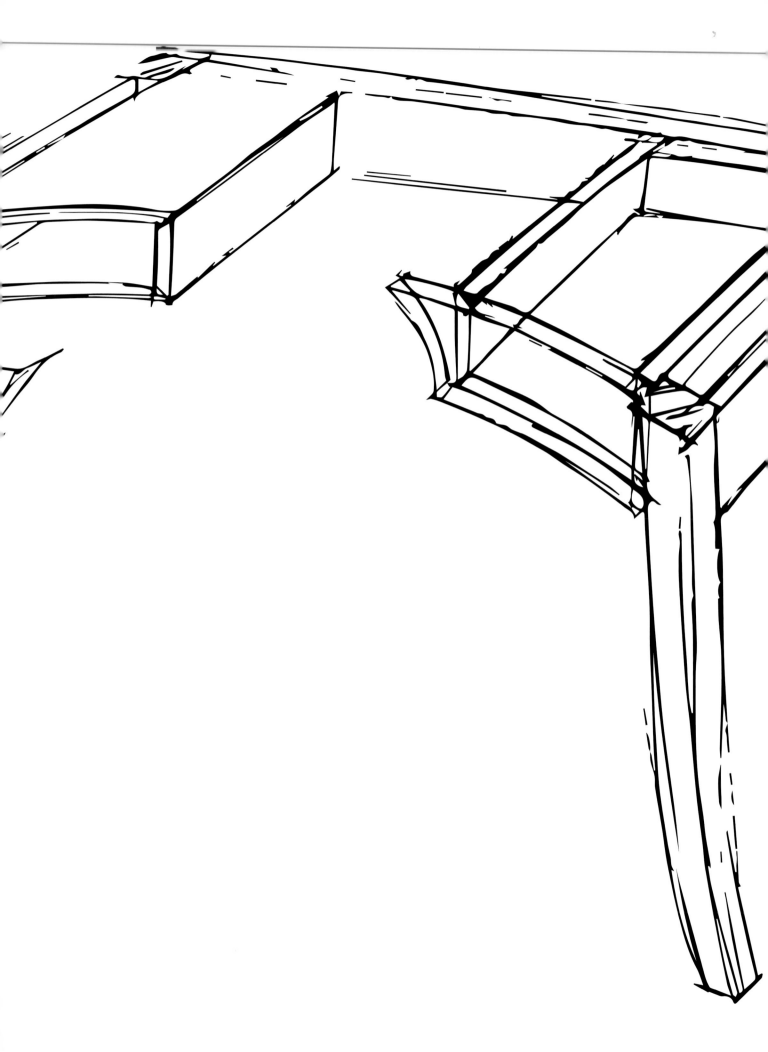

PLANS, RODS & TEMPLATES

Fig. 35.1. A general sketch of the desk.

Now we are in trouble; we have to make the damn thing! This is Daren Millman's workspace. You can tell by the tidy, well-organised space he occupies what kind of a maker Daren is. When Daren sits down and works out a project, he can tell you almost exactly how many hours it will take to make. He does this with our students as they move from projects to learn techniques to designing their own pieces. He reviews their ideas to see if they are makeable and, if so, helps them develop a process list. Go get timber, cut boards to length, etc., with times allocated to each process.

So, with my drawings done, I have gone to Daren to identify the bugs in my design. His job is to work out the process for making it. But he won't make it – he is too busy, too clever and too expensive. Steve will make it for us. Steve has been a student at Rowden for about 18 months, first doing a year-long course, then six months of renting bench space here and developing his work.

Steve lives on site in a caravan with Laura, his very tolerant wife. Steve's workspace is just opposite where Daren works, and it is where we will see the desk and chair come to life.

But first, the work belongs to Daren. I ran into Daren in the shop, and he began telling me about drawings he had done, sketching on a router catalogue as he told me about the hinged lid.

"This is going to determine the construction," he said. We both know this middle section is going to be tricky. It's thin and could bend under usage if Carol bangs down on the keyboard. "I've got other drawings if you want to have a look," he said. And here they are.

Look at how he is using the drawing to think through the construction. Some are life-size, on which he works out the actual thickness of a component. See the sketch at right – three layers of aero ply and two layer of veneer give him a component thickness of 5.5mm.

Figs. 35.2 & 35.3. Daren's workspace (left) and Steve's bench, opposite it.

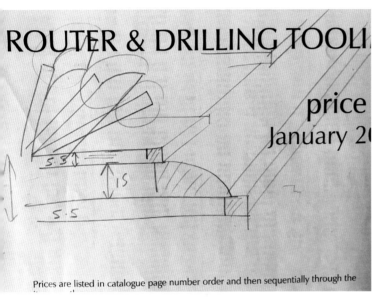

What he needed me to decide was how the opening lid comes down onto the desk. Does it have a moulding on the front of the lid, that either replaces or fits over the moulding at the front of the desk?

My preference is for the middle course. If I lose the moulding on the front of the lid, I have a skinny and mean-looking lid. If I lose the moulding from the front of the desk, I might lose structural stiffness. So my favourite at the moment is the one where the lid has a soft, round moulded front that slides over the moulding at the front of the desk. That's not easy to make – Daren won't like this. The process we go through with every complex piece is a bit like a good tennis match. You need a partner who can hit the ball back as hard as you hit it.

"I must have fixings in that corner." Love-15.

"How many fixings, Daren?"

"Oh at least three." 15-15.

"Can we keep the thinness of these components?"

"Yes, well, if we position them here." 30-15.

"But we do need the strength." 30-30.

"Can we keep the structural strength and just have two fixings, that are wider apart?" 40-30.

"And make the fixings that bit longer." Cross court drive to the baseline, and game.

But Daren's response was very reasonable: "And how

Figs. 35.4. & 35.5. Daren's early sketch on a router catalogue drawing (above), and his later variations.

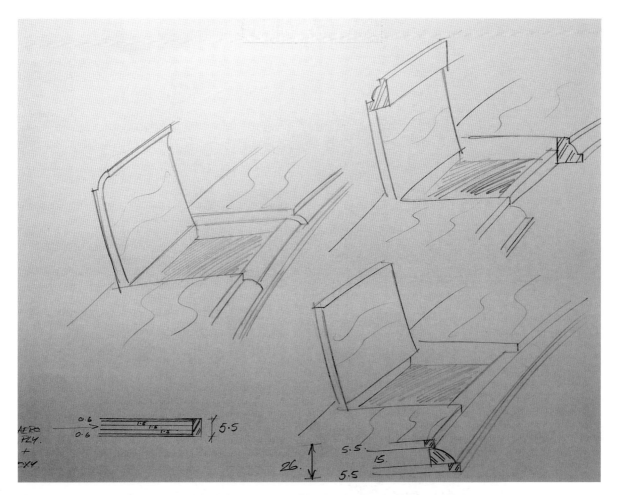

Fig. 35.6. Eventually all these sketches led to a proposed lamination for the desktop.

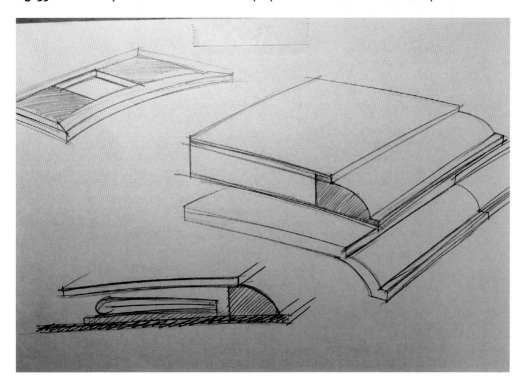

Fig. 35.7. What he needed me to decide was how the opening lid comes down onto the desk. Does it have a moulding on the front of the lid, that either replaces or fits over the moulding at the front of the desk?

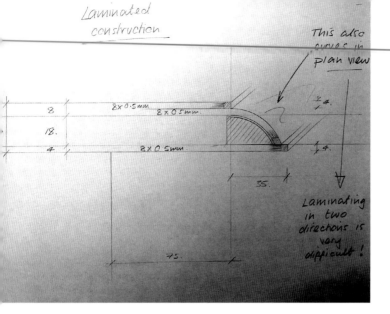

This also
curves in
plan view

8 × 0.5mm
8 × 0.5mm
8 × 0.5mm

Laminating
in two
directions is
very
difficult!

8
18.
4

35.

75.

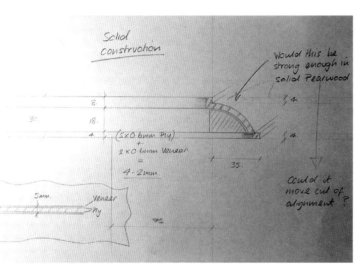

Solid
construction

Would this be
strong enough in
solid Pearwood

(5 × 0.6mm Ply)
+
2 × 0.6mm Veneer
=
4.2mm

Could it
move out of
alignment?

8.
18.
4.

35.

75.

5mm.
Veneer
Ply

30

Figs. 35.8 & 35.9. A sketch showing a laminated lid (above) and one using solid wood.

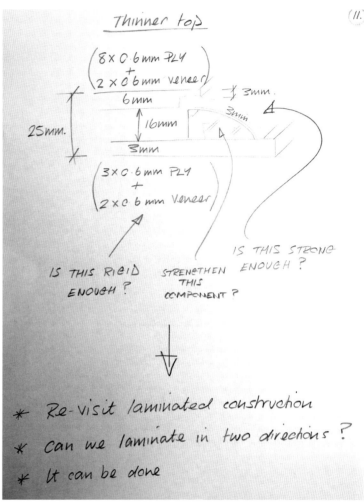

Thinner top

(11.)

(8 × 0.6mm PLY
+
2 × 0.6mm Veneer)

6mm

25mm.

16mm

3mm

3mm.

3mm

(3 × 0.6mm PLY
+
2 × 0.6mm Veneer)

IS THIS RIGID
ENOUGH?

STRENGTHEN
THIS
COMPONENT?

IS THIS STRONG
ENOUGH?

* Re-visit laminated construction
* Can we laminate in two directions?
* It can be done

Figs. 35.10 . Exploring a thinner top.

do you propose to open that lid?" Hmmmm… I am sure we can come up with something.

And that's an interesting statement. Time and again, I see myself putting off decisions until I have an answer. I know that sooner or later Daren will come at me with, "We need a decision on that lid," and I will have an answer, a good one. I don't right now, but it will go on to the back burner in my head, and I will have an answer very soon.

The way we do this, and the way we are showing you how to develop the process for a making a complex piece, is exactly the way we do it with students at Rowden. They learn how to use hand tools and woodworking machinery, and they have made a bench and a nice box , but now it's, "OOOOOOOh – scary!" But once you have seen it done, and done it once yourself,

you can see the process and apply it to almost any piece you then want to make.

If you want to eat an elephant, the way to do is a bite at a time.

So, I went back to Daren, and showed him how I was writing up what we did together and sharing his drawings. "I should have done better drawings," he said. "No, don't worry – they do the job."

I wondered why Daren began with the front lipping of the desk lid – but I suppose it doesn't really matter where you start to eat the elephant. Once that is resolved, he will ask Steve to make full-size templates, then move on to look at the hinging of the lid. Daren seems to work on the moving parts and the thin, high-risk areas first.

The drawing at top left shows a laminated version of

the lid – but this was abandoned as Daren sees that you can only laminate in two dimensions with great difficulty. So, a solid-wood version follows. This is the way ahead. Note how Daren is still exploring options for construction. Will it be very thin ply or carbon fibre? (I am not keen on carbon fibre, given the cost.) We are looking not only at construction, but at materials – can we get 0.5mm plywood? If so, can we laminate that with epoxy to a very stiff but thin sheet?

This shows Daren thinking out how the solid form could be worked on the shaper. When we talked about it, I said, "That's great if we have to do 10, but we are doing one here – can we consider hand work, as the bend is in two dimensions but it's small? Spokeshaves and Swiss pear will work nicely together." Daren muttered OK, but I don't think I convinced him.

Now I come back to getting the thinness I want. So far, you will note that Daren has drawn these cross sections at two or three times life size, just to get the accuracy. I wanted to get the construction resolved before I started to moan that he had blown it up to a 30mm thickness. This was not something I could compromise on; the thinness was important to the piece.

So here we are. We settled on the lower version with a 4mm thickness at the bottom for added strength and we compromised at a 26mm overall depth. The worry we both had was with strength. The way the lipping of the lid fits to the lid itself is supported by my original drawing. With mouldings, it's very easy for makers to return to old ways and compromise the design of the moulding they want. I developed a new and fresh version of a very old and common moulding – a cove – and wanted my version, not something more "normal." It's easy to lose these details in translation. Always keep looking at the original design drawing.

Next, Steve will make full-size templates of the plan of the desk and the legs. Daren, being smart, wants to make templates before the full-size drawings, as he can then easily transfer from one to the other with accuracy. You draw around a template; doing it the other way is less accurate.

"But how do you see the full-size and make changes?" I whinge.

Well, I will get to see templates; I should be OK working those to a finished shape.

The drawing shows how Daren transfers my small-scale drawing to a larger scale by creating a grid over

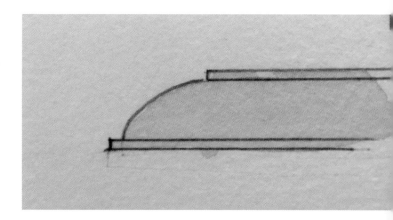

Fig. 35.11. Detail of lid from presentation drawing.

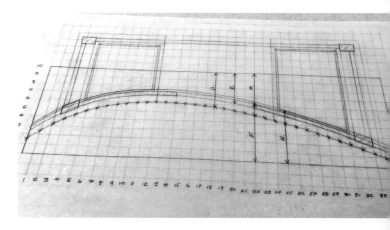

Fig. 34.12. How Daren transfers my small-scale drawing to a larger scale by creating a grid over the original, then enlarging the grid and plotting the intersections on the new scale.

the original, then enlarging the grid and plotting the intersections on the new scale.

Another step is choosing and ordering the timber. I settled a while ago on Swiss pear. This has been a favourite of mine for forever. I made my first serious cabinet in pear, and Jim Krenov talked about pear in his great books. The Swiss grow these trees as shade trees along main roads and have a decent crop every year. They steam the timber to kill large boring beetles that live just under the bark. This steaming slightly changes its colour to a slightly more pinky red. The lovely thing about pear is that is has not got the graphics – the grain lines of other timbers. What it does have is a subtle colour shift. Daren will tell me who has got the timber in stock, and I would normally go to see it – but this

Figs. 35.13 & 35.14. I settled a while ago on Swiss pear. This has been a favourite of mine for forever. I made my first serious cabinet in pear, and Jim Krenov talked about pear in his great books.

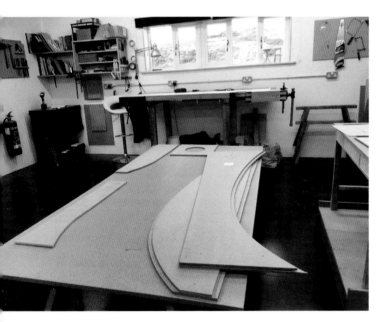

time it's Bob at Timberline. I have been buying timber from him for more than 40 years. (He had a great stack of timber that he calls his pension pot: "No, you can't look through it; you can't afford it.")

Because it's him and because I have not the energy to drive, we order it unseen and get super timber. You should not do this; you should go and make your bones with the timber man. Learn from him. Look at boards and piles of timber and see your components in each piece. Choose your boards, then buy a bit more. Bob sent us lovely stuff, and I am happy to pay his horrible prices because we are mates; we have history. I have this kind of relationship with a small handful of woody men and women. Occasionally, it moves on to a relationship with the next generation of young yard-men and women. Choosing the timber that contains the piece that you have in mind is one of the better parts of this job. It's not plastic, this stuff.

The next part to be worked on is a full-size "rod." A rod is simply a drawing at full scale. (They are called rods because drawings of windows and door details were traditionally full-sized and made on sticks that collapsed down to narrow wooden rods then were

Figs. 35.15 & 35.16. These full-size sheets of MDF with drawings are our templates (above). Below, Daren works out details of the construction with components being placed on the full-size rod.

Fig. 35.17. Here's where the desk will live.

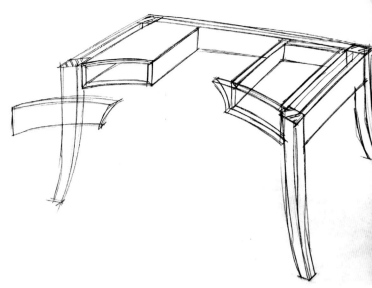

Fig. 35.18. A general construction drawing of the desk.

then stored for later use.) These full-size sheets of MDF with drawings on them are our rods (which don't collapse).

"I didn't think it would be so big," Daren said. That struck me like a smack round the ears – a note that I didn't want to hear. I went totally deaf for a while because Steve was in full swing making templates and if it's too big…!

This was a crisis. But if it all goes smoothly, something isn't quite right. After a few days, we looked at it again, and I began to believe that Daren was correct – it is too big. Not that it couldn't function at that size. The proportions were really nice – just, it wasn't smaller and more concentrated, and it was not as delicate as I wanted. This is a lady's writing table; she would want it delicate. It's bit like you are cooking and the sauce is good, but it could be more intense if you reduced it by a third. First stop was, could it be scaled down? Phil, my digital assistant, came to the rescue with different reductions.

I took them to the space the desk will live in, and came back with new and smaller dimensions. Just scaling down did not work, so I had to redraw the whole piece. But it's not a big job now – we have the overall concept and an opportunity to refine and look again. At this stage of a design, it's all tightening up proportions and getting the details right. None of Daren's work is wasted, but most of Steve's will go in the bin.

A particularly rude student called this a "vanity project," as it wasn't for a customer but for my home. It hurt my feelings for a few hours before I realised he was absolutely correct. It is a vanity. Without vanity, nothing exceptional, nothing special would ever be made. It requires an element of vanity to dream a different dream then try to bring it to life. Vain, maybe; arrogant, sure. I put my hand up to all of that. But this is about inner belief more than anything. I think this piece will be worth all the effort to drag it screaming into the daylight of existence. If I am wrong, it will end up in the dumpster of history. If I am right, someone 200 years from now will appreciate the effort we took to get it "right."

Don't be afraid of the dumpster of history. I can see my children or grandchildren working through my old folios of drawings – thousands of them – and chucking most onto the fire. What do they want musty old drawings for? Nothing like a good warming fire to clear out the rubbish.

So, this is where we are now: a new drawing of the old idea, but smaller and more intense. The legs are better. Look at the right-hand leg. This has a 1° splay that pushes the foot out by 25mm; I tried a 4° splay on the left leg, and it became too obvious. This is the art of fooling the Mark One Eye Eyeball. She's fickle and sensitive; we want her to look at that leg but not immediately see what is happening. This will make her look again until she works it out. Four degrees would have been too obvious. "Oh – that's what's going on.

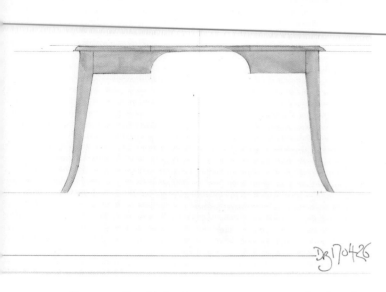

Fig. 35.19. So, this is where we are now: a new drawing of the old idea, but smaller and more intense. The legs are better. Look at the right-hand leg. This has a 1° splay that pushes the foot out by 25mm

Fig. 35.20. Daren prepares drawings for the next stages of the project.

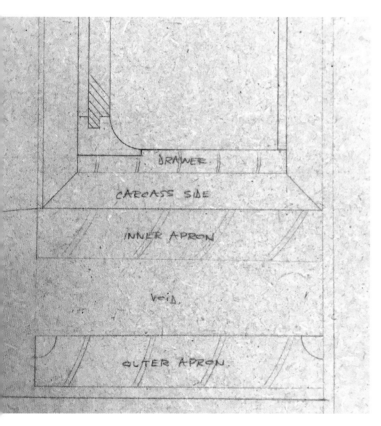

Fig. 35.21. a cross section of one side of the drawer and the inner and outer carcase aprons.

How tedious."

This photo (above) is Daren in the next process, which is developing detailed drawings of the tricky bits of the piece. It's not necessary to detail the whole piece (though we ask students to do so). A skilled maker will only do the bits that need to be worked out. But having said that, look at the detail he goes to resolve each problem area.

This is a detail shot (left) that shows a cross section of one side of the drawer and the inner and outer carcase aprons. The drawer is an example of how Daren and I work together. He drew this up first as a more conventional drawer with thicker sides. I came back to him, asking that he use a thinner drawer side, as this is a lady's desk. This meant using a drawer slip at the bottom of the drawer side to house the drawer bottom. Thicker timber would take a groove, but thin stuff needs a slip. Look at that slip — it has a lovely rounded soft shape. This is something we developed on an earlier cabinet. It's a Rowden special, but it is essentially a development of a drawer slip that Alan Peters put in one of his last pieces. Daren talked about the careful use of timber here, so the timber for the drawer slip came from the adjacent piece of timber used in the drawer side. Note how the slip is housed into the side by 2mm to avoid the feather-thin edge; this is a maker thinking and drawing to avoid issues down the line. We are settling here on 8mm-thick veneered drawer boxes with a 22mm drawer false front. We are talking at this

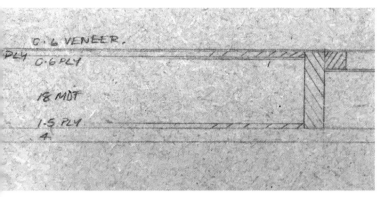

Fig. 35.22. We are using very thin plywood laminated together with epoxy to give us stiffness — hopefully enough stiffness to do the job.

stage about using sycamore sides and slips, with cedar of Lebanon drawer bottoms.

The drawers are to have a piston-fit construction, which is the Rowden way of doing things. This will allow us to have the drawer handles on the very corner. Carol will just need to reach down and put a finger behind the corner of the drawer front and it will ease out. I know this works, and I know the pleasure this gives having lived with pieces of my own furniture that do this. Easy open, woof, scent of cedar. Mmmmm. Furniture makers do not live, often enough, with good examples of their own work. Sadly, we seldom experience the joy that we give to others.

The drawer handle will have to play this important part. It will be shaped to the finger like the neck of a violin. It will be tactile and lovely. It is the most important part of a piece of furniture. It's the bit your customer touches; fingers engage with it to experience how nice your work is every time they touch that handle.

The double aprons are there to allow for a more stable glue-up and to provide a surface to attach the drawer carcases to the main desk carcase. I wondered if this could be a good place to put a secret compartment. But then it wouldn't be secret.

Look at these two drawings. We are using very thin plywood laminated together with epoxy to give us stiffness — hopefully enough stiffness to do the job.

VERY PATIENT MEAT EATERS

This is where you make your money: the machine shop. If you are smart, you think once and cut many times. You develop a design that people like, then work out how your machines can get you that result easily and quickly. It's called "jig thinking." A jig is a workshop-made thing that holds the job in a fixed attitude to a cutter. So that chair leg comes out exactly the same time after time. At Westcombe, my Bideford workshop, we even had a jig room. At the end of a job, all the jigs were gathered up, notes were made on them and they were carefully stored. When,

Fig. 36.1. Steve at the band saw.

five years later, you thought you might need a table leg like the one we made five years before, the jigs were buried beneath years of MDF. The maker who knew the job had left and the notes were no longer intelligible. I have never managed to get this right: think once, do many times. But you can do it!

My wife has just taken up beekeeping. We went to buy her first hive from a nice elderly man named David. He had long silvery hair, curling in ringlets around his shoulders. He looked as if he'd stepped out of a "Lord of the Rings" movie. He lived north of Exmoor, and had once been a builder but ended up making Western red cedar beehives. David's workshop consists of a very large shed with piles and piles of beehive components. I mean everywhere – there must be thousands of components stacked up to 6' high. Between the stacks are narrow passageways, each with components to shoulder height to the left and right. Thousands of components. Between the ever-present stacks, the narrow passages each lead to a single machine – in one case, a tenoner, in others, a different hidden machine set up for a key operation. David

works here alone, though he has a helper come in to pack his orders and take them to the mail. David had no website and now does only one show a year – but he sells well-made, beautiful cedar beehives day after day. Think once, set up once and cut many times. This is what I have failed to do.

I get asked which machine one should buy first, and I think my answer is some form of grinder to sharpen hand tools – but that is closely followed by a band saw. I am amazed, however, by how badly band saws cut stuff up. I watch students struggle as the cut goes off line. Here is the problem – and the solution. When you start woodworking, you probably have a pretty small band saw. The length of blade on this saw is quite short, so it will get dull very quickly. The problem is that you are not responding to this and putting on a new blade. You then push a little harder to overcome the dull edge, and it all goes wrong. When a band saw tooth enters the job, the gullet behind the tooth fills up with dust, all right and proper. But if you push too hard, the gullet packs with dust and spills onto the side of the blade, driving the saw off line. The answer is to change

Figs. 36.2, 36.3 & 36.4. The safe execution of a cut at the band saw. At end of cut, Steve moves his hand in front of blade.

the blade, become more sensitive and just allow the blade to eat the job. Chunka, chunka, chunka.

We require students to go through a machine shop training, which is aimed to keep them permanently attached to their fingers. I regard fingers in the same way; count them as I start and again when I finish. Woodworking machines are very dangerous, they are like extremely patient meat-eating beasts. One slip – not now, but 15 years from now when you are more experienced – late in the afternoon when you are rushing and a bit tired and ZAP! No fingers.

My favourite safety measure is the "red zone." Each machine has one. You see it in your head as you approach each task. While the red zone is different on every machine, it is always an area your hands should never enter. Use push sticks or simply keep your fingers back from the red. And always make sure that the floor is swept clean, not slippery with shavings.

The photos at right show Steve beginning to machine some pear for Carol's desk. He's wearing boots with steel toe caps, ear defenders and eye protection. We didn't set up this photograph with the safety equipment; Steve dons this every time for his own protection.

Here, Steve is cutting on the band saw; the board has one planed face and a planed edge, which is against the fence. The movable top guides have been lowered to just above the job.

As the job reaches halfway, Steve is able to pause. He can then set up a support to the exact height and position under the job behind the band saw. This becomes more important as the job is pushed out of the band saw and the support takes more weight.

As he approaches the end of the cut, Steve takes up a push stick – a notched piece of scrap with a soft rounded handle – to finish the job. It keeps his fingers out of that red zone.

The next meat eater I'll introduce you to is what we in the United Kingdom call a planer, but in the United States is called a jointer. This is usually the machine that puts a flat face side onto the job – and it can take your

fingers off in a flash.

Look at the setup here at left. It's not perfect but it's not bad. The vertical fence could have been shifted to expose less blade, but the yellow bridge guard is down as low as it can be. It's around this bridge guard that the machine's red zone lives. My hands would never go within an inch on either side of that guard. The pressure is placed downward on the job on the "infeed table," but as soon as we can, we want our pressure on the "outfeed table" – the one on the other side of the cutters. Changing your pressure from one side to the other side, lifting your hands over that yellow guard, is safe use.

Make certain that dust extraction is running and the blades are sufficiently sharp. When the blades are dull you get a "hammering" feeling as they whack into the job – not sweetly cut it. We keep three sets of blades: one in the machine, one with our saw doctor, Brian Mills, and one set ready to go into the machine as needed. Between blade changes, Daren touches up the cutting edges with a small oilstone. The setup of new blades is with a "carry forward" stick. This small length of scrap timber sits on the outfeed table, projecting over the cutters. We take a measure of how much the stick is carried forward when we turn the cutter block by hand. The check is done at three points across the cutters. This avoids clever and unnecessary aftermarket tools and keeps set-up time down to a few minutes.

Figs. 36.5, 36.6 & 36.7. The safe execution of a cut at the planer/ thicknesser (what is called a jointer in the U.S.).

Fig. 37.1. Making a model is a good idea; if that is stiff then chances are the real thing will be OK. But we are not doing that on this job; time is against us, we have an exhibition in October and it's now July.

THE DESKTOP

The essence of Carol's desk is its thin middle. That also is the technical challenge – can we make it stiff enough at the front edge to be usable? Now we are not structural engineers; all of our knowledge is based on what we have seen and done. So, you take a punt. Making a model is a good idea; if that is stiff then chances are the real thing will be OK. But we are not doing that on this job; time is against us, we have an exhibition in October and it's now July.

The rear of this desk will have a rail between the back legs; the front rail will have a solid support in pear at the front of the carcase – not a big one, but I hope enough. The base of the centre is 3mm – very, very thin.

To make this work, we use laminations – thin layers glued together are inherently stiff because of the glue lines. So, we used five sheets of 0.6mm plywood (made from three layers of 0.2mm timber) and glued them together with epoxy (which contains no water) to make a stiff, thin sheet. We then lipped the lamination with solid pear and taped it on, because using cramps would be too aggressive. It sets overnight, but hardens up over a six-day period – so we leave the component flat for that time.

The long curved lips were template routed so the fit was perfect. The photo on the next page shows Steve making one of those templates. Planning ahead saves you loads of time.

Fig. 37.2. To make this work, we use laminations – thin layers glued together are inherently stiff because of the glue lines. So, we used five sheets of 0.6mm plywood.

Fig. 37.3. Routing the template curve for the desktop.

Fig. 37.4. Numbering the ply sheets.

Fig. 37.5. The lamimation after veneering.

Next, after the lips are flushed off, the board is veneered with pear. Steve checks the veneers and makes sure each sheet is numbered so they don't get out of sequence.

Now we are starting to get the component into shape. This (bottom right) is the lamination after veneering. Again, we left things to cure for several days, as the epoxy stiffens up in that time. This will be the

thin sheet that we build upon, the centre of which be exposed and form the base of the storage for the laptop. The sheet Steve is lifting in the image above right is the laminated lid of the laptop storage; the lipped MDF components on either side will make the top of the desk on either side of the lidded storage.

In the image top right, you can see drawn on the rod (the plans, if you missed the last chapter) the mould-

Fig. 37.6. Lid components arranged.

Fig. 37.7. Details of the moulding on the rod.

Fig. 37.8. Showing the components to the rod.

Fig. 37.9. Stickering the components is essential.

ing that will surround the desktop. At the bottom is the 3mm sheet, then the solid moulded curved edge, with a tiny raise to the central field. This is a cove moulding seen on furniture everywhere. I have just developed it to a slightly different form, extending the curve of the radius and making the steps tiny and carefully considered. Less is more.

Now we are considering the front lipping; Steve will rout this exactly to the curve of the two components. Then he will separate the centre section. This will later be attached to the centre-section lid. He wants the colour and figuring of this one piece to run through the three components.

A whole range of components have been cut to rough size and stored in the warmth of the workshop to acclimatise. The walls of the workshop are heavily

Fig. 37.10. A dry-fit is essential for a complex glue-up such as this. Note how carefully the clamps have been applied.

insulated and we keep the door closed so the humidity is relatively low even on a wet day – perfect making conditions. See (on the previous page) how the components are all kept stickered. That allows air to circulate over all four surfaces of each component. We once had a student leave thin box component on the benchtop in the sunshine over a tea break. By the time she returned, the sun had dried one side of her thin piece so that it cupped by an alarming amount.

"What do I do now?"

Jonathan Greenwood picked up the component, looked at it, turned it over and replaced in the sunshine on the bench. "Go have another cup of tea; it will be flat in 10 minutes."

What we have now are the two components, MDF core with pear lips, which will sit on top of the thin 3mm-thick pear sheet on either side of the laptop compartment. See how carefully the clamps are applied (above). The setup has been worked out before glue goes anywhere near the job. At right you can see the Festool Dominos that have been put in less for strength and more for help in locating the piece correctly.

Fig. 37.11. Dominos aid in alignment and strength.

Fig. 37.12. The result: Everything is tight and in alignment.

The front rail has now been cut into three components. If the colour and grain is to run through as we want, we need to trim as little off these junctions as we can. See above how Steve has fit a shim of veneer under the caul? That's to allow that front lipping to move just enough – no more.

DESKTOP MOULDINGS

Get the router out; now we are into territory you all know about. These router bits, bought specially for this job, are monsters. They are the kind of router bit we keep locked away, just in case some ignorant student puts them in a hand router and switches it on. At a screaming 9,000 rpm, they would then be holding onto a gyroscopic nightmare that drags them all over the workshop. These dudes are meant to be used only in a fixed router table, at low rpm. In effect, a mini shaper, or as we call it in the U.K., a spindle moulder.

Mouldings are great. They control light and shade – to provide visual interest, darkness, with a pinpoint line of highlight. Play with them; they are tools that give visual delight and entertainment for the sniffy, easily bored Mark One Eyeball. Use mouldings from the router catalogue and you are asking for trouble, as she will have seen that shape "sooo many times, darling; it's so dull." But I wanted a simple classic moulding, and I am relying on the small raised detail to give what is a straightforward radius moulding some distinction.

Daren's drawings show Steve the curved component on the front of the lid, and the matching component at the front of the desk. These mouldings will help to support Carol's wrists when she is typing, and will support the thin centre section of the desk.

Shown clearly in the drawing on the next spread is a cross section of this moulding, as seen in the laptop compartment. Just forward of the word "tray" is the 3mm plywood veneered sheet everything is built upon. The moulded piece of pear will give support and strength at the front of the compartment, and last to the front of the lid, which is moulded on the outside and on the inside. This fits closely over the first component as the laptop storage lid is lowered. This is pretty spiffy routing!

Fig. 38.1. The large bits required for this desk.

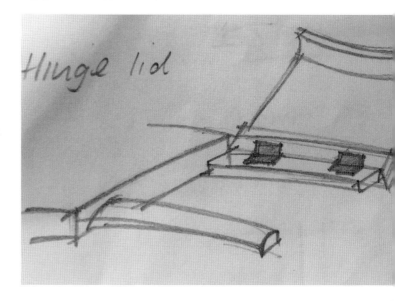

Fig. 38.2. Daren's sketch of the hinge support. Note the large cove shape on the inside of the lid.

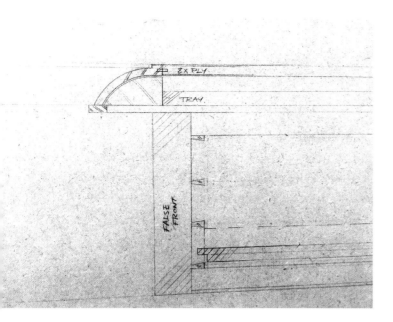

Fig. 38.3. A cross section of the moulding profile.

Fig. 38.4. The Rowden plywood router table. Simple.

Fig. 38.5. The router hangs in the tool well of the workbench.

Fig. 38.6. Starting the cut.

Which brings us to router tables. Now, students have been buying expensive router tables and proudly bringing these to the workshops for years. But we don't own a purpose-made router table. This big sheet of plywood shown above is our router table. It fits on a benchtop, often held between dogs or clamped where a clamp won't be in the way. A Trend router hangs underneath the board, and is adjustable from above. Steve

is checking the surface here top right to even out the wax and enable the job to slide over it. Note that if you don't have a tool well with a removable bottom in your bench design, you will need to support this in another way. Tool wells are pretty much a necessity.

Above is a shot of Steve running the job over the cutter, increasing the cut by 1mm increments each time, which he does by turning that handle by a

Fig. 38.7. The point fence.

measured amount. He is running a test piece here, making note of how much he increases the cut each time. The router is cut back on speed to allow for the large-diameter cutter.

See the shop-made, adjustable-point fence? The job is running against it, guided by the greenish MDF template. (I told you we made a lot of templates!) The actual job being cut is beneath the greenish template, fixed to it with screws. In fact, technically this is no longer a template; it is a jig. The handles atop it keep fingers well out of the firing line.

This point fence was purpose-made by Steve to guide this job; it is called a point fence because when the job runs against this one point, you get a full cut. You can back off and take a finer cut by pushing against a point on the fence just behind. This gives you control and safe use. The point fence also helps to cover the cutter to stop that damn big cutter from hurting people.

We will also mould some scrap on the same cutter setting; those scraps will become useful sanding blocks

Fig. 38.8. The point fence in place over the bit.

Fig. 38.9. Spline groove tooling.

Fig. 38.10. Dry-fit of top assembly.

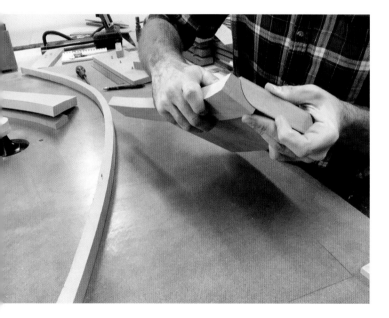

Fig. 38.11. Testing mating parts.

Fig. 38.12. It helps to have a glue-up partner.

to fit difficult components. You can then attach abrasive to the moulded block with double-sided tape to use later in the process. So much of this is thinking ahead.

Next, we need to fit the edge lipping to the laptop compartment's lid. Because it's only 3mm thick, a spline was fitted between the two to increase the glue area. A spline cutter is used to make the spline groove. The tooling accepts different-sized grooving cutters. I was delighted to see this guy was still being used; I

remember buying him 20 years ago for a specific job, and I wondered if the huge expense I incurred would ever be paid back.

Here's the dry-fitted assembly, which shows the care that goes into a glue-up. This component is curved and thin, so it's bent easily under cramps. Look at the setup, with four cramps underneath and cramping blocks. The job fits into a three-sided box that stops the lipping from sliding left or right. The glue line has been

Fig. 38.13. The top lipped and sanded.

routed, guided with either a male and female matching template. These are bearing on a curved block that matches the curve of the job, but allows the cramp to pull up square. Cramps only work square.

Look at the back of the setup. There, the cramps are bearing on a thin strip of MDF positioned in the middle of the cramping block and dead in line with the 3mm MDF job. This way, we overcome any slop in the heads of the cramps and keep them from going out of square.

Glue-up sessions are critical – they have to work, and so much of your effort is under test at this moment. We always have a buddy to help, so Daren is there to lend a hand. We also always do a dry run and gather up all the cramps, glue, blocks and brushes we need. When the glue hits the job we are rehearsed, so any slippery stuff does not cause a problem we cannot sort out. But it is still high stress.

So here we are with the desktop laid out. The panels to left and right have been lipped and sanded flat to remove a dome in the centre of each of the panels. The lid has been lipped and is ready for fitting. Next will be the hinging of the lid to the desktop, followed by

veneering the desktop. But Daren is on holiday for two weeks, and Steve has instructions to do the hinging and store the components ready for his return.

So, let's finish this lid and get it hinged. The first step is locating a strip at the rear of the component that will take the hinges. Without it, the lid is so thin that screws would come through the desktop. Steve has made grooves in both components with a tiny strip of aero ply to act as a locating spline.

Next, he polishes the inside face of the lid with shellac followed by wax. I am not after a high shine (more on this later). On the next page you can see Steve cutting the recesses to accept the Brusso stopped hinges we chose to avoid putting a stay on the lid.

Next, we have a bit of silliness. You'll recall I said we do that extra bit nobody notices? Well, here it is. This component is lipped all around – the problem is that you can see a teeny bit of end grain where the side lippings end. So, Steve has covered them with a thin veneer.

When we do a job like this we sometimes get held up. Daren is the hold up, as he is on holiday, so we work on another part of the job. In this case, it's the

Fig. 38.14. Figuring out the hinge rail.

Fig. 38.15. Cutting hinge mortises hy hand.

Fig. 38.16. Lipped up.

Fig. 38.17. The overall cramp setup for this operation.

Fig. 38.18. The top assembly – together and working.

Fig. 38.19. Sanding smooth for surface veneering.

Fig. 38.20. Testing epoxy.

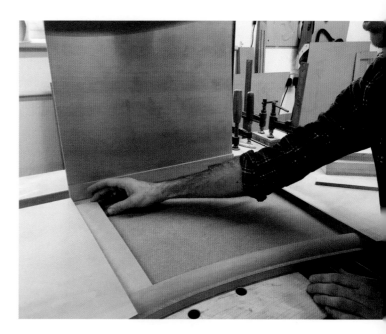

Fig. 38.21. Fitting out the areas that will hold pens.

legs and frame of the table. Make lists, work out the process and write down the steps. Feeling listless? Make a list!

Shown below left is the assembly of the desktop, and you can now begin to see what we are making. The moments when we put parts together and they fit and work together is what keeps us going. Making a piece like this one is a long climb – we need moments when we can glimpse the finished piece.

Steve is at the stage now of preparing surfaces and applying final primary surface veneers. He has three surfaces to match up. The veneer must run across these so that when the lid lifts up, you see an uninterrupted flow of pear. It's another one of those "why do we bother moments" – well, we bother because it matters, because countless generations of craftsmen and women have been getting it right before us.

Steve also has the challenge of making sure all the surfaces are flat, especially where the lid and desk meet. So, he is sanding the ground with paper backed by hard MDF.

Next is the problem of veneering just one face. I know the convention is to also put veneer on the back to help with moisture equalisation and keep the job flat, but we cannot do that here. Rules are there to be broken. Above right is Steve testing epoxy on one surface of 3mm MDF – because the process and the epoxy itself involve no water, it is a good candidate here. (We use lots of different glues for different purposes.) He's also testing the thickness of epoxy required to stick while preventing bleed-through (glue coming through

Fig. 38.22. An overall look at the desktop assembly.

Fig 38.23. The desktop assembly with the lid open.

Fig. 38.24. The final profile and the cutter.

the veneer and spoiling the surface). To overcome this, he'll add "colloidal" (a kind of fluffy white powder that makes the glue thicker as needed), testing the amount little by little.

So, at last we can see what this desk area will look like. We had quick, scribbly drawings that gave us some idea, but this is the real thing. Now I can see the soft curved piece at the front of the desk that will give me stiffness where I need, and will provide wrist support for Carol as she works at the keyboard. At the sides are two areas, one of which will hold pens, paperclips etc., and provide storage for the stuff that collects around a desk. So far so good. We say that a lot – so far so good – but we can still make a cobbler's of it. Having invested so much time in each component, it's important to not make a mistake that wastes all that valuable time and sends you back to square one.

The moulding here is a good example of an element that can set you back. We have the desktop all veneered, and Steve has cunningly matched up the veneer to run through the three components seamlessly. He did this by putting pencil marks across the joints, then cutting them out with a Japanese knife and laying the centre section. He then matched up the position of the two outside leaves to the centre.

He has built the centre lid and fitted it. Now, we need that moulding to run around all three components.

You can see at left the cutter and its moulding. Getting from the one to the other took a little doing. First, the centre section needed to be placed solidly in the centre, with no potential to vibrate. The back was hinged and the sides were fitted with veneer spacers to occupy the slight opening gaps, and a solid baseboard completed the set up for routing.

Routing that top took Daren and Steve nearly two hours; each cut was one millimetre. Run the job around the cutter, pause, raise the cutter one millimetre, do it again. As they approached the final profile, they took off only half a millimetre. Slow but safe. We cannot risk that top at this stage.

DANCING A FINE JIG

Fig. 39.1. Magnolia test leg blank in jig.

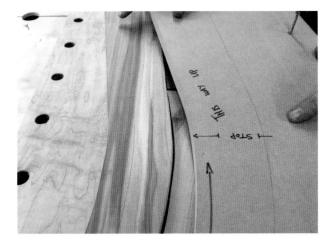

Fig. 39.2. Directions on the jig keep us routing in the correct direction at all times.

There are times when I wonder what is going on. That's a pretty usual state of mind for me. I seem to get nearer and nearer to waving my stick at the seagulls and shouting at passing cars. But when it comes to "making," this disconnection usually involves piles of expensive jigs and the spindle moulder (or shaper, as you guys call it). I see a pile of jigs made beautifully and look at the product – in this case four desk legs – and wonder why the desk legs were not made by hand, just as quickly.

I have never been able to win this argument with Daren, and my last workshop sought to become more efficient by making more jigs. We even had a room full of these useless implements. "Ah we should keep the jigs; we may make a chair leg very similar." That's how the argument goes, but by that time three things have happened. One, you can never find all the bits of jig for the necessary complex and clever sequence of machining; they are hidden beneath the pile of subsequent jigs. Two, the maker who invented this clever contraption has long since moved on and exactly how these bits of MDF fit together moved with him. Three, your old jig never quite does the new shape and you end up making a new jig.

Many makers love making jigs. Jigs keep us out of the firing line. Making even four identical forms by hand, can of course be done, but when there is a machine that will replicate shapes, most makers will dive for the cover that a jig provides. And jig design enables us to show how clever we are. Well, here we go.

Steve has made a box jig (so-called because it looks a bit like a box and the job fits inside it). The idea is clever and sensitive to the material and the design. (Note that in the photos at left, Steve is running a test leg in magnolia, which is why it looks greenish.) In this case we have legs that curve out at the bottom. This means that the grain of the pear would be roughed up if machined in one direction. So, he made this jig, which enables him to turn the

Fig. 39.3. Fitting the blank in the jig.

Fig. 39.4. Securing the jig.

Fig. 39.5. Making the cut.

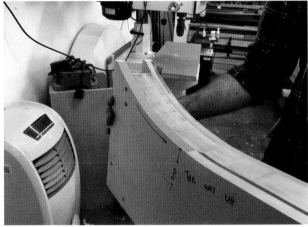

Fig. 39.6. The finished cut on one section of the leg.

job over and machine the short curved ankle from one end and the long straight leg from the other direction. That is because he has two identical guiding surfaces, one directly above the other. You can see in the photos the red line that tells him to stop and turn over. Clever jig, this be.

The photo above shows the cutter block running above a guide ring. The jig is in contact with the guide ring, and the cutters trim the job above to the exact size.

Spindle moulders really are great tools. They do the same thing as a router inverted in a table, but they do it better. The heavy mass of the cutter block provides heft through the cut, so the block spins at lower speed than a router and gives a cleaner cut.

Don't look so surprised, Steve (see above). Hand-

work was called "Workmanship of Risk" by David Pye in his wonderful book "The Nature and art of Workmanship" – what you are doing is "Workmanship of Certainty" – this is the industrial process of replication coming into small workshops.

OK – back to the bench shop. This pair of legs with two rails is what we are after; these will be the outer frames joined by a rail at the back. Each of the two frames has two side rails – a bit of overkill, but our structure is potentially wobbly in the middle so we need stiffness at the side structures, and we need to transfer that stiffness to the centre. We will do that with the addition of the drawer carcases joined to the leg frame. We don't know for sure that it will be stiff enough – had we made a maquette we could have checked that out – but we are pretty confident. Fur-

Fig. 39.7. The completed cut on one face of the leg.

Fig. 39.8. Underframe with spacer to hold aprons apart at correct heights.

Fig. 39.9. Spokeshave the legs smooth.

Fig. 39.10. Dominos join the aprons.

niture makers don't have structural engineers to tell us the tensions involved. We only go on what we have done before, the stuff that hasn't yet fallen down.

First Steve has to take the machined surface off the legs. Above, he's working on the twisted surface of the front leg. Careful shaping with a spokeshave is needed. The components are joined together with Festool Dominos – small loose tenons. They give us enough strength for the joint and eliminate a deal of semi-complex joinery.

This, at right, is our disc sander, which gets a lot of use. Steve sets it up square to sand the top of a leg component, as shown. He then takes the leg to the table saw and puts it in another jig to cut the foot to length. All the legs will be cut in this jig, so it is essential that the stop's end is sanded square so we get accurate leg

Fig. 39.11. The disc sander setup for the top of the legs.

Fig. 39.12. Disc sanding the top of the legs square.

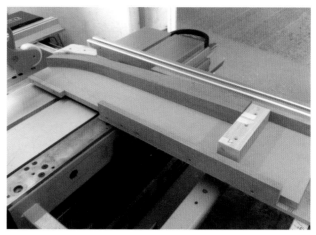

Fig. 39.13. Cutting the feet to their final length.

Fig. 39.14. Checking the feet to ensure they are in the same plane.

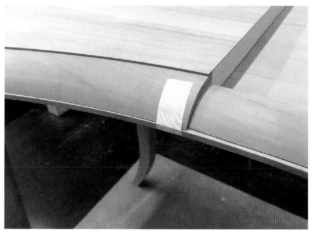

Fig. 39.15. Detail shot of the moulding taped to the desktop.

lengths. We learnt this by making batches of two dozen chairs that didn't wobble!

This is a big moment – getting the job to stand on its own feet so you can have a good look at the proportions and see what needs fixing. So far so good, but we next need the drawer compartments made and fitted.

The exhibition date is looming large, and both Daren and Steve are working weekends – my wages bill is eyewatering. But Daren has not yet booked the van to deliver the piece to the exhibition, which worries me. When he does that, I will know we are going to make it.

OK, last lap. Now it's on to the final joinery and polishing before assembly. This is critical; you do not want to be polishing into corners if you can avoid it. Above,

Steve using our standard shellac and wax finish for secondary and inside surfaces; apply it with a rubber that is kept in a glass jar. The rubber has a lambswool or wadding interior and fine cotton exterior. This holds the polish. As Steve moves the rubber and presses down, the polish is released. The shellac polish in the small bottle is very dilute, maybe less than a 1 lb.-cut (one pound weight of shellac dissolved in one gallon of alcohol). The other bottle contains mineral oil – use just a small dab to keep the rubber moving.

The aim is not a full shine, but to seal the surface and finish with a good wax polish. This is a quick and easy finish in the workshop, as shellac flashes off very fast. You wouldn't want to polish with someone sanding on the next bench, but you can generally polish in the

Fig. 39.16. Now add polish.

Fig. 39.17. Polished legs.

Fig. 39.18. Side assembly glue-up.

Fig. 39.19. Fitting the drawer carcases.

workshop without too many special measures. If I had a high-shine job to do, I would try to find a dust-free room, or I'd do the polish at the weekend when the dust had settled.

Let's take a careful look at the glue-up above. There are eight cramps and only four components. Look at the angle-clamping block at the top of the far leg. Notice the support blocks between the double rails to stop them from bending under pressure. Notice also the small paper-faced clamping blocks to stop the blocks

from marking the new polish. Ye Gods – the care these guys are now taking as they get near to the finish line.

Now we can see the drawer carcases fit. These are critical to the structure, providing stiffness to the front of the desk. Note how we avoid work that is not necessary; lippings on MDF components that are never seen after assembly are omitted. If, however, this area would be visible, even to a 4-year-old crawling underneath, it would get lipped, then veneered and polished. That 4-year-old could grow up to be a customer.

DRAWERS TO DIE FOR

Now we'll make the drawer boxes that hang beneath the desktop. I know some of you might be uncomfortable with veneering, but bear with me, will you? Veneering has a feeling of dishonesty; you expect a timber surface to be the same the whole way through. Veneers are a thin surface layer.

But bear this in mind – most of the finest furniture ever made was not solid wood but veneer.

Veneering is a technique that allows us to avoid the movement of solid wood. It also allows us to take a wonderful rare log and spread it across our surface, rather than using it in one place only. Once you know how to do it, it's a nice, controllable technique that is small-workshop friendly. You'll need a couple items of specialist equipment, including a vacuum bag and a glue hopper, but other than that, it's straightforward, good, simple making.

My focus on veneering in this chapter comes from watching Daren and Steve in a mass glue-and-pressure session with all the drawer box components. All four parts of each component are carefully laid out in order: the lipped MDF ground, two veneers (one for the outside, one for the inside) and a pressing sheet of thin board that is 5mm larger in width and length than the job. Note at right that the lippings are small; big lippings would move and telegraph though a veneered surface

In the images at right Daren is mixing the two-part glue (Easy Bond UF-R Formaldehyde Liquid Resin and UF-H Powder Hardener). The scales, which measures the weight of the two parts, are invisible beneath the

glue bucket. The ratio is 10:1; this glue gives us a critical open time of about 15 minutes. Stir it well, then put it into the glue hopper. This hopper gives you a wide, fast, even spread of glue over the surface, which is what you want.

Look at the sequence and the set-up shown in the photos. The job is laid out so that both Daren and Steve can move around the table to do different jobs without getting in each other's way. First, Daren applies the glue on the ground, then moves to the next panel. Steve comes in behind to place the veneer on the glue, then turns the workpiece over to expose the underside. They then go around the job a second time to veneer that surface.

Finally, the pressing sheet is placed on top of the top veneer. This protects the surface of the job in the vacuum bag, and its slightly larger size prevents the veneer from being bent over the edge. Notice that it is marked UP in the centre to cut down on confusion. Masking tape is applied to the edges to keep everything in place before each assembly is moved to the vacuum bag. Remember, we have only 15 minutes of open time – this is the critical time it takes to get the job under pressure…so let's hustle here, fellas!

A good vacuum bag is a great tool. Unlike a big steel press, it only takes up space when it is in use. It works on the principle that if you take all the air out of a bag, atmospheric pressure is exerted on the surfaces of the job. And that's more than enough to hold your veneer in place.

A vacuum pump (a normal pump running in reverse) is attached to the bag, the edges are sealed, then

Fig. 40.1. Drawer pieces ready for veneer.

Fig. 40.2. All arranged for glue-up.

Fig. 40.3. Each veneer assembly has four components.

Fig. 40.4. Mixing the liquid resin glue for the veneer.

Fig. 40.5. Loading the hopper.

Fig. 40.6. Applying the epoxy.

Fig. 40.7. Stick 'em up

Fig. 40.8. On top goes a pressing sheet.

Fig. 40.9. Veneer packet.

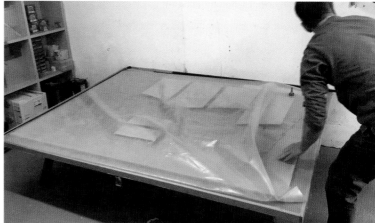

Fig. 40.10. Into the press.

Fig. 40.11. A good vacuum press is critical.

Fig. 40.12. Drawer carcases.

Fig. 40.13. A dry-fit of the drawers.

Fig. 40.14. The drawer pieces atop the drawer box.

the pump sucks out all the air. You leave it there until the glue cures.

Back to the workshop. These (above) are the two drawer carcases – the veneered components that were in the bag – laid out before assembly. These are simple boxes that we're fixing together with Dominos. The essential thing is that the sides of the carcases are parallel; without this, fitting a good drawer will not be easy. Veneered carcase components help ensure this. A solid-wood carcase is prone to movement, and you may well need to dress the inside surfaces with a handplane. I remember the bruised knuckles from doing this.

Cramps, lots of cramps, and more cramps. This is a typical Rowden glue-up; we take no chances. Two well-fit surfaces, a little bit of glue and a little bit of pressure. If you find yourself bending the handles of the cramps,

something is wrong.

Drawer fitting is where Rowden gets even more anal retentive. I know there are lots of modern metal drawer runners. I have them in my kitchen, and they close softly to perfection. But we teach a drawer-making process that began well before I was born. I asked Fred, who learned his making in Germany before the war, about drawers, and he showed me his method for best-quality drawers. I asked Alan Peters, who learned his making during the Arts & Crafts movement at the Edward Barnsley workshop just after the war. Both showed me basically the same method. Alan had a slight tweak that might save a step, but essentially this is a system developed by many minds over a considerable period of time. It gives a lovely fit that is generally unaffected by weather or heat.

You begin with a good carcase, then gather your drawer

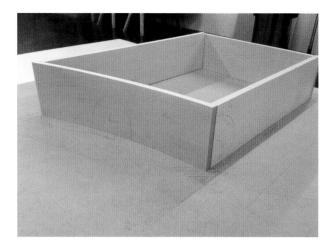

Fig. 40.15. The drawer assembly.

Fig. 40.16. Shooting the parts to size.

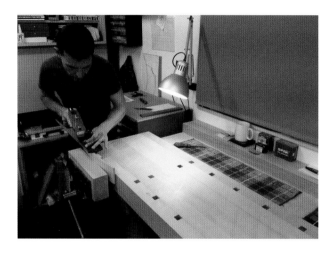

Fig. 40.17. Planing the drawer part without a shooting board.

Fig. 40.18. Fitting the sides to the drawer box.

components. All four – front, two sides and back – are individually fit to that carcase before cutting the joinery and before assembly. So, mark them out so you know where they fit. The drawer front gets a semi-circle drawn on the outside centre on the bottom edge. If there are two drawers (or more), mark them so you know which parts go with which drawer. So here the Ls on each part indicate not only which part is which, but that they're for the left-side drawer. A drawer back gets the same mark as the front, but you know it's the back as it is narrower. Drawer sides get a quarter-circle marked on the outside front-to-bottom edge. This tells you front and back, top and bottom, inside and outside: all the essential information when it comes to glue-up.

We are making tricky angled drawer fronts for this desk – but I will describe our process as if it were a simple,

square dovetailed drawer box. That is tricky enough.

Start with the drawer sides. Fitting them to the carcase is a shave-at-a-time business. A good shooting board can be used for trimming end grain or long grain (provided the shooting board is long enough to take the full drawer side). Planing the top with the job in the vice as shown is slightly more difficult but can be done.

Shooting is a regular job and it can be hard on the hands as the grip on the plane is not comfortable. Daren got this workshop-made implement from Alan Peters's workshop after his death. It's a wooden handle that slips over the side of a No. 8 to provide a comfortable and secure grip. We hope to some day offer exact hardwood replicas to those of you with a pile of shooting to do.

Shoot the ends of the drawer sides square and to

Fig. 40.19. Fitting the back.

Fig. 40.20. Work one end. Aim for a tight fit.

Fig. 40.21. Fitting the front.

length (and in a square carcase, they should both be the same length). Then shoot the top edge until each drawer side will just slide in the carcase. No slack – just a nice fit. Don't get too anal retentive about this; the fit is most important in a drawer's width, not its height.

Next, fit the drawer back to the front of the carcase. We have a curved carcase here, so it's more complex. But essentially you fit the back as tight as you can. Fitting this component is maybe the most important thing in getting a good overall drawer fit. Bear in mind that the drawer back is shallower than the height of the carcase to accommodate the drawer bottom, so it's the width and angle of the ends that are at issue. You're fitting to a carcase that may or (most likely) may not be square. So, the ends of the drawer back should be shot at the angle of the carcase. To do this, you can put

a pink slip of paper between the shooting board fence and the drawer back. This just slightly changes the angle at which the end of the job is presented to the plane – 89.5° not 90°. Move the slip in nearer the plane and it's 89.2° – a very sensitive way to adjust that angle.

Work one end first to get the angle right, then trim the other end to fit. You really want a tight, tight fit here. Why? Well, drawer components expand and contract with the weather so the height of the drawer is no help and can cause the drawer to jam. The width of the drawer box, however, will give you a good sliding fit if the box fits tightly in the carcase.

Now fit the drawer front. You can, if you are careful, use the drawer back as a template for the front. You then have marks to which to shoot, but still test the job against the carcase. (With the curved front here, we cannot do this.)

There is an added wrinkle when shooting a drawer front: Don't get it to fit right in the opening. Most of us would aim to have a drawer front with ends that angle 89° (if squared from the inside face). The slight "reveal" or gap around the drawer is created by this angle. Tricky stuff this drawer fitting. Keep with me now.

Daren has fit his drawer front tight but has allowed it to go deeper into the carcase because the drawer will have a false drawer front. If this is your actual drawer front, you need to have something to trim off after assembly and in the fitting process that will leave a clean edge to the drawer front in relation to the carcase. The front is a primary surface and should be spot on.

Now we come to joinery. You all, I guess, know

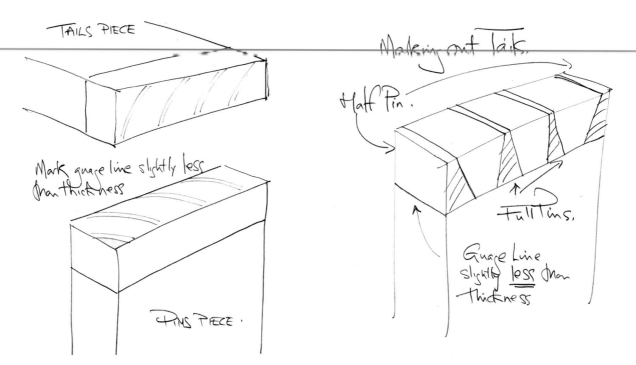

TAILS PIECE

Mark gauge line slightly less than thickness

PINS PIECE.

Marking out Tails.

Half Pin.

Full Pins.

Gauge Line slightly less than thickness

Fig. 40.22. Mark the dovetail baselines.

Fig. 40.23. Mark out the tails.

everything about dovetailing. No? Well, I will run you through the process as it relates to thin-sided drawers and through-dovetails. Here, as noted, we are fitting a false drawer front, so it's through-dovetails all around on this job.

Start with the components marked up and fit so you know top and bottom, inside and out, what fits to what (getting this wrong trips up a lot of people). Set a gauge to just shy of your components' thickness and gauge all around both ends of the tail pieces and pin pieces. Setting it "just shy" is terribly important. Almost all dovetailed joinery needs cleanup with a plane after assembly; this way, you clean up to the end grain of the pins, which are slightly below the surface. With drawers, the end grain of the pins (the drawer front and backs) are fit perfectly to the carcase. After gauging the baselines, put the pins pieces to one side; almost all our dovetail work at Rowden is done tails first.

Mark the tails out with a half pin at top and bottom, and, in this case, two full pins in the centre. We might use dividers to plot these out. I would use a knife to mark these, but we are quite relaxed about it if you use a sharp pencil at this stage. Later it becomes more critical and a knife is essential.

Now this is where your sawing is examined. Alan Peters always said, "Have a practice in a bit of scrap to warm your hand up and get into the rhythm of sawing." Concentrate, turn the radio off and stop any

possible interruption.

Your stance is important. Your back leg should be positioned to allow the sawing arm to clear your torso. The saw, wrist, arm and shoulder should all form a straight axis that swings straight from the shoulder. Look at yourself as you do this and correct; moving that back leg around often helps a lot. We teach sawing by giving a demo, then tell you to do lots and lots of practice cuts. Each time, the cut gets straighter, and that leg moves a little farther around. Your body is a wonderful tool holder.

Start the cut at the far side of the job, tickle, tickle, tickle, and lift the weight of the saw. Establish the saw groove just inside the marked line. Now lengthen the cut, rah, rah, rah, and as you do, bring the saw to horizontal. You are now in position.

Now you go down to that baseline. Depending on how you set up the job in the vice, it will either be vertical or slightly angled. It matters not – you should be able to follow that line. Rah, rah, rah. Take it easy and use the full length of the saw, but do not rush or drive the cut down. Allow the saw to do the work. Hold that saw as if it were the hand of a 4-year-old granddaughter you were guiding across a busy road. Gently, but with purpose. If you grip it too hard she screams and it all goes to hell. Same with the saw. Doing this is very Zen – all about focus and not attempting to physically guide that saw. You think that saw down the damn line.

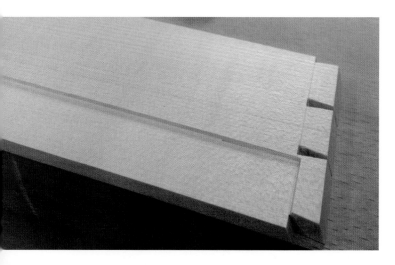

Fig. 40.24. The drawer side, with the joinery cut (the routed sides will accept drawer slips – more to come on that).

Fig. 40.25. Transfer setup.

The only thing that really, really matters about these cuts are that they are straight and they are at right angles to the face. Oh – and they stop above the gauge line.

Now clear the waste. We use a nice coping saw to remove most of it (if the blade is too coarse to enter the dovetail saw kerf, tap the blade with a light hammer to take some of the set off).

Now chop back to the line. Daren would have made his openings for the pins to fit one of his chisels – smart dude. Tap the blade with a mallet to approach the baseline from both sides; the job is not clamped down so you can flip it over quickly. The essence is to approach the line with a series of cuts to just past halfway in depth. When you cannot get another cut in front of the line, you can safely chop into the gauge line. Carefully fit the blade in the gauge line and tap to establish the cut, then tap, tap, tap down to just past halfway with the blade held carefully at right angles to the job.

Turn it over, repeat and clear the corners and Roberto est ton Oncle.

So far this has been not too demanding, but now we need to fit one set of pins to the tails. The marking out is critical and cutting to the subsequent line is where the fit is made or rubbished. Good dovetails are from the saw with a touch of the chisel here and there to the pins – that is the work of a skilled maker. Above is the setup for marking the tails from the pins you

have just cut. When things are in position, hold the tail piece there with one hand in the centre – light pressure between the plane and the job will hold it firm whilst you mark out. Use a marking knife that will get right into the corner. I favour a knife with a sensitive thin blade; I don't want to cut the tails, but I want to run that blade along the tail and mark its position on the pin piece below. You need a clear mark that you can see. A good bench light helps here, and a decent pair of spectacles.

Having got the angled marks across the end grain, transfer straight lines down to the gauge line on either side. Mark the waste – lots of people cut to the wrong side of the line.

Now set up to saw the pins. This time saw to just barely leave that line on the job. This "leaving the line" is essential to a good fit. Clear the waste, chop back to the line, and you can consider fitting the pins to the tails.

Offering the job up and tapping the pieces with a small steel hammer will give you an idea of which pin is going to go down and which is not. The sound from the hammer will tell you. A higher note will tell you about stiffness and warn you to relieve the side of the pin. There is a myth that dovetails only should go down once. Every serious maker I have talked to admits that they take their dovetail joints down at least halfway just to check the fit.

DRAWER SLIPS

You must have been wondering about the rebates on the inside faces of the drawer sides. Well, we do a posh kind of drawer slip, and that's where they fit.

First of all, what is a drawer slip? Its original purpose was to enable a maker to create thin delicate drawer sides, sides too thin to accept the groove for the drawer bottom to fit into.

Instead, you fit a drawer slip that accepts the drawer bottom and doubles the bearing surface of the drawer's bottom. It's a refinement, and I see students doing it when really it should not be there. Where you should see them is in a lady's dressing table or a similar delicate piece.

So, we are OK in using them here. A conventional drawer slip is shown in the diagram. The "Rowden slip" is one I adapted from one Alan Peters did in one of his last pieces; it makes the junction smooth between slip, drawer side and drawer bottom, but it is a bit of extra work.

It's part of that nonsense we do in that ridiculous last 5 percent. I know, I know; it's silly but words like "spoiling the ship for ha' pouth of tar" ring in my ears. It's something that sometime in the future will matter. A hundred years from now, my great, great grandchildren will be clearing out granny's house and someone – I hope – will say, "Let's keep the desk; it's like nothing we have, but I quite like it." Therefore, I hope, keeping it out of the great dumpster of history.

The photos show the process of making these slips. Daren was careful to select timber that was quite similar – maybe adjacent boards to the drawer sides – so they matched. From right to left: Run the mould-

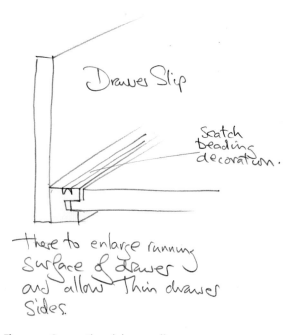

Fig. 41.1. Conventional drawer slip.

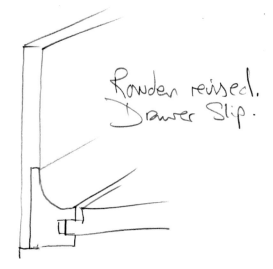

Fig. 41.2. Rowden drawer slip.

Fig. 41.3. Routed to accept drawer slips.

Fig. 41.4. Slips run on a motherboard.

ing, rout the drawer bottom's groove in the slips and drawer front, then separate the slip from the board. Note that two slips per board give some economy of material and handling.

At right is how the slip is separated on the band saw. We are not worried that we have a band-sawn surface on the bottom of the job. These are fitted deep below the drawer, so they are handplaned flush in the drawer-fitting process. Note the MDF back-up board to help stop spelching.

Cleaning up these coves can be done with a large dowel of suitable diameter and abrasive. You can see from the photo at right below that the mating surfaces are smooth, and the joint is invisible. This is all about Daren's very sensitive timber selection. A gooseneck scraper can help with that final pull of a few shavings down to the line.

Drawers at Rowden almost always have cedar of Lebanon drawer bottoms, because of the fragrance that then perfumes the room every time the drawer is opened. It's an assault on the senses (it also repels moths, so my socks are safe). Below right is the setup Daren used for final planing of his drawer bottoms to exact thickness and finish. He is using a Record No. 7 with a Clifton forged high-carbon steel blade; we wouldn't get the sharpness we need for this from A2 steel. We use a small Festool orbital sander, then apply a thin shellac seal coat – but no wax on cedar, as it clogs the grain and blocks the perfume.

This is the drawer after assembly, with glue in the joints. A dovetailed drawer is one structure that should not be clamped – a drawer should simply be tapped together with a steel hammer to hear the ring as the joint bottoms out. In this case, the drawer is placed above the carcase to make sure the shape is kept during drying. A typical, square drawer would be checked for equal diagonals, then left on a flat surface to dry. Note how Daren glued up the drawer with its bottom in place rather than fitting it later.

Shown on the following pages is a "drawer board"; it is essential to fitting the drawer, which has already been fit in height in individual components, but is tight in its width (I hope!). There are three drawer boards in this case – one that fully supports the drawer in each of the different dimensions. One is for final planing of the drawer back; the other is for final planing of the drawer sides – note the angle of the junction

Fig. 41.5. Sand the cove while the slip is attached.

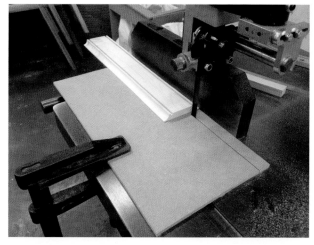

Fig. 41.6. After the routing and sanding, rip the slips free.

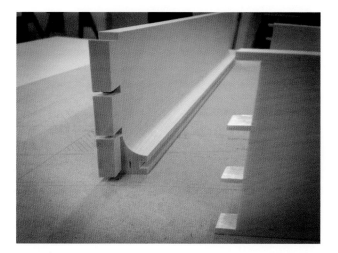

Fig. 41.7. A slip fit.

Fig. 41.8. Scrape the transition smooth.

Fig. 41.9. Plane the drawer bottoms.

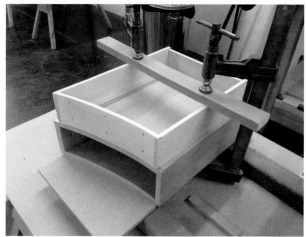

Fig. 41.10. An assembled drawer clamped to dry.

Fig. 41.11. Drawer board.

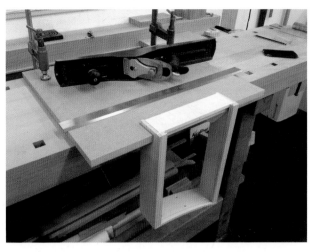

Fig. 41.12. Drawer board with back.

of drawer side to the drawer front.

Look closely at the drawer side setup in particular – do you remember I said to scribe your gauge lines for dovetailing a tad less than the thickness of the job? This is why: The final planing flushes everything up as you fit the finished drawer.

In this case, it's a few careful strokes down to the end grain of the mating joint surface. When you do this on the drawer sides and plane just to the end grain, the drawer will (should) suddenly fit perfectly in the carcase. If it's stiffish, push it in and out to burnish the drawer side. That burnished area will be where it's too tight. Engage your brain before the plane, and plane off just these burnished areas. And it will fit.

At right is a detail shot of the drawer back with the bottom removed; the slip will be trimmed flush. Note how the drawer back is lower than the sides, and that its top is slightly domed. There are half pins at the top and bottom, and the convention would be one full pin less than the drawer front. The top of the drawer side then gets tapered from back to front to ease the entry of the drawer into the carcase.

Fig. 41.13. Drawer board with front.

Fig. 41.14. The drawer from the back.

Fig. 42.1. We wouldn't use shellac for a family table that will see more heat and alcohol. But for a desk, dressing table, chair or cabinet, it's a reasonable choice.

PEAR DESK FINISHED

We use shellac a lot at Rowden. I learnt the benefit of this finish years ago, when I had a table being made in burr black walnut veneer. Terry was making it for me in an unheated barn not far away. Being a former farmer, Terry didn't need heating – but the tabletop did. I had eight leaves of this walnut burr and extravagantly suggested to Terry that we put four leaves on the top and four on the underside, then we could choose the best surface. All went well until the finish went on. Terry sprayed lacquer on one side. As it dried, it pulled at the glue lines and opened them. Damn.

OK, we can put those veneers down, but let's not use lacquer on the other side; let's use shellac…which we hope will have less pull as it dries.

When I compared the two sides of the table I was stunned. The shellac side had greater depth, I could see more and see deeper into the complex burr veneer than I could with the lacquer. Same bundle of veneers, same layup, same maker. The difference was the finish.

We wouldn't use shellac for a family table that will see more heat and alcohol. But for a desk, or dressing table, chair or cabinet, it's a reasonable choice. We apply it with a rubber made from a wad of springy fabric

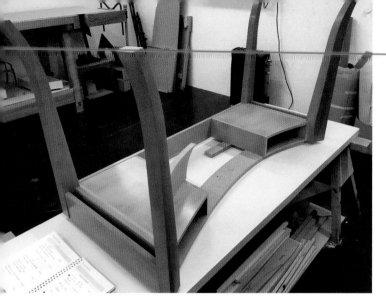

Fig. 42.2. Upside down for assembly.

Fig. 42.3. Final clean-up and leveling of the top.

Fig. 42.4. Final finish of the interior.

Fig. 42.5. The surface before the final French polishing.

rather like sheep's wool (in fact, if you have a sheep handy, its wool would do the job really well). Wrap the wadding in fine cotton cloth; old, good-quality, well-washed white T-shirts are great. We use a clear or transparent shellac, with as little colour as possible, though it will still be slightly yellow. A good polisher will use a 3-lb. cut. That is, 3 pounds of flakes in a gallon of spirit – that's a heavy polish, which takes skill to apply.

Ours students start with a 1-lb. cut, and might still add spirit to that. This builds slowly and gives them control of the process. Writing about French polishing is like writing about sex; it is almost impossible to get it right. There are so many variables: the temperature of the room, the polish's thickness, how much polish is

on the job and how hard you press with the rubber.

Start applying in circles, then figure eights, putting polish onto the raw wood. You'll start to see the colour of the wood emerge. Circles overlap and melt the previous layer. The spirit dries out fast in the warm room, setting up on the surface almost as fast as you apply it.

As you go on, you find that the pores of the bare wood are filling with polish and the polish is building to a semi-shine. Keep it even. Where it is still dull give it a few more licks. You will reach a stage where you have to stop as there is too much polish on the job. The rubber drags and grabs. Stop. Put the rubber away in an airtight jar.

Now make your mind up: If this is a break to just let

Fig. 42.6. Polishing is always up against the clock. We have to deliver this piece to an exhibition on Monday. The days before all fill with finishing.

it set up, then you can apply more in a half-hour. Or you can call it a day. Usually, you should be able to give five or six "Goes" in a day – that is, in each Go, passing the rubber eight to 10 times over the surface. Those five "Goes" make up a session. A skilled polisher will complete a session in a day and complete a full polish in three sessions. Each full session will not have taken more than 30 minutes total over the five "Goes."

Now allow the polish to harden; leave it at least over the weekend and keep the heat on. When you come back to it, perform a light de-nib with #320-grit sandpaper, then you go again.

The polishing rubber will need feeding as you work. You can apply a small dab of mineral oil to the rubber to help it keep working longer. How much is a small dab? "Well, the oil on the side of your nose is probably enough for a day."

We don't aim for a fully filled piano surface (with all surfaces equally polished); three sessions for secondary surfaces is usually "good enough."

But "good enough?" Well, let's be clear. That surface is still important to your piece's final quality. It is through the surfaces that the customer experiences your work. But there are primary and secondary surfaces. The top is a primary surface and we want that spit bonk. Legs and the back rail, well, those are secondary and might well get a bit less time.

Why? Polishing is always up against the clock. We have to deliver this piece to an exhibition on Monday. The days before all fill with finishing.

Then we are finished. It's gone and we all feel a little low and empty. Steve has taken on what turned out to be a challenging piece of work, and he brought it to a really good conclusion. A huge round of applause for his work skill and application. Daren helped prepare cutting and process lists at the start to set him on a pathway to success. Daren was always there to help – especially near the end when the drawers needed making to get in under the deadline. One of my former students, Rose, described him thus: "Daren is a bit like Yoda, but before he got wrinkly."

In the end, the piece was stiff and strong and maybe we need not have worried about structure as much. But we didn't know for sure – and as nobody had made a piece like this, we had nobody to ask. That's what designers do.

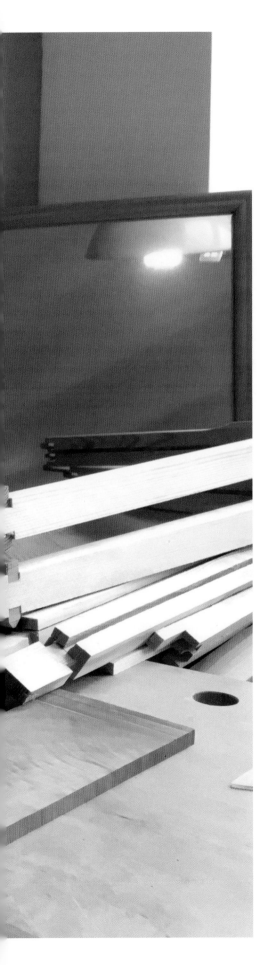

CHAIRS: THE FURNITURE MAKER'S CHALLENGE

Most chair design demands that you make a full-size prototype then sit in it, then make the chair. We should do that, but having made a few chairs, we tend to go straight for the finished chair. It's swinging from the chandelier by your fingertips.

On the following page, take a look at the seat shape – it is a little unusual, so take a moment to get used to it. It starts off as a thick block of ply-wood laminated to give me the thickness I need at the leg junctions. It is then shaped. The middle is cut out, and the shape of the seat developed to the form you want. The benefit of this method is that I can make my seat any shape I want, without complicated joinery. Legs can be notched into the seat and fixed easily with good long screws or Parnham fittings (I will tell you about those a bit later).

Have a good look at this. This is the process Daren has developed to transfer my drawings, which are usually quite small, to a larger scale (in this case, one-third of full size). He then makes an accurate model from dimensions he takes directly off the drawing. First, look at the accuracy of the model; it's spot on. He knows I see slight changes, and he knows that this stage of transferring the drawing into 3D is the critical one. He takes the drawing at one-third scale and cuts it up, using it for templates for the legs, sticking the drawing on the timber then shaping it out to match the drawing.

Ignore, please, the foolish-looking seat block of MDF on which the back legs are sitting. Look instead at the support block the seat is sitting on, which

Fig. 43.1. Chair design is about comfort and creating a light, strong structure that looks good from every angle. And the shapes have to seem new and all work together.

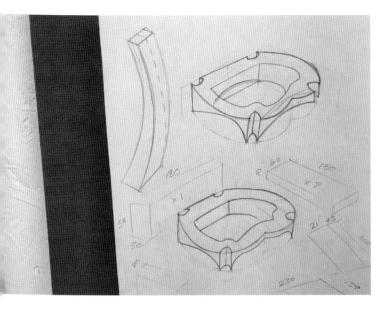

Fig. 43.2. Chair seat sketches.

Fig. 43.3. Model on support block.

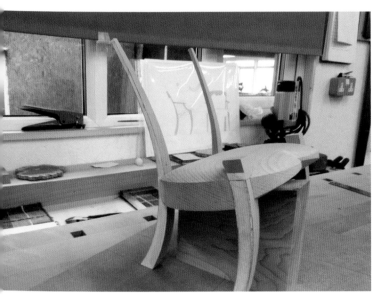

Fig. 43.4. Model on support block, another view.

Fig. 43.5. Model on an angle.

holds the seat at the right height and angle while we develop the position of the legs. We do this when making full-size chairs, too; the relationship of the seat to the ground is critical.

Then he makes a seat block. Please try to see past that huge lump of timber (the seat) which is currently at the wrong angle and the wrong height. You have to get things wrong at times if only to change them later. This seat will later be shaped and formed into a sensual, fluid upholstered shape. Worry not.

The point now is to get something down that is accurate from the good parts of the drawing. The side elevation and front elevations are not great – but they are what I have. As the model evolves, I can develop and tighten up the design. You see from the photos that Daren is starting to shape the top of the seat upholstery and the seat's front shape. He works from lines carefully drawn on the seat, taken from the drawing.

You can see in the two drawings above a development. Until this point, the seat was pretty circular in plan. Here,

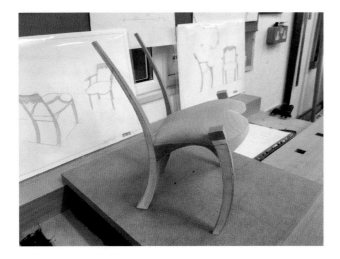

Fig. 43.6. A three-quarters view.

Fig. 43.7. Sketching in the crest rail and propping up the back feet to change the seat angle.

I change that, cutting into the seat shape to take two great bites – one on each side. Huge improvement. When you do this, it's called "going off piste" – it's where all the excitement lies. But you need to be able to get back to your old idea just in case the new one fails. Use photos at each stage.

Work through these developments a step at a time. Try to change one thing, assess, then move on. If necessary, write a list of changes and work out the order in which you will make those changes.

My next change is to the back rail of the seat, then the crest rail, then the rake of the whole chair seat. At the moment, the chair leans back too far. I did it in the drawing to add speed and aggression to the pose of the chair; I wanted the side view to feel like it was under tension, was resisting a huge wind. Now that is working against me, making the chair too cool, too leaned back – and probably quite uncomfortable. The answer is simple. Lop an inch or so off the front feet to bring the whole chair more upright. We tested this by putting the rear legs on an 18mm sheet of MDF and the front legs on the benchtop.

Now we have the crest rail. And I had to resist the temptation to change it. Changes at this stage should generally be taking stuff away, simplifying the image – not adding complexity, but creating a more resolved image.

Chair design is about comfort and creating a light, strong structure that looks good from every angle. And the shapes have to seem new and all work together. Edward Barnsley said a good viewpoint for a chair is of

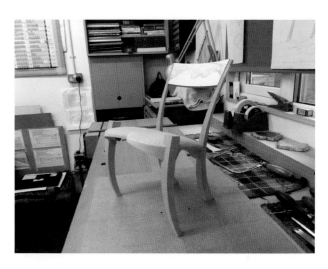

Fig. 43.8. Changes at this stage should generally be taking stuff away, simplifying the image.

Fig. 43.9. Model from back.

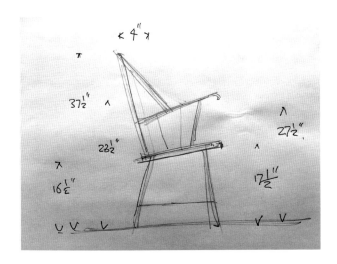

Fig. 43.10. Profile drawing of Windsor chair.

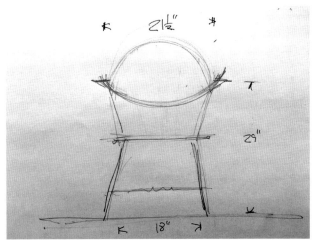

Fig. 43.11. Elevation drawing of Windsor chair.

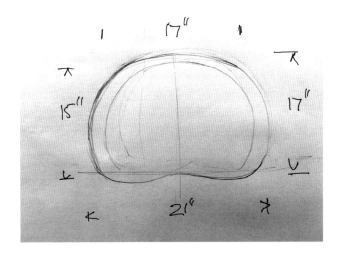

Fig. 43.12. Plan drawing of a Windsor chair seat.

the back three-quarters from about 15' away. No question. A chair is a furniture designer's most difficult task.

This chair is running into trouble. We are working on a decent solution for the angles, but it has a seat that is too low to be usable for a working chair. A salon or drawing room chair can be as low as 15" from the ground; it looks comfortable and inviting to sit in and is slightly more difficult to get out of. And that's what we have with the model at the moment – a salon chair not a desk chair. This kind of chair is not related to a working surface such as a table or desk. A desk or dining chair should be about 17-1/2" from the ground, so our seat has to come up the equivalent of two whole inches.

It's design slippage – you need to always compare your model to a real-life comfortable chair. This is hard. There is no easy answer to this, as we are all different shapes and sizes and find chairs comfortable or not in lots of confusing ways. The best approach I suggest if you are a person of average size is to make a comfortable chair for yourself and let everyone else go hang.

So where do these magical figures come from? As I mentioned in an earlier chapter, I have a Windsor chair in my studio, probably made in America, that I find comfortable. When I need seat and arm measurements, I measure this chair then carry those measures over to the new chairs I am making. We all stand on the shoulders of those who went before. This chair has been with me as a studio chair for more than 30 years, and I

still love it to bits. It creaks and groans and needs regluing now and again. But it is light, flexible and comfortable, and it is good to look at. If I can help produce as good a chair I will be a happy man.

So, let's look at these drawings and see what that chair tells us. Seat height: 17-1/2" falling back to 16-1/2". Elbow height: 27-1/2", with the arm raising to 28-1/2" at the point the hand falls over the end of the arm. The chair back falls away 4". The overall width of the seat is 21-1/2", but the inside sitting width is 18", the depth is 17" and the usable depth is only 15". Engrave these dimensions on your chairmaking soul and move away from them at your peril. Do not think that if you make a good-looking chair, people will find a way to sit at comfort in it. They won't, and you chair

Fig. 43.13. Shaping the back for the model.

Fig. 43.14. Considering the arm supports.

will be chucked into the great dumpster of history – rightly so.

Back to work. The chair seat has now been raised by the 2" necessary. The seat is now not leaning so crazily back, and we are starting to see a chair design that might work. What we do is keep working around it, tightening up visual relationships, changing this, improving that. Each change has an effect on other parts of the chair, so it's important to make one change at a time and be able to step back again. Simplify at this stage; don't add new stuff in. Take stuff out. It's harder to be simple, but much better. Go around and around the piece, doing this until it is visually a tight as a drum.

You want to reach the point where nothing can now be changed without changing everything. It's like finishing a drawing: You are climbing a pyramid one pencil mark at a time. Revising, refining, simplifying, getting nearer the top, getting nearer to the finished image. You are almost finished; one more pencil mark and you are at the top. But two more pencil marks and you are back to base camp. So, watch it.

The images above show the next step we took. The forward visual push of the legs has the effect of demanding that the arm support is pushed back. See how Daren is using the one-third scale drawing to get exactly the shape I want. My instructions at this stage were to go straight back at right angles to the ground. This kept the arm support simple, with a vertical line going up the outside of the leg and up the arm support. Next, we tapered the inside face. With luck that whole component can now be cut out at one go – arm

Fig. 43.15. The support blocks below the arms.

support and leg – happy days.

Doing the arm is another matter. Daren took copies from the drawing that are too curved. This is a taste thing. A bit like tasting soup, it needs a bit less curvy herb. Curves are great but you can have too much of a good thing. You can have floppy, indolent curves and curves in tension. I tend to draw curves either from Mr. Chandler's Unique Templates or by bending a steel rule to eyeball the curve while getting Daren to draw the line. Now, please, Daren – before my fingers give up. Without straight lines and tension to work against, curves are just floppy and dull. So now we need new arms.

Fig. 44.1. We are going to show you the development process we used on the model, but now at full size. The process of a shaped plywood seat and solid legs is one that can be adapted for many versions of this kind of chair.

CHAIRMAKING

The chair that goes with the desk didn't make it to the exhibition. So, we sent Perseus instead. Now we know the way we designed the desk chair, with low arms at the front, was correct. They will not clash with the desk drawers as Perseus does.

What we do have is the maquette or model made accurately by Daren to develop the ideas on the drawings to a one-third scale model. This resolved many of the design issues, so making the chair should be a relatively straightforward thing. Chairs are not easy to make, but this one should not be difficult. If you want to make this chair, get the plans from our store. In fact, get two copies; one to study and one to cut up and use to create your leg and seat templates.

We are going to show you the development process we used on the model, but now at full size. The process of a shaped plywood seat and solid legs is one that can be adapted for many versions of this kind of chair. The plywood seat can be any shape, so there is lots of room for you to develop your own ideas.

We begin with the seat, as this is the single component all others join into. We use plywood and stack laminate it to a thickness of enough to support the legs (about 80mm). Keep the seat component square for as long as you can; marking out joinery is so much easier on a square form. The illustrations show the development of the full-size plan by squaring up the smaller drawing. Then, we mark out on the seat.

Next, you have the challenge of fitting the curved leg component to a housing cut in the ply seat. You can see Steve test-fitting the leg template to an offcut from

Fig. 44.2. Our working model.

Fig. 44.3. The model from behind.

Fig. 44.4. The working drawings.

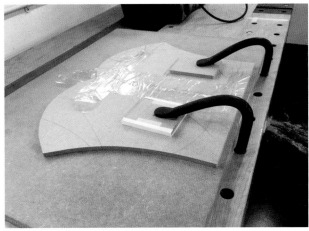

Fig. 44.5. The seat template.

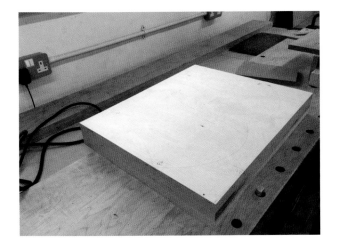

Fig. 44.6. Stacked plywood for the seat.

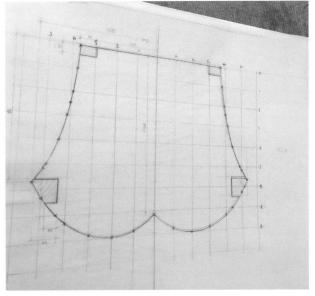

Fig. 44.7. Graphed-out seat.

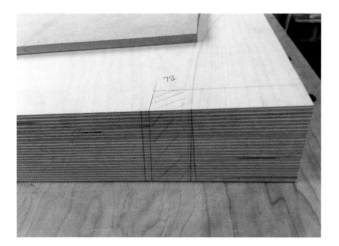

Fig. 44.8. How the leg is let into the seat.

Fig. 44.9. Experiments to fit the leg into the seat.

Fig. 44.10. Creating the jig for the curved groove.

Fig. 4.11. How the jig helps to create the housing in the seat.

the seat material. To do this, you need to make a jig for your router. First, shape MDF pieces to the curvature at the top of the leg. Then use those to create the sides of your router jig. They are screwed to the top left and right sides of the jig. Then a router, with a top-bearing bit, is used to trim and adjust the size of the opening. This in turn creates the housing in the plywood seat to accept the chair leg. Phew!

Now we come to two more tools that in our shop are essential to modern chairmaking: A plinth to stand the job on, and a seat support to hold the seat at the correct height and angle relative to the floor.

The plinth is a version of the plinth that most pieces of furniture are assembled upon. It provides an accurate flat surface and brings the job off the floor so overlong legs can be measured and trimmed to length.

The seat support is critical. It holds the seat, in this

Fig. 44.12. The seat blank atop the plinth.

Fig. 44.13. Finding the leg angles.

Fig. 44.14. Leg blanks acclimatising.

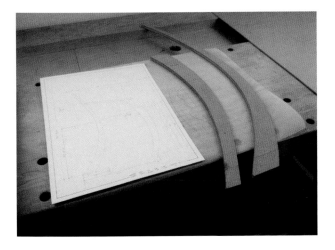

Fig. 44.15. Leg templates.

Fig. 44.16. The leg jig.

case located on stub dowels, at a fixed height and angle relative to the ground. All this stuff is important – especially if you are making a batch of a dozen chairs. One wobbling chair can be fixed with a disc sander and a bit of patience. Twelve wobbling chairs are a serious pain. I know – I have been there.

Above you can see Steve has worked ahead, cutting blanks for the legs and arm supports oversized, then leaving them stacked under his bench. This is one of the big differences we see between short-course students and makers. The short-course people have a pile of components that warp and twist; the maker has a carefully stickered stack of components acclimatising to the workshop's humidity.

Your templates for the front and back legs will have been developed either from a small drawing

and squared up, or they will be copies taken from a full-size plan then stuck on the template and cut to exact size. Squaring up is a classic process of drawing a grid on a small drawing, then a larger full-size grid on another sheet. You then transfer points in each square where your job intersects with the grid.

The templates are then used to create jigs. Templates are not jigs themselves and should not be used or confused with jigs. Jigs are a means of holding a job still whilst it is shaped or cut to size. You can see the template in the foreground atop the spindle moulder jig. But the jig is what the actual job will sit upon when it's being cut to the exact shape. The toggle clamps are there to securely hold the job in position.

Once shaped in one direction, the legs will be tapered in the other direction. Here, a thin lath is bent

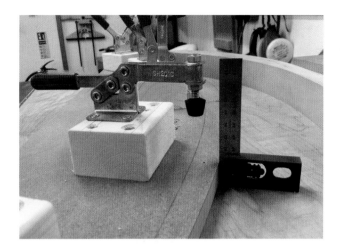

Fig. 44.17. Make sure things are square.

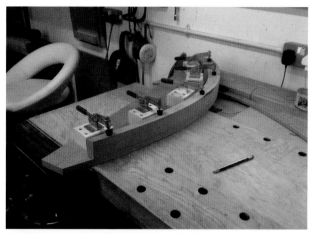

Fig. 44.18. Secure the leg stock in the jig.

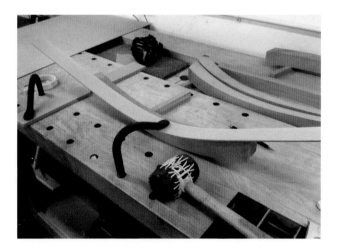

Fig. 44.19. Offcuts add protection.

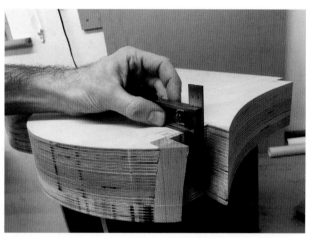

Fig. 44.20. It's only a mistake if you can't fix it, and Steve did.

inside the curve and a straight line marked down the job.

Now to show that even the best make mistakes, here's one Steve made (above right). He was carefully cutting a recess in the seat to accept the front leg when he realised that it was going to be in the wrong place. OOOOH. We all do it – it's not possible to make anything without sometimes making mistakes.

I made a walnut dining table for a client with a small defect in the centre. I thought I could polish it out but I was mistaken; I needed to let in a patch and repolish. I told the client what I had done and he didn't seem to mind, though it drove me nuts. Several months later, I got a case of good claret from him.

"Thank you," I said. "What have I done to deserve this?"

"Ahh," he said, "I have been betting dinner guests that they cannot find the repair you made to the dining table. It's a great after-dinner game, after a couple of bottles, shuffling around the plates and stuff on the table, and I have made huge winnings. Thank you!"

The essence is knowing that you can repair it. A good repair is good making, good craftsmanship. The photos show the solid blocks Steve glued in before recutting the joints in the correct locations.

Now the legs can be fitted to the seat. A flat is planed on the back leg to marry with the straight surface on the seat. Then, it is carefully fitted to the seat. Finally, the front legs can also be let in. The routed recess is a tapered curve, so the leg slides in then down to tighten in the recess.

Dowels, screws or Parnham fittings – one or all of

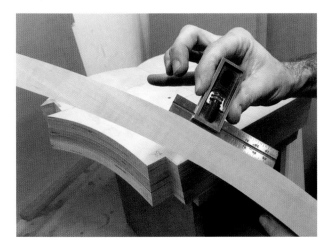

Fig. 44.21. Plane the flat.

Fig. 44.22. Fit the leg to the seat.

Fig. 44.23. Detail of front leg fitting.

Fig. 44.23. Clearance holes drilled in the jig to install Parnham fittings.

these are generally found in my chair joinery. Dowels are old school, and for them, we almost always use a workshop-made jig, a block that will guide the drill and locate the holes on both parts of the job.

Screws are amazing fixtures that give great strength to a joint and pull it up tight. When chairs are difficult to get a cramp on, this is of vital importance. In these joints, Steve has put two dowels that later will be replace by Parnham fittings. In other chairs, we have used screws capped with a neat wooden plug. The screws will be great here for trial assembly, as the screw eliminates the need for complex cramping setups. Chairs are really hard to get cramps on. Screws also allow you to put a longer screw in for final fix.

Parnham fittings are a fixture developed by John Makepeace when he had a workshop at Parnham House. This is a threaded rod that replaces the dowel. Degrease the threads and use a good quality epoxy. These do not require the accuracy of dowels joints as the epoxy takes up the slack, so it is a quicker and easier method.

I would have done this differently, making the arm support as a part of the leg, but Daren and Steve chose to make the arm supports as separate pieces and fix them to the top of the leg with Parnham fittings. Anyone who has designed chairs will flinch at the mention of arm supports. They are Tricky Woo. I think it's because they are usually curved components that transfer weight bearing from one place to another. In this case, it's from the top of the leg to the front of the armrest.

Fig. 44.24. The fixture in place.

Fig. 44.25. Use dowels for initial fitting.

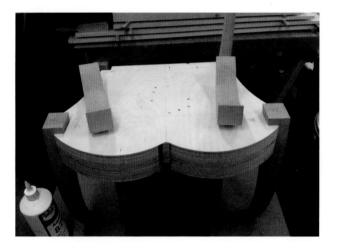

Fig. 44.26. Arm supports.

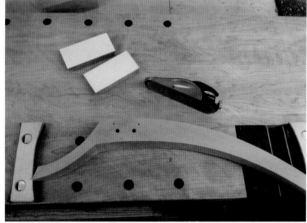

Fig. 44.27. Arm support connected to leg.

We generally press down just there to ease ourselves out of a chair.

Here is a good example of how tricky they can be. These arm supports were made and fitted on the chair nicely developed from the model. But they looked rubbish. It took me a weekend of worrying about it to figure it out. The inside curve was flat but was describing an arc. The component looked fat and wrong. However, put a 6" rule touching the top and bottom corners and you see that the rule describes another arc down the front face of the support, going into the support by 5mm in the centre. Draw a line on that, cut to the line and happy days.

Now the back splat can be made. It's a curved component and quite deep, so band saw to the line then use a compass plane down to the line. This can

Fig. 44.28. Measuring the arm support.

Fig. 44.29. Measuring the arm support with a steel rule.

Fig. 44.30. Steve fitting the crest rail.

Fig. 44.31. Bird's mouth in arm fits around rear leg.

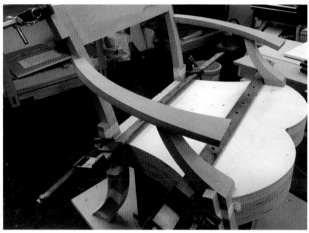

Fig. 44.32. Heavy plywood seat.

be done on both sides.

The photo above shows Steve in the final fit of the crest rail and rear leg. We are now moving into the final phase, but the arms of the chair still need fitting. We have a simple arm support that tapers in thickness from where it joins the rear leg to the front where it is supported by the front arm support coming up from below.

The arm has a bird's mouth cut in the end that fits around the rear leg. The photo above shows Steve fitting the test arm in magnolia. He inserts a screw from the rear of the leg, aiming it out and slightly down to pull the arm onto the corner of the leg. There is no housing in the leg; it's just pulled up really tight with the screw. A small housing could be cut in to give greater support. The front of the arm is located on the

arm support with a stub dowel.

Now the massive plywood seat is going to be reduced to a slender shapely form. This huge plywood form is only there to give strength to the joinery of the four legs. The centre and most of the sides can now be cut away to a shape that will define the shape of the leather upholstery. Be sure that you leave enough strength behind when you do this — but it is possible to safely remove more than three-quarters of the mass of the plywood.

The next phase is to clean up and polish all the components. The joinery is done, and all the final shaping is coming to completion. Now is when you need your spectacles to have a good critical look.

The components are then sanded up to #240 grit. The image above shows Steve with a sanding block

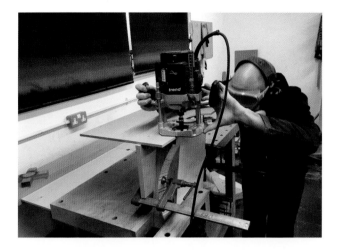

Fig. 44.33. A router takes off some of the weight.

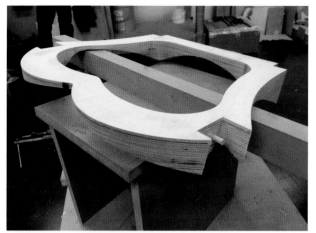

Fig. 4.34. The lightened seat.

Fig. 44.35. Sand the legs with a block matching the curve.

Fig. 44.36. The assembled chair.

curved to match the shape of the chair leg. When it comes to polishing, the pear will benefit from a thin shellac polish. We use a 1 lb. cut (one pound of shellac in a gallon of clear alcohol). This is a good starting point, but if you are inexperienced it may be too stiff a mix. The aim is just a few thin coats before knocking it back with #320-grit paper, then applying wax. Shellac is a good finish when it comes to dealing with epoxy squeeze-out – just wipe off the excess glue with white spirit.

I don't want to tell stories…but Daren had to stop Steve from doing a late-night glue up. This is the end of the job and Steve is moving on after nearly two years at Rowden. He needs to get the car back for Laura to use on Monday. Deadlines and end-of-job tasks such as a glue-up don't work well together. We have seen lots of

potentially great pieces lost at the last, rushed minute. Daren, as usual, was there with beady eye and firm hand, and we managed to reschedule. But be warned: it's a bear trap waiting with every job.

The chair will now go to Mary Holland for upholstery in red leather. Mary knows what I want; she has upholstered many of my chairs. Working with an upholsterer can be difficult. They usually want to inflate all your forms with a bicycle pump to make them round when your image is tight, lean and smooth. Mary knows what I want…but I will have to go down there a couple of times to get that exact shape.

So here we are at last – we can see the shape of the seat and sit on it for the first time. It's a funny time, this finishing of the pieces – finally seeing the result of all the work. I feel too close to the piece to be objective. I

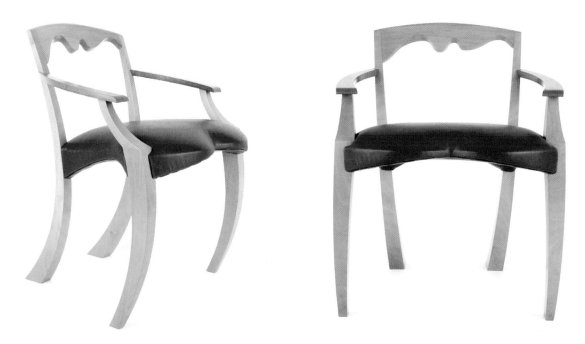

Fig. 44.37. I feel too close to the piece to be objective. I will need to see it in an exhibition to see how it stands up to the way the world views it.

will need to see it in an exhibition to see how it stands up to the way the world views it. But I know it's a comfortable chair, that it is light and strong and doesn't look bad from all the angles. So, I guess it will have to do, until next time. Thank you Steve for a wonderful piece of work. Thank you Daren for running shotgun on the job, and keeping it going in the right direction.

Fig. 44.38. Carol's chair and desk.

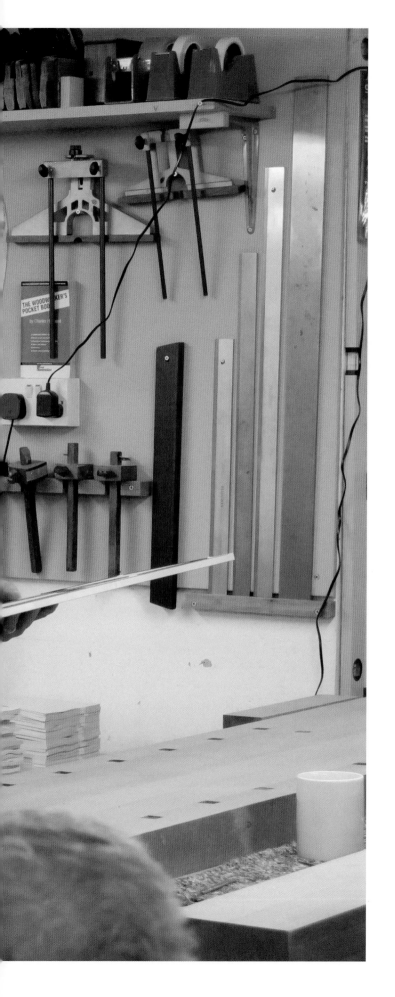

THE LAST WORD

Well, at last, we are both here at the conclusion. Mind you, it was a close-run thing. If I had paid any attention to my dear oncologist I would have never made it. But I am "smouldering" which I gather is a rare state to be in. But, I could catch fire at any minute and go into the deep pit of chemotherapy, or I could smoulder on, who knows?

The disclosure of my forthcoming end has had a very positive effect; I now value every moment I am given. Personal things are on the job list that would have never got done. Succession has become a big issue for me. It's one of those things that small business people put off until it's too late. I have had smouldering time to set up new young ambitious directors for Rowden in Ed Wild and Matt Lacey. Both have been trained here and "get Rowden," which is important.

It's wonderful to see their drive and direction; they approach the issues at Rowden from the viewpoint of a different generation – one that embraces social media to develop a new vital idea of the future.

We have a five-year plan that will see four more long-term students and another member of the teaching staff. New workshops are planned to go where the old piggeries were. These overlook a long meadow down to the lake and will have big windows down one wall. CNC is coming to Rowden shortly and plans are to set up a second- and third-year apprentice scheme to take a small group of young makers to a standard of work so they can step straight into jobs in top workshops. This great task is necessary as the shortage of skilled makers has become apparent in our industry.

My work, now that the book is done, resides in a large box of drawings. In it are 35 years of client pre-

sentation drawings – some of them were built, many are crazy ideas that were never made. The idea is to combine CAD/CAM with a group of designs developed from the box. These can be sold as a collection from our new gallery. Prices will be kept modest and quality high, pieces will be restricted to small edition numbers and Rowden customer service will, we hope, be second to none. Ed and Matt will be going to war selling these and other pieces in the coming years at selected exhibitions. It's all very exciting.

The desk and chair will be at home very soon. They came home for a short stay before whizzing of on exhibition. Carol is delighted, and they both look great in the space they were designed to occupy. Steve has moved on to a workshop in Sussex, I think. Daren is working on a marquetry chest I have drawn up. When he has completed that, I have four great boards of burr elm that I want made into a chest. I got these at an auction at the workshop of

the late Trevor Pate. Each year, Trevor would make a wonderful chest and exhibit it at the Devon Guild; each year it would sell. Trevor chose timber so well and made with such simple integrity. I want to make a chest in his memory. We have a drawing, and we have Trevor's timber. All we need is to make it. Craft politics these days is all about youth and newness.

Now then, what about the Why? At the beginning of this book, I asked why do we bother? Why should we bother with all this quality stuff? Well let's just look at that. Just why do we do it? It's madness. We pound our heads against those last few percentage points of quality that nobody really sees or cares a fig about. Most people would not recognise it even if it got up and bit their leg. It costs us brain cells that we cannot spare, it costs us hours, days, weeks of sweaty work that would be best avoided. Weeks that we probably won't get paid for. For pity's sake, why we do this? It is surely the most foolish thing?

This approach may be viable in the world of the amateur. She is restricted by nothing short of knowledge and skill. She has no deadlines or price restrictions. She can go for real quality without compromise. Sadly, however, the lack of knowledge, skill and talent get in the damn way.

I have attempted to do this quality stuff and to feed my family with the profits of my production, which is very different. Jim Krenov inspired me to make to the best of my ability. I took his example and, inspired by Ernest Gimson, turned it into a commercial workshop. OK, I took students to help pay the bills, but for the greater part of my working life, it was work for customers that did the bread-and-butter work – the students were the jam.

It's not possible always to get it right all the time. Some pieces went out with problems we couldn't fix. But the aim at the start of the job was always to make it as well as we could. I was blessed always with teams of gifted and conscientious makers. Neil Harris, Malcolm Vaughan, David Woodward, Graeme Scott, Chris Heywood and many others all played a part. Later, Nick Chandler and Daren Millman came, made wonderful contributions and took on the culture of the shop: You do it as well as you can. You bust a gut or just don't bother coming in.

Once you are able to see work of supreme quality (and you are able to create it), you are unable to "unsee" it ever again. Call it a drug or an addiction, it becomes a compulsion. You know the difference between good work and truly exemplary work. And thanks to places like Rowden and the people there, you know the path to take. So, you have to take that path. If you don't (and commercial restraints might prohibit you from doing it at times) you feel the less for it.

You want to look back on your life and see a line of well-made pieces stretching off into the distance. Each one not perfect but made as well as you could

have, given the circumstance. You want to be like great designer-maker Tom Hucker. He was once asked why he sweated over that last 10 percent and said, "If I didn't, I would not know myself."

When you become this person, you gain control over things that most people have no control over. Freehand sharpening is a tiny example of this. You have gained control over your body to shape steel. On the larger stage, learning to draw grants you access or control over the creative hemisphere of your brain. This gives you a tool more powerful than a table saw. The ability to pick up and put down images, to throw down five well-placed lines that represent exactly the idea inside your head, now that is cooking.

Training, skill and knowledge give you control over machines in a world where machines seem to control us. You gain understanding and some control of timber, a complex and challenging material. A material always changing, warm and responsive, or downright ornery. Stepping back even further, furniture making gives us control over the nature that inspires us, over trees and the forest, which were a forbidding and dangerous place for most of human evolution. And here we are, shaping the fearsome place to our pleasure.

And here, perhaps, is the biggest Why: You are no longer a cog in a machine. You are the entire machine – the entire system, if you will. You generate ideas from nothing. You pull new images out of dark obscurity into the daylight. You make them real. And you sell them to feed yourself and your family. Repeat until you die. Few people in the industrialized (or post-industrialized) world can claim to inhabit the entire circle of creation.

Each one of us must pick this up or leave it be. It's not for all of us, and I take my hat off to many who just need to pay the bills and feed the family and know that the job must stay put. Maybe we can do this weekends and evenings and bring together our thinking and our doing, if only for a short time. That alone would be worth doing.

But there are a small number of you, the cussed contrarians, who will not allow your thoughts and actions to be separated for all your working life. You want to look back on an exciting fulfilled life, a life well lived. With a mighty health and safety warning I am the first to say: Yeah, go do it. Work to become the best version of yourself, the best version that you possibly can become. All Hail the 873 or whatever it was.